Praise for *He Called Himself a Barnstormer*

"While reading *He Called Himself a Barnstormer*, a biographical novel, it is difficult to distinguish fact from fiction, but what rings true throughout is how God involves himself in the affairs of man through written revelation as well as the seemingly random circumstances of one's life that are guided by divine providence. As the reader enjoys the story, hopefully they will also reflect upon their own life to see how God is at work there as well."

—Joe Williamson

Joe Williamson is the author of *Finding YOUR Place in the World*, a book about discipleship which he has facilitated the teaching of in several countries.

The author has given us a delightful historical narrative in her book *He Called Himself a Barnstormer*, set in Middle America with adventures along the way from Ireland, the Caribbean, New York, and ending in Indiana. Those who enjoy history, migration, romance, and religious faith should travel along with the author on this important early American journey.

—Stephen B. Plaster, PhD

Stephen Plaster is the author of several books of history, among which are *Islam Anthology*, *Manuscripts Remembered*, and *Islam and Bible Prophecy*. He also teaches adult classes at First Baptist Church in Naples, Florida.

―――

"The December air was bitterly cold and the ground was covered with a dusting of freshly-fallen snow. Gnarled branches of black leafless trees were silhouetted against the grey somber sky. There was an eerie, yet peaceful silence in the old Limberlost Cemetery as I stood reading the grave stone:

> 'ELD. JAMES SCOTT, DIED JULY 19, 1891,
> AGED 90 Y. 9 M. 9 D. FOR SIXTY YEARS
> A MINISTER OF THE GOSPEL HE DIED
> AT HIS POST.'

Looking at the obelisk of my great-great-great-grandfather, I had many questions about him and his life. *He Called Himself a Barnstormer*, a historical novel based on the life of this ancestor, proposes to answer many of those questions. Beautifully written and filled with imagery, it reiterates the principles upon which this country was founded, the hardships and heartaches suffered by our forebears, whose determination and devotion were steadfast."

—Bruce Barron, MD

Bruce Barron is an ophthalmologist. He lives in New Orleans and has authored and co-authored several medical publications. He, also being a descendant of James Scott, has passionately done much research on his family roots.

He Called Himself a
BARNSTORMER

A Novel

By
Charlotte J. Reynolds

Rena,
God bless
Charlotte
"Joanne"

Deep River
B O O K S

ISBN – 13: 9781632694706
Library of Congress: 2018956378

Printed in the USA
Cover design by Robin Black, Inspirio Design

Table of Contents

Prologue

Searching for answers can sometimes be overwhelming, especially answers to questions the world seems not to have answers for. Questions like: Is there a God, and if so, does He really work in the affairs of men? Those were questions I labored over, praying often to find the answers.

One day, when I was on my knees seeking, asking for wisdom, I ran across a book declaring to have the answers. It was an apologetic, a book in defense of the Bible. Reading through its pages, I must say, it was very convincing. For example, it said that most of Jesus' followers were executed in torturous ways because they could not deny who Jesus was. Those men had seen Him die and then witnessed His coming back to life again. If they were willing to face that kind of death, I reasoned, surely Jesus was who He said He was. As I continued my search, I found other convincing evidences, and, in time, discovered that one of the most compelling apologetics for believing the Bible is America. Why? Well, let me explain:

In 1620 a ship called the *Mayflower* faced near-disaster as a storm, relentless in its fury, caused the main beams of the boat to bow and crack. That was the beginning of America, for out of that disaster the Mayflower Compact was formed—not by men seeing the world through fear-filled eyes, but by men who had an undisputed conviction that the God of the Bible should be at the center of their lives.

It was intended to be only a temporary agreement between men who were encountering a wilderness where there was no law and order, but it became so successful that eventually that historical agreement would come to influence the men who established our government, laying a foundation of "law and order" that has been passed down to us today. No, it was not a democracy based on the changing whims of people, but a constitutional republic established on the "absolute laws" of the Bible, producing more "freedoms" than the world had ever known. Those men believed what Christ said in John 8:32 (NIV), "you will know the truth, and the truth will set you free." And then Jesus told us, in John 14:6, that He was the "truth."

They also must have known what Noah Webster, the author of our English dictionary, once said: "All the miseries and evils which men suffer from vice, crime, ambition, injustice, oppression, slavery, and war, proceed from their despising or neglecting the precepts contained in the Bible."

Knowing that those men obviously held to a firm foundation which sprang from a belief in the Bible seemed to solidify my faith; however, I questioned, "What happened after that generation was no longer living, when the next generation came along?" I had read that many of their descendants were leaving the states along the Eastern Coast and moving west, into an uncharted territory—territory that knew nothing about Christ or the Bible. As I read further, I learned too that, leaving their churches behind, life became difficult. Morals started to decline, as corn liquor flowed freely. Thievery and murders seemed to penetrate the land, and without a legal court or people to raise a protest, guns and ropes, more often than not, settled disputes.

But God, it seems, was not through with America. For I soon found, that without computers or cell phones or other modern devices, He was able to raise up men willing to carry the cross of Christ and His gospel into that wilderness, preaching and teaching people His statutes, helping to preserve the union and the "freedoms" He had established there. Some became well-known evangelists; many more were just simple, humble men who felt His call, and were willing, beyond all cost, to be used to rescue the sheep and bring them back into the fold.

Chapter 1

Autumn 1822

James Scott shielded his eyes with his arm, as the brutal wind relentlessly blew the salt water straight into his face. Standing on the deck of the ship with his father, struggling to keep his stance, he suddenly heard a loud thunderous boom. The pirate sloop hit a reef with a tremendous blow, sending them both flying into the water.

Now, trying to stay afloat, he searched the wreckage, yelling "Father!" as the wind seemed to rip up the word, throwing it back into his face. "Father!" *He's got to be around here somewhere!*

"Here, James! I'm here!" James turned toward the voice as a huge wave lifted him high above the wreckage that was beginning to drift apart. Lightning flashed, and he could see, for a split second, his father desperately clinging to a piece of wood too small to support his weight. He was moving away from him at a fast pace. James started after him when he heard him cry.

"No, Son! Try for the shore."

"Father, I won't leave you," James yelled, as he continued swimming toward the voice, desiring not to see the hopelessness of the situation.

"I'm old! I can't make it. You can, lad. Save yourself. . . ." With every word he spoke, his father's voice faded until James could not hear him at all. As more lightning flashed in the sky, James could see the piece of wood his father was clinging to slip from his grasp as he disappeared into the mist.

A wave came crashing down on top of James, pushing him under, pinning him for a moment onto a reef. Pain shot through his back, as flesh gave way under the sharp edges of the coral.

Now, fighting merely to survive pushed all thoughts of his father from his mind, for it seemed as though his lungs were on fire when he finally struggled to the surface. He took a quick breath of air as he felt himself being dragged under again; but reaching out, in a last, desperate attempt to save himself, he grasped a large plank from the deck of the ship and was able to pull himself up past the surface. With every bit of strength he had, he struggled out of the water and upon it. He didn't stay there long, as the water surged around him, but in the distance he could see the darkened silhouette of an island, not more than a kilometer away.

His heart was beating now more rapidly than he had ever experienced, and with the memory of his father's voice piercing the wind, saying, "Go, Jimmy, go . . . you can make it lad. . . . Save yourself," he laboriously put one arm over the other and swam.

There was some solace knowing he had tried to save his father, but he struggled in vain, as the wind and the waves were physically impossible to overcome. It was all James could do to save himself; so he swam, concentrating on nothing else—nothing, that is, until, riding the crest of a big wave, he looked back. The moon had just slithered from behind a dark cloud, its silvery light reflecting on the tall mast of the *Bald Hornet* where the skull-emblazoned flag was still flying, as if to say, "I'm down, but not forgotten." The boat was caught on the rocky reef below the waterline. Moments later it was gone. Justice seemed to prevail, but holding sway was a sadness that gripped the heart of James Scott, for with all vestiges of the pirate's sloop went the hope of ever seeing his father again. . . .

What a grand fellow his father had been. Coming to America from the County Down, in the province of Ulster in Northern Ireland in the late 1700s, John Scott grew up during a time when most of Ireland was coming under the heavy arm of religious persecution. For laws had been forced on them from every conceivable source, producing a life of despair; still they clung to their faith, even as the shroud of darkness spread across their lives.

Although many of the Irish were Catholic, still there were some who were not. The Scott family was Presbyterian; however, Catholicism held a strong influence.

John Scott, a tall man with a kind heart, loved the sea. He owned and captained a ship which transported flax from New York to ports in Northern Ireland.

But it was the songs he sang that James treasured, and those stories—those wonderful stories he told, with their imaginary words, whether true or not—held a fascination that captivated James' heart and soul.

"Always remember, my son, that 'Scotia' or 'Scot' was one of Ireland's earliest names, for it was that name, our name, that was and is as much a part of Ireland as are those rolling green hills bathed in the mist of the early morning dew. For you see, a thousand years before Christ, Milesians—people who came here from Spain—invaded this land. One of their ancient ancestors, a beautiful woman she was, or so they say, her name was Scotia, queen mother of the Milesians. Those people must have been so bewitched by her that they became known by Scotia or Scot. That name, our name, was to be a part of our land then and long afterwards, even up until the time of the Celtics. It was eventually carried into what is now called "Scotland," after a famine hit the South causing people to flee northeast and eventually into that land taking with them the name."

Then with his stories came the songs. . . .

> They came from a land beyond the sea,
> And now o'er the western main
> Set sail in their good ships, gallantly,
> From the sunny lands of Spain.
> Oh, where's the isle we've seen in dreams,
> Out destin'd home or grave?
> Thus sang they, as by the morning beams,
> They swept the Atlantic waves.

"And so they came, the Milesians, to our beautiful land we now call Ireland."

Thus his father's stories did go, and James took in every word, always eager to learn more about this land—a land he seldom saw, yet one for which he held a fascination.

James learned from his father that Scotia/Ireland was, at one time, a pagan land, existing about a thousand years before the birth of Christ, or before history found its writing. Years later the Celts, a warlike people who nonetheless knew the art of a more sophisticated life, restrained people wherever they went, and many found their way to that beautiful island of Scotia. He remembered tales being told of humans eating humans, and how evil saturated the land. But, centuries later, after Christ walked the earth, it began to change.

"It changed because of a man the people called Saint Patrick, who was first shipped to Ireland as a slave, but later escaped, only to come back, after he had traveled the Mediterranean learning about the faith. He came back to tell the people about Christ. Yes, an awareness of Christ seemed to transform their very lives," his father said, "so much so, that centuries later, it became impossible for the people of Ireland to turn their backs on the church Saint Patrick brought to them. Yet, in the years ahead, Ireland would pay a great price for this endeavor, as it seems the devil, relentless in his pursuit, would use men to created havoc, causing undue heartache, forcing people, even today, to leave the island."

History had always been a passion for John Scott. He loved it and because he did, he never grew tired of telling others, especially his sons, what he knew. He had learned much of that history from his uncle, who first owned and captained a ship called the *Nancy Grace*. Grateful to have the knowledge, he became even more beholden to his wife's parents, for after he married he was to learn much more from them; they were Catholic, and had lived through countless days of difficulty in their beloved Ireland. So difficult, in fact, that in time it would leave him with no recourse but to take them, along with his family, to a new home many miles across the sea. Yet the years of living in another land could not, nor would ever, erase the fond memories he held for Ireland.

John remembered the year his uncle died. It was in 1794, the year John turned twenty-nine. His uncle had always insisted that, upon his death, he would be turning the *Nancy Grace* over to him. Now, recalling how he struggled to make a decision whether to sell the boat or not, John remembered thinking, *If I do sell her, I could use the money to enhance my farm, or, perhaps give it to Margaret's parents who, I know, could certainly use it; but then, it might be good to keep the* Nancy Grace *and continue in the shipping business.* Considering those possibilities, he remembered how his uncle had always insisted that he follow in his footsteps, since he had made numerous voyages helping him as first mate.

John loved the sea. He was as much at home on a sailing ship as he was walking those dirt roads to Newry where his uncle resided. The excitement of seeing the ports of the various countries in which they sailed was beyond anything he had ever dreamed. And taking the helm of, what seemed like to him, a giant ship, feeling the waves beneath the prow and knowing he was in command, was exhilarating. Under his uncle's guidance, he had learned the mathematics and rules of navigation, how to keep account of the ship's course. The fact was, if he needed to, he could do it all.

The *Nancy Grace,* he remembered, was named after his grandmother, who herself was a grand old gal and deserving of a craft being named after her. The boat was a three-mast sailing ship with a full suite of square-rigged sails. She housed a gaff sail on her stern most mast, and with her canvas in full bloom, John thought, *She surely is a beautiful sight.*

His uncle was British and had sailed several vessels in his life—the first when he was quite young and still lived in his native homeland. But when he met and married John's mother's sister, he then decided he could run a shipping business from Newry. It was located in the County Down in Northeastern Ireland, in the Province of Ulster, near where his wife had lived most of her life.

"She'll probably be my last ship, John; and when I die, I'll be turning the *Nancy Grace* over to you. You're my nephew, but you've always seemed like a son to me, and the only son I'll ever have," his uncle said.

Since he had no sons of his own, John was fully aware of how delighted his uncle had been at seeing him so captivated by the sea and to sailing.

"It gives me a feeling of satisfaction, and great pleasure to teach you all I know, John, and from being in the shipping business through these many years, I guess I know quite a lot," his uncle said, with a smile on his face.

Having made numerous trips transporting flax, John knew that, at that particular time, Ireland was knee-deep in the business of making linen, for he had heard that England, who had created numerous problems for the Irish though the years, was still encouraging the growth of that lucrative enterprise in Ulster, so that by the late 1700s it accounted for seventy percent of all Irish exports, and it continued to expand throughout the 1800s until production reached unprecedented levels. It seems that Ulster, in Northern Ireland, was the only province that had been totally obtained by the British.

John remembered his uncle talking about a set of laws that the British had established there, more than a hundred years before. "Those laws forced the Irish Catholics out of Ulster; however, there were some who did stay," he said. "They continued fighting the British, but eventually they failed as well, and were soon forced to leave the territory. After those people were gone, the Province of Ulster was virtually in the hands of the British government.

"During those years, years that became known as the 'Plantation of Ulster,' the British encouraged the Scottish, and

English men as well, to come into that region and occupy its fertile valleys, surrounded by that maze of hills." His uncle looked toward the mountains, which were now clothed with misty clouds. "Those settlers, who were mostly Protestant— Presbyterian I think—were then given land in parcels of one thousand acres or more by the British Crown. And, so that's how we got this land."

Having that knowledge, John could better understand why Ulster was the main supplier of linen, and why most of its farms grew flax. Still, it seemed, the need for flax was greater, by far, than what those farms could produce, so ships like the *Nancy Grace* had to transport it from America, to make up the difference.

"We anchored the *Nancy Grace* at the mouth of the Clanrye River in Newry," his uncle said, "since that's where my home is. Newry is the fourth largest city in Ulster, and it's well located as it's between Belfast and Dublin, the two largest seaports in Ireland."

In an effort to make a decision whether to sell the *Nancy Grace* or not, John took a long walk on the hills that overlooked the town. He loved that walk. It was refreshing, especially in the early hours of the day. Now though, he hoped the morning air would clear his mind, and help him make a decision: Should he keep the *Nancy Grace* or offer her up for sale?

Observing the scene beneath him, he thought about the small farm he owned that was not far from Newry. How thankful he had been for that farm, for it certainly had helped sustain life for him and his family through the years. *But, I can't think of that farm now; I have to make a decision. Should I sell the Nancy Grace or not? If I do sell her, I could use part of the money to help the Kellys,* John considered, as he remembered his wife's parents. *If ever they needed me, or the money I could provide, it certainly would be now!*

John knew that his father-in-law, Douglas Kelly, was a proud and at times obstinate man. John had often wondered why the Kellys had not left Ireland years before. *Of course, being a "pompous ol' bloke," he just wouldn't do it! And knowing him, as I do, he probably won't take the money either!*

He constantly felt a need to help Douglas and Ann Kelly, as they were tenant farmers. They lived outside of Ulster, yet their farm was not too far from Newry. It was in a county where the production of linen had not been as profitable, so he was aware how difficult it had been for them to scratch out a living on such a small amount of land. It left him with the responsibility of helping them pay their rent when it came due in the spring. It was a well-known fact that the Catholics in Ireland were the most wretched persons on earth. *Yes! A few years earlier, I wouldn't have been able to help them at all, since it was against the law for any Protestant to help a Catholic. Fortunately, those laws are changing and have now become more tolerant.*

John compassionately remembered the stories he heard about how the Catholics had suffered under the "Penal Laws," laws that the British had forced on them. "Those laws were designed to disarm, disinherit, and discredit anyone who was Catholic, in the hopes it might exterminate them, especially the aristocracy," Douglas Kelly said, "and for the many Catholics who remained in Ireland, it did exactly that!"

It was sad, as John remembered how that religion became a crucial social divide, and that the Kellys—whose family, at one time, was considered among the social elite—now, because they continued to cling to Catholicism, were among the downtrodden.

"Catholicism in Ireland was not as corrupted as it was in Rome," Douglas Kelly said. "And that was, probably, due to the fact that Ireland was so far away from Rome. It didn't feel its influence. Yes, it stayed pretty true to the faith."

As John walked the misty moors, he couldn't help but reminisce, remembering what Douglas Kelly had told him.

"Countless people, over the years, left Ireland for what they hoped would be a better life. Many joined battles in other countries far away, for they felt laying down their lives for a worthy cause was far better than staying here, where they would certainly die of starvation and humiliation. They left by the hundreds of thousands, as laws were being forced on them, laws that forbade them the right to receive an education, to enter a profession, to purchase land, to vote, to keep any arms for their protection, to buy land, and the list went on and on. They couldn't inherit land or rent any land that was worth more than thirty shillings a year, and they were forbidden to attend Catholic worship. Priests were banned and hunted with bloodhounds, and bishops were forced to leave the country," Douglas Kelly told him, with sadness in his voice.

Yes, it is sad, for the church Saint Patrick brought to this country, which changed Ireland from the pagan land it once was—giving its people a peaceful life, a good life—is now under attack, and because it is, people are being forced to leave this land by the droves!

He remembered his father-in-law talking about a set of laws which Saint Patrick had established in Ireland. "Those laws were based on precepts written in the Bible," Douglas Kelly said. "But the English turned their backs on those laws as well, and have slowly replaced them with an 'archaic feudal' system, a system that deprives us of our rights, treating us as though we're less than animals."

What is difficult to understand is how anyone professing a belief in Christ could treat another human being in such a way.

"It's a well-known fact," he remembered Douglas Kelly saying, "that about the time Henry VIII came to the throne in England, France and Spain became a real threat! It was felt that if either of those two countries took control of Ireland, they could use this island as a base for an attack against England. So, it seems, fear drove Henry VIII to extend his government into Ireland. Strongly influenced by Christianity, most if not all of Ireland was free land, but when Henry VIII stepped into the position of its primary lord, cleverly convincing the Gaelo-Norman lords and the Gaelic chieftains to accept him, they literally gave him the property rights of their people. It wasn't long until well-trained English officials took control of the government, and Catholic Ireland was on its way to serfdom.

"When Henry's daughter Elizabeth came to the throne, she spared no expense gaining military control of the island, as Spain, by that time, had proven to be a real threat. Within one century, from the time Henry VIII first sought control of Ireland, to the end of the century, the entire country was effectively ruled by the British, with each—England and Ireland—finding hatred and distaste for the other."

Well, it does seem that religion is the major stumbling block! And it certainly has brought unimaginable suffering to many Catholics, like my in-laws, who, not only stubbornly stayed in Ireland, but also had the fortitude to hang in here. John surmised this with some feelings of gratitude, for had they not stayed, he would have never met their daughter Margaret, who eventually became his wife and the mother of his two children.

Now, though, I have a decision to make. Should I keep the Nancy Grace, *or put her up for sale?*

"You know, John, your uncle was so excited knowing you would be in control of the *Nancy Grace*. I think of all the ships he's owned he loved the *Nancy Grace* the most, and that was because he had you right there beside him."

John stood with his aunt, looking out across the garden and the broad expanse of grass that encompassed her Newry home. The clouds, having parted for a time over the Cooley Mountains, allowed a ray of sun to beam down on them, bringing with it a feeling of peace. With her arm through his and a tiny tear forming in her eye, she made her plea.

"Please, John, keep the boat. I know he would want you to sail her again. He had planned that, I think, from the moment he first took you with him, when you sailed to England with that first load of linen. Do you remember? You were pretty young then. How old were you?"

"I don't know for certain. I think I was about eleven or maybe twelve, but I do remember feeling a bit of fear, and at the same time, I was eager to board that ship to see for myself what she was like. It was exciting, though a bit frightful too! I remember she hit some pretty strong headwinds, and was being tossed about as huge waves hit her prow, but Uncle soon had her under control. It was amazing what he could do and how much he knew. No need to fear when he was on board, that's for certain."

"Yes." Letting her arm drop, she bowed her head and closed her eyes. John wondered what she was thinking. *She's probably thinking about Uncle, missing him, but, of course not nearly as much as she will after the people are gone and she's alone.*

Well, that's that! How can I do anything less? He would keep the *Nancy Grace*. After all, owning it, and being the captain in control, he could now make the financial decisions. Later, when he had the time, he would look over his uncle's ledgers to see exactly what the expenses were and how much he could make shipping linen to the mainland, picking up flax in New York, and bringing it back to Ireland. And of course, there was always the "people"—those poor Irish souls, who were now fleeing the country to go to a new world they knew little about. Well, he certainly couldn't turn his back on their flight either!

Perhaps, if I kept the ship, there will be enough money to help my in-laws and to do all the other things I was thinking about. Well, only time—days, weeks, perhaps months—will tell. I'll have to wait and see. But I will sail the Nancy Grace*!*

Chapter 2

James Scott lay on the sandy beach exhausted, caring not if danger surrounded him. It would be better to face death, he thought as sleep inevitably overtook him, the sound of the surf fading as he gave way to unconsciousness.

When he awoke, the day was bright and beautiful. The sun, hitting his face, was high in the sky. *Must be about noon*, he thought. *I must remember this and be sure to write down what day it is.*

With that thought in mind, James pushed himself up on one arm, only to realize how sore he was. Sitting up and then standing, it pleased him to note there were no bones broken.

The beach was beautiful; he had never experienced anything like it. The color of the water was beyond his description, and the air was warm with a taste of salt in it. *God's creation,* he thought, and then it hit him—the shipwreck, his father's last words, and the thought that he would never see him again!

Here, surrounded by a beauty he could not put into words, was grief tugging his heart so much that it forced him to his knees and to cry out, "Oh God, what have I done to deserve this?"

When he opened his eyes again, he saw something floating in the water. *Part of the ship,* he thought, and then he saw more rubble washing upon the sand. On further examination, he could see the foremast, which had been cut away during the worst part of the storm to keep the ship from foundering.

Remembering that, he also remembered the terrible shaking of the boat as the wind hit the main mast, tossing the boat onto the rocky reef that surrounded the island where he now found himself.

Trying to reconstruct the scene, he searched in vain for anything that might bring back some semblance of what had taken place in the last twenty-four to forty-eight hours—anything that would give cause for, and thus help alleviate, the grief he now felt.

Here he was, only twenty-two years of age, and now finding himself on an island somewhere in the southern Atlantic Ocean. It was late October 1822. His father had drowned, as had all the others aboard the ship. He seemed to be alone on the island, as there was no evidence of any other human life, at least none that he could see.

But then, maybe I'm not alone. Part of this island could be inhabited, perhaps by people of a stranger kind—an uncivilized creature of sorts, doing God only knows what!

Well, he couldn't think about that now. There were other things more pressing, like the insatiable hunger he was now experiencing, and the pain. The bleeding had stopped from the wound he had received when his back hit the sharp edges of the coral, but would the pain ever cease? Fortunately, it only hurt when he exerted himself. As long as he took care not to push himself, it was tolerable; and so he walked the beach, searching for anything or anyone that would or could make some sense of it all. But the longer he searched, the more desperate he became, and soon found himself yelling, "Hello, is anyone there?"

Over and over again he shouted, hoping against hope there would be someone, some creature who might hear his cries and come to his rescue, but he did so in vain, and soon realized it was useless.

When he turned to walk back to the place where he had first hit the beach, a thought entered his mind. It was as though a voice was speaking to him: *"James, pick up the rubble. You may never need it, but pick it up anyway. Put it in a safe place away from the surf."*

Finding it painful to bend, James used his feet at first, kicking the lighter objects away from the water. Bending his knees and lifting the heaver things, with his back as straight as he could keep it, he managed to clear the beach. There were still larger objects floating. *"Don't worry about those. They will soon land on the beach. You can get them later,"* the thought pierced his mind again.

He found many things on the beach from the wreckage. Most of it he could not identify, but he did recognize a small box. Surprisingly, it belonged to him, but he left it with the rest of the stuff, realizing, suddenly, how thirsty he was.

I must find water.

So he left the beach, desperately looking for water—fresh water, water he could drink. In so doing he headed toward the strange-looking trees that lined the sand. Leaves from odd-looking plants covered the ground, and they were filled with rainwater from the storm the night before. *Thank you, God* flashed through his mind, as he, momentarily forgetting the pain, bent over and grabbed leaf after leaf and started drinking. Everything went down, including a few small black objects floating in the water. Having pushed the pain from his thoughts, he now drank until he was satisfied, but with the water came a chill, a sudden shuddering feeling of coldness. He wondered if it was not caused by the cool October air, or perhaps from the overwhelming despair he felt. It seemed strange to feel cold, since he was naturally a warm-natured sort of person.

It was getting later in the day now, and the hunger was beyond anything he could have ever conceived. Looking at the beach he had just cleared, he saw something shining in the late afternoon sun, half-buried in the sand. On closer examination, he saw it was a bottle. He picked it up, only to find it partly filled with a liquid he could not identify. Perhaps it was the "rum" he had heard the pirates talking about the night before the storm. There were two of them on deck, fighting over a bottle filled with some sort of liquid. *Yes it was rum, they called it "rum."*

Pulling it out of the sand, his thoughts were of using the bottle to capture some of the water before it evaporated—water he could use for drinking until he could find a better source.

The sun was low in the sky now, and James was growing weary. He needed rest, but he also needed to find a place where it would be safe for him until morning. He wanted desperately to fill the bottle before the water evaporated from the plantings, but what to do with the "rum"? Alcohol had not played a major role in his life; still, he was cold and he was hungry. It was tempting to open the bottle and at least take a swallow of the liquid. Perhaps it would help him sleep. Night was coming, and he knew the darkness would be all-consuming. So, opening the bottle, lifting it over his arm, he took a big swig of its contents. Wow! He was right, it was "rum," and he could feel a burning sensation all the way down into his stomach. Well, at least his stomach had something in it now, even though it felt as if it were on fire. *Maybe another swallow won't be as bad,* he thought, as he took another big drink or two.

After a time he began feeling a bit warmer and perhaps not quite so weary, less stressed too and therefore less threatened, so he decided to push himself into the thicket of bulging plants to look for a place where he could lodge for the night. He gingerly stepped over some tangled roots he supposed were from the strange-looking trees that encircled him. He found a clearing there, among the plants. *Here would be a good place*, he thought as he surveyed his surroundings. Perhaps he could take some of the ship's planks he found on the beach and make a shelter in case it rained again. With those thoughts in mind, he walked back to the pile of wreckage to look for anything he might find suitable, and there on top of the rubble was the box. He had taken it with him, when he and his father and some of the seamen who had survived the attack were forced aboard the *Bald Hornet*. It was a small box—not anything that would attract much attention hidden in the blouse of his shirt, but in it were some treasured items. For one thing, there was a small pocketknife, which he knew would certainly come in handy now.

Seating himself on the sand at the edge of the thicket, crossing his legs, he opened the box. Yes, there was his pocketknife and some smaller items he might find useful, but digging deeper his hand fell on something hard and round, something he had all but forgotten. What was it? *Oh, my God! How could I have not remembered?* Lifting it from deep inside, reflecting the late afternoon sun, was a small gold locket. As he pulled it from among the other items, it sprang open and out spiraled a ringlet of beautiful strawberry blond hair. A little bit of mist filled his eyes now. Perhaps it was the aftereffects of the rum, he thought, but deep within his heart, he knew that this loss would be the greatest—and remembering now would only add to his misery and his desperation. At the same time, his heart kept saying, *How could I have forgotten? Was there any sound reason why I would not, could not have remembered . . . Mary?*

Chapter 3

Mary White leaned over the gate as far as it would allow. It connected with the palings that surrounded the yard of the boarding house where she was now living. If she stretched far enough, she could see South Street, the port, and pier number seven. It was down the street, only a few blocks away, and on beyond the pier laid New York City's East River. That is where she saw him last. Sadness gripped her heart. Although she had not known him well, still she knew, deep within her heart, that she had felt something for this tall, genuinely generous, good-looking Scotch-Irish fellow with the laughing blue-gray eyes that she had never felt before. As she stood there, the words of a song came to her mind. It was a song she had sung many times, never realizing that those words would one day hold a meaning that would spring true for her.

The day was long and the day was short when you left to go to the sea.

The wind did howl and the wind did sing, what was it telling me?
That though I thought I knew you then, I never knew your heart.
And now I know the wind and cold since we are now apart.
The night was long and the night was cold when they told me of your fate
And though you seem so real to me, you were not at the gate.
And though I thought I knew you then, I never knew your heart
And now I know the wind and cold since we are now apart. . . .

Mary White, who was also Scotch-Irish, had hoped to come to America with the last ship of immigrants from Belfast, but as it turned out she came on the *Nancy Grace*.

One evening, as she sat before the supper table with her father, he said to her, "Mary, my daughter, you know how hard I've worked trying to keep this farm and all my other holdings together. Certainly we have been blessed over these last few years, as there hasn't been any outside threats or problems with the authorities for a long time. It seems that, maybe, life, here in Ireland has finally found some stability. But it is tenuous, seeming always to depend on the political weather, which, for many years now, has kept me on the defensive. Mercy, I remember when most of our farms supported only one family, but, as you well know, since your brothers are married now, this farm is struggling to support several families. I'm saying all of this to say to you, go—go to America. Any place is better than staying here, but Mary, my daughter, before you leave you must have a husband. I can't let you go without someone to look after you, someone to care for you, as I would do, were I going, too."

Mary knew it would be difficult for her father to let his daughters go. She remembered him saying, "I realize, Mary, if you and your sister leave, there's a grave possibility I will never see you again. Of course, I also know that if you stay here, there's a good chance I will lose you anyway! Most young girls who marry have to leave their family farms to move many miles away, or are forced, along with their husbands, to leave the country. So sending you away to a foreign land, though it certainly isn't something I had planned on doing, I do believe is the best thing for you, especially since you want to go. I'm just thankful there is family in America, and that somehow you will be able to connect with them, especially if you need their help."

That certainly took Mary by surprise. She remembered the many conversations over the last several months she had with her sister Rachel, when she found out Rachel was leaving to go to America. She knew Rachel and her husband Will had postponed their trip three times, in the hopes that she might be able to find a way to go with them, but now they could not, nor did they want to, postpone their trip any longer; and so, with sadness, Rachel had told Mary, "We'll be leaving soon to go to Belfast to catch the next ship for America."

She remembered saying to Rachel, "I would love to go with you, but what would father say if he found out that I want to go, too?"

"I don't know, Mary, but you had better be prepared for a struggle, as I don't think he will take kindly to the idea. He wasn't very happy when I told him *we* were leaving."

Mary knew how fortunate she was to have four older brothers, all of whom were able-bodied. They were married, with families of their own, and had been a godsend for her father, who struggled to produce flax for the linen market. She wondered if it wouldn't be easier, now, for her father to let her and Rachel go, knowing it might be a better life for them, and especially since he still had his sons at home to help with the planting and the harvest.

Later that evening Mary and Rachel talked again.

"Oh Mary, I am so happy for you," Rachel said, as she gave Mary a hug. "It seems father isn't going to stop you."

"Yes, but he said I must have a husband. He won't let me go without one. How will I ever accomplish that? The only laddies I know are the Kelly boys, and of course, those men they hired to help with the farm, but they're not anyone I would be interested in marrying."

"Well, Mary, perhaps you can come to Belfast with us, to at least see the boat we will be taking, and to just be there to say our last farewell. Who knows, maybe by some miracle you might meet him, the lad you will marry. We will pray, and see if our prayers will be answered. You must know how very much we want you to go. It just won't be the same without you."

They did pray, but Mary didn't believe it for a minute. *It would be nice, but I know it won't happen. I'll not meet him, that man, whomever he is, that I am to marry!*

⌒

They met quite by accident. Who would have guessed that she being merely eighteen, and he almost twenty-two, could have met that way? What were the chances, beyond divine intervention?

Mary and Rachel had said their last farewell. As Mary stood on the jetty, watching her father helping her sister board the ship, with tears swelling in her eyes, spilling out, soaking her rosy cheeks, she saw him. He was just standing there with a curious look on his face. *Why,* she asked herself, *is that fellow looking at me?*

Frustration drove her to ask, "Sir, you're staring at me! Why?" She turned to face him fully, with her blue eyes sparkling behind the moisture from the tears.

"I think I've seen you before, in Bellikiel."

"Oh?"

"Yes, my father used to own a farm not far from there. I'm sorry for staring at you, but I would like to help, if there's anything I might do. You seem so distressed!"

"Oh, no, sir, I don't need your help! You see, my sister is leaving. She and her husband have boarded the *Jupiter* and will be sailing in a few hours for America. I wanted so much to go with them, but my father will not allow me to go by myself. For you see, I'm not married."

"My, a pretty lass like you, I wouldn't think that would be a difficult task to accomplish."

She liked the way he talked—unabated, beguiling. Who was this seemingly refined gentleman? She wanted to know, so she asked.

"Sir, I'm Mary White, but I don't believe I know who you are?"

"I'm James Scott. My father John Scott owns the ship, the *Nancy Grace,* and I'm his first mate in charge of the crew, and if need be, taking the helm. We arrived a few days ago from New York and will be sailing again within the week, as we need to return there as soon as possible."

"Your father owns the *Nancy Grace*? I've heard of that ship. I like the name!"

"Well, she was named after my great-grandmother. I never knew her—that is, my great-grandmother—but they tell me she was a fine lady. So tell me, Mary, do you live in Bellikiel?"

"No sir, my father owns a farm not far from there, but I do have an aunt who lives in Bellikiel that I sometimes visit."

"My father's farm was near there also. Perhaps our fathers know each other," James said. "I was born in America. I never lived in Ireland, but I love hearing about it. My father lived in the County Down most of his life, but was gone much of the time, as he has been at sea since he was twelve."

Suddenly, Mary heard her name being called. As she turned, she saw her father running toward her.

"Mary, Mary, COME! Rachel, she's waving from the ship. You can see her. Go that way, down the boardwalk to the wharf.

The ship is anchored in the bay. Hurry and wave your good-byes before the boat leaves."

Mary turned again to look at her father, and then looked back, yelling as she ran toward the quay, "Father, that's James Scott. I just met him. His father owns the *Nancy Grace*. He used to live in the County Down."

James was dismayed Mary was leaving so suddenly; he felt a tug at his heart, for it flashed through his mind that he may never see her again.

"How do you do Mr. Scott? I'm Jacob White," Mary's father responded, holding out his hand to the young man now standing before him. "Hope my daughter hasn't been too brazen. She's feeling a bit sad right now. Her sister is leaving and she so wants to go with her, but I cannot permit that. She's by herself and it is just too dangerous for her to go without a mate."

"Sir, she was just telling me. I feel bad for her. Perhaps. . . ."

James never finished his sentence, for he saw his father approaching.

Recognizing Jacob White, his old friend, John Scott reached out with his arm, first to take the hand of Jacob White, then to embrace him with it.

"My, my, it is so good to see you, Jacob. How are you and how's the wife and family?"

"Well, well, I wondered, when my daughter Mary said that Mr. Scott, here . . ." James saw him nod his heard in his direction, "that his father owned the *Nancy Grace*, if it wasn't you. I didn't think you'd sold it, but I haven't seen you in years. My wife is as great as ever, and do you know I have four sons? Yes, and they're all married, and I now have seven grandsons, but only one granddaughter," Jacob said.

"My, my, how time passes. Well, we're living in New York now, in America. I sold my farm in '98 after that siege near Newry. I'm sure you remember the Britons, along with the Orange Yeomen, burned a great many homes there, and then when the English government proclaimed Martial Law, I knew it was over, and time for me to leave the country," John Scott said.

"Oh, yes, how well I remember. They were trying to stop the 'United Irishmen.'"

James, totally captivated now with the conversation that was taking place, looked at Jacob White with anticipation, for he wanted to know more. He had heard about the trouble in Ireland, but certainly had not been a part of it, as most of it took place several years before he was born. Now, though, here he was standing with two men who had witnessed it firsthand.

"Bless his heart and theirs," Jacob said, as he looked at James. "I believe it was in '96, wasn't it John, when a son of a Presbyterian minister reached out to the Catholics in Ireland, declaring that the Protestants and Catholics needed to set aside their differences and unite for the good of the country."

"Was he able to gain their support?"

"Yes he was, James. He gained a good amount of support from many Catholic priests and Presbyterian clergymen in Ulster as well. They were all hoping they might get some control back for the Irish and some concessions for the Catholics, too, as they had suffered horribly under those Penal Laws."

"So were they able to do it?"

"Well, it seems England wasn't going to allow that to happen, and so they set out to dismantle them, and they didn't care if every crime, every cruelty was committed in the process—and well, I must say, they certainly did stop them!" Jacob White said.

"I believe the Britons had their headquarters near Newry, didn't they, John? It was a bad time, and it only added to bad times, too dreadful to think about now!"

James looked at Jacob White and could see his eyes fill with sadness. Then he heard his father say, "Yes, and it was then that I knew I had to get my family out of Ireland, and it was an easy feat, since I owned my own ship. I decided to take them to America. America was like home anyway, since I had made so many trips there. But not only did I take my family, but I took my wife's parents too, Douglas and Ann Kelly, and my grandmother's sister, who by the way lived in Newry and experienced some shameful, horrible days during those times.

"My in-laws have a large home in New York now. They turned it into a boarding house where they can take in passengers when they first arrive in America to help them get settled. It seems to be working out well for them. Of course, those passengers have to be Irish, you know, nothing but Irish."

Suddenly James heard Mary's voice, screaming "Father!" Running toward them, she yelled "Rachel's ship has been delayed. It isn't sailing until the morrow. They're getting off the boat."

Jacob looking puzzled, quietly, as if thinking out loud, said "Oh, goodness, now what do we do? It's too far to go home."

"Tell you what, Jacob—why don't you all spend the night on the *Nancy Grace*? We aren't sailing for several days. You can take your time. Decide what you want to do. There's always room on our ship for friends." John Scott offered.

While Jacob White and Mary made their way through the crowd disembarking the *Jupiter* to find Rachel and her husband Will, James and John Scott left to prepare for overnight guests on the *Nancy Grace*.

"Father, I want to marry her."

"What? What are you saying?" John Scott was now giving his son his full attention, as they walked toward the longboat that would take them to the *Nancy Grace.*

"Oh father, it has been difficult to find a fair maid to marry. I'm always at sea and though I see many a lass, there hasn't been one like Mary. The first time I saw her in Bellikiel I knew that I had felt something for her. So I really do want to marry her, if she will have me; and she needs to marry, as she wants to go with her sister to America, but Mr. White won't let her go without a husband. Will you marry us?"

"Well, James she does come from a good family, that's for certain. Yes, if she will have you, I will marry you, but you must be sure this is what you want to do."

There was time now—a few precious hours to talk before the *Jupiter* sailed—and that is what James and Mary did. They talked until the wee hours of the morning, and then he asked her,

"Mary, if you and I were to marry, perhaps your father would let you go with us to America when we leave next Thursday, and we could take your sister and her husband as well! My father knows William Hutchins, the master of the *Jupiter*. We'll talk to him and get your sister's husband's money back. But Mary, since we don't know each other well, we can be married in name only, or until we know each other better. I will let you decide when the time is right to consummate the marriage. If you should decide you don't want to be married to me, we can have the marriage annulled, and you can be on your way. I care enough for you to wait, to let you have some time to make that decision."

Mary quickly turned her head toward him, and when she did, he could see surprise was written across her face.

"Oh James, I didn't expect a marriage proposal. If we were to marry, then I could go to America with my sister. She and I have been praying for this very thing to happen, but I didn't believe it would, no not even for a moment did I believe.

"But, I'll have to give you my answer on the morrow, James, for I must have time now to think, and I will have to ask my father for permission, you know? And you must speak to him as well, or he will never give his consent."

James and Mary were married, but in name only, for James made good on his promise, and never even once told Mary that he loved her. *I'll wait until she knows me better, for I feel certain that perfect, special moment in time will come! Yes, it will happen!*

And so Mary waited too. . . .

Chapter 4

"All aback forward!" James yelled, standing on the forecastle of the ship.

Facing the high winds, which had pushed the ship backward, he suddenly became aware the line had broken, causing the sails to flap around violently.

"Worst of all fears would be for those winds to tear that mast down," James said to one of the seamen standing beside him, as he pointed to a tall pole rising from the deck of the ship

As he looked up, he was relieved to see that the sailors had the rigging under control, but a feeling of sadness encumbered him. Still he was pleased, knowing the *Nancy Grace* was able to set sail within the week, and that Mary, her sister Rachel, and Will were all on board, along with nearly a hundred others—desperate people, people willing to be crowded together on his ship. For most of them, from Northern Ireland, were seeking asylum in the new world, escaping a life too difficult to endure, and the crisis had been made worse by a harvest failure, followed by a slump in the linen trade.

Now, though, he worried, they could be facing an arduous journey crossing the sea, and there was nothing he could do about it, other than what had already been done.

His greatest fear was that the trip, which usually took about six weeks, could be made much longer, for the headwinds that were quite strong had caused the *Nancy Grace* to fight to gain even a small amount of time. It became a concern for him, as it was now August and the flax season was fully upon them. Soon the harvesting of the fibers would be completed and the flax, coming from the Hudson River Valley and the fields of Pennsylvania and Maryland, would be arriving in New York, ready for transportation to Europe. He knew the timing was crucial, for if the *Nancy Grace* could make it to the New York Port in time, they might be able to pick up a large load before the season was over.

Struggling to keep his stance with these heavy winds blowing about him, he remembered his father saying; "It's important to harvest the flax, James, when it reaches a certain color, for if it is removed too early, while still green, the fibers will be very fine and weak; however, if it overripens the stems will be strong and brittle, and the fibers too short. It's essential to capture them when they are yellow, for then the fibers will be long and supple, ideal for processing."

James was aware that in America the yellowing usually started in early August, making the flax ready for harvesting, drying and transportation to Europe by the middle to the end of the month. It was now the middle of the second week in August. He wondered, could they make it back in time to pick up a large load? Concern now filled his mind. But right now, of course, there were *the people*. Getting them safely across the sea, he knew, would be a challenge.

As James stood on the deck, struggling to keep his stance with the high winds whipping about him, he thought of Mary. Since the ship was experiencing stronger than usual headwinds, it had forced him to attend to the ship, leaving little time for her. He was pleased that he and Mary did have a few hours to spend together before the ship left the quay; but not knowing her well, nor having the time to talk at any great length, he was careful, almost reticent, about what he said to her. When they did speak, it was about the essential things—his concern for her safety, as well as the other passengers, which was always upper-most on his mind, for he knew that on such a long journey there could be hazards ahead.

Now, with the ship experiencing stronger-than-usual head-winds, a more anxious feeling flooded over him, for the voyage could be delayed, making the threat of danger an even more likely possibility.

To get themselves out of the high wind, Mary, along with Rachel and Will, were being pushed now into the steerage, as people, nearly a hundred, were crowding into the between-deck. She wondered how she might survive in such a small area, which was not more than six to eight feet high. She could see that bunks had been placed along the sides, leaving room for only a small corridor that ran between them. As many as three to six people now scrambled to sit on a single bed, along with the fleas and lice which made their homes in the straw mattresses.

"Our captain is a hard and impulsive man!" Mary heard the person next to her say.

"Yes, but he does have our welfare at heart," she responded, "for we could be on deck being swept overboard."

Mary looked at Rachel, as they covered their mouths with their hands. "The air is stifling." Mary muffled the words, as she strained to see Rachel through the darkness.

She remembered James saying that because of the high winds and waves, ventilation could become a serious problem, as the pipes used to ventilate the ship, would have to be closed to prevent water from leaking into the steerage and other parts of the ship. Mary wondered what might happen if the awful weather persisted. Would they have enough air to breathe?

Since the vents were now closed, darkness enveloped her; the vents were the only source of light. "Oil lamps can't be used, for with the pitching and tilting of the ship they could easily spill, causing a fire," James had told her. She strained to see even the smallest amount of light, light which forced its way through the cracks and crevices over her head.

With the tilting and pitching of the ship, Mary could sense people being jostled from their beds, as they went sliding about, knocking each other over. Many were now experiencing sickness, complaining of headaches and stomach pains, which soon gave way to vomiting. Those who were not sick were now made sick from the stench of others. This went on for more than an hour, before Mary saw one of the seamen coming down the steps with a bucket in his hand.

"Ho! I've come to help clear the air." He said as he grabbed a red-hot iron and dipped it into the tar in the bucket he was holding. The smoke and steam from the bubbling tar began to penetrate the smell and did seem to help with the stench; at least it deadened the worst of the unpleasant odor. However, Mary noticed that the smoke was as bad as, if not worse than, the foul air.

In such an atmosphere it was not long before Mary too began to experience nausea. Grabbing her stomach, she wondered what she might do if she threw up, when somewhere—amidst the coughs, sighs, and wails of the other passengers—she heard her name being called. Straining to see through the darkness, she suddenly became aware that James was standing in front of her.

"Are you alright, Mary?"

Mary could barely answer him, and he could tell she was hurting. He bent down, and whispered in her ear, "Follow me!" He motioned for Rachel and Will to follow him as well.

Soon they found themselves in a small room on an upper deck; James called it the chart room, or roundhouse. It was in this small room, she learned, that the planning and plotting of the ship's progress was initiated. The air here was much cleaner, as a fresh breeze filled the room every time the doors opened.

"I'm so sorry, Mary, that you have to go through this. Are you alright?" James leaned over to ask her again, making certain she heard him.

"I am a little seasick," Mary said, trying not to complain, as she placed her hand over her mouth, for she really didn't feel well at all. Sitting down in a chair near the door, she said to James, "It helps being here, for I do think I am feeling a little better now."

"I regret you all have to endure this. We weren't counting on the weather being quite this bad! I feel sorry too, for all those people in the steerage," James said, wanting them to know he did have compassion, but also had a handle on the situation as well. He knew what they were going through, as it had happened before, many times, but there was nothing that could be done, nothing more than what they were already doing.

"I don't mean to frighten you, but we could have an outbreak of black fever. Do pray that doesn't happen, for it has, on many of these ships in similar circumstances. We've been fortunate so far, as it hasn't happened, yet, on ours. I do hope you will be more comfortable here. I'll check on you again soon." As James left the small room, she saw him force the door closed, as the wind continued its mighty fury.

As it turned out, she saw little of James for several days. However, Will, out of curiosity, did open the door from time to time to see what was happening on deck, and then reported his findings to Rachel and Mary.

"I can see James! The sails have been badly torn. Some have even been ripped from their spars. He's directing the men repairing them, and is now telling those sailors to trim them back. I guess they have to set them at a certain angle in order to take advantage of the wind. What a job! The waves are like mountains of water." Will told them, as he gripped the handle firmly to keep the wind from pulling the door out of his hands.

"You know," Will said, closing the door again, "it's difficult to believe that we all are putting ourselves through this. I'm feeling a little of the nausea myself now." He quickly found a chair, sat down, and put his bare feet upon the chart-table. "I'm sure, though," he continued, "that most of those people in the steerage would rather take their chance of surviving on this ship than staying in Ireland. What a shame that life there for many borders on slavery, perhaps even death. Thank God for America. That country is truly a blessing."

With the strong winds and vast waves Mary, Rachel, and now Will had become sick, but being in the roundhouse seemed to help. There, at least, they had room to move about, and certainly plenty of fresh air to breathe.

On the few occasions when James did look in on them, he could tell they were miserable, but there was nothing he could do; he prayed for the wind to become manageable, and within a week it did. Finally the air shifted, calming the sea. The air current, which was now coming out of the southeast, allowed the *Nancy Grace* to pick up speed, moving her steadily across the sea toward her destination.

With a more moderate wind, the sails properly trimmed, and the ship on a steady course, James and his father had time now to relax. So many evenings found them at the master's table enjoying a meal with Mary, Rachel, and Will. They were family now, so it was good having time together, getting to know one another. Will, with his quick wit, entertained them, but it was not long before the conversation turned to an explanation about the place where they were going.

"Because of its easy access to the sea, New York is a great city," Captain John told them, "and with the completion of the Erie Canal, which is in the process of being built, it will probably become an even greater city."

"What and where is the Erie Canal?" Will asked.

"They built the canal in the upper part of the state of New York. Their hope is that it will connect some large bodies of water called the Great Lakes with the Atlantic Ocean, by way of the Hudson River which flows along the west side of New York City. When that happens, more produce and goods from the Midwest will be pouring into the New York harbor," John said.

James and John had found it fascinating learning about the country and were more than willing to tell anyone who was interested about what they had learned. Now, it seemed, the new arrivals were captivated by what they were hearing and wanted to know more.

"There's hope that the Erie Canal, when finished, might make some needed social and economic changes, as they say it will open the door to the West, giving people access to rich farm land, and other resources, on the other side of the Appalachian Mountains," James said. "We've heard the Northwest Territory is rich in timber and minerals and is great land for farming. Of course getting to that area can be a challenge. I've heard it's a bit dangerous too, and certainly time-consuming, but with the opening of the canal, the trip to and from the West will be easier and, hopefully in the long run, less expensive. And, it will probably make New York one of the greatest commercial cities in America. I can just see it now, barge-loads of farm products and raw materials coming into the city, and manufacturing goods and supplies leaving its shores."

"I have family in the West," Will said, "I wonder how difficult it would be to find them?"

"That's a good question. Unfortunately, I don't know that there is a good answer. They say it will take only a little more than two years to finish the canal. Actually, a portion of it is already completed. But when it's done, it will open the Hudson River to the states in the interior. Of course we're happy about that, as one of the major crops in that region is flax," James said.

＝＝

It was the twenty-fourth of September when the *Nancy Grace* pulled into New York Harbor. It certainly was later than John and James had planned, but at least they made it safely across the sea. Since the ship was two weeks behind schedule, it left them little time to waste.

The harbor near the lower end of Manhattan was deep, allowing most ships to dock larboard, or portside. So they pulled the *Nancy Grace* into the dock on the larboard side, which kept the right, starboard side free. Doing so prevented damage to her rudder, but James knew that it would also make it easier for them to load flax.

＝＝

As Mary stood on the deck of the ship waiting to get off, she looked out across the East River port. The sight amazed her, as the port was booming. South Street, which stretched several miles along its bank, was full of activity. There were a hundred or more sailing ships, either anchored in the harbor or along its miles of wharf. Most of their sails were gone, as they were either folded or being repaired; she could see a jungle of ropes hanging from bare spars, looking like a giant spider-web. Their bowsprits, pointing upward and outward, seemed to her to command attention, as if giving an image of soldiers waiting for orders—or perhaps, she thought with a smile on her face, *they're just saluting the people passing by.*

And there were many people passing by, as the East River port was a busy and an impressive sight; everything was in constant motion. Hundreds of sailors were bustling by, carters driving in every direction, laborers engaged in or in the process of engaging work, and merchants and their clerks wagering deals. The coffeehouses were teeming with people. And waiting to be picked up were bales, barrels, tubs, boxes, and cases sitting on or beside the wharf! Mary wondered what might be in those containers, as she remembered the flax the *Nancy Grace* was picking up.

John and James had little time to spend with family, as they said their "hello" and "goodbye, sorry, but we have to be going." The family understood, as it had happened before many times, but it always made it easier knowing that soon they would be reunited again when the *Nancy Grace* pulled into port for the winter. It was a time to look forward to, as it made a harsh winter tolerable, and helped the fall pass quickly as well—for when they came back, they would not be leaving again for several weeks, or perhaps months, depending on the weather. It was always a comfort knowing that, but for now they had only one evening to spend together, and so they made the most of it.

Mary walked with James along the cobblestone streets of the city toward Battery Park. She was feeling much better, and said to him, "It's good having both of my feet on solid ground."

The nausea had left, and the thought of a more secure environment gave her a feeling of warmth, for she would be staying with James' mother when he took off the next day for Ireland. Still, sadness gripped her heart, for James was leaving. Mary was pleased that her sister Rachel would not be far away, as the Kellys boarding house was down the street only blocks from James' mother's home.

She wondered how long it would take Will to find work, get settled, and perhaps even buy a house one day. Of course, that house might be in Pennsylvania, or some other place! *Oh, dear, and I will have to stay here, in New York, with James—or rather, with his mother, as he won't even be here most of the time.* She could not think about that now. James was leaving. A feeling of fear and sadness overtook her for a moment, then she said, "Your mother is a delight to know, James. I'm so thankful to you and to her, for letting me stay there while you are gone."

"I'm thankful too, Mary, you like her, and that you're feeling much better. When I come back from Europe I will bring a ring for your finger. I'm sorry we didn't have time to purchase one before we set sail. If you like, perhaps, we could be married again here, in a church. I was hoping we would have more time now to spend together, but the *Nancy Grace* must sail on the morrow, as the flax will not keep forever."

She wanted him to know that while he was gone she would be thinking of him, missing him, but finding it difficult putting those feelings into words, she said nothing. It seemed, how-ever, that she could not put a damper on her thoughts. *He's a stranger. I don't know him at all. We certainly did not have much time together on that boat, coming to America, and now he's leaving. I wonder; does he love me? Maybe he married me because he felt sorry for me.* Those thoughts hurt! Still, she continued to wonder, *If I have no feelings for him, then why am I so sad that he is leaving? Could it be that I do care for him? But how can I tell this complete stranger how I feel, and how can I find out what he's thinking about me?*

With an ache in her heart, she realized there was no way she could tell him what she was thinking, and now those thoughts, coupled with all the chaos, emotional stress, and disorientation of the last several months—leading up to and along with the arduous journey crossing the sea—was almost more than she could bear. The journey was not at all like what she had dreamed it would be. Mary was thankful Rachel was with her; still, she missed her father and mother. *I probably will never see them again.* With sadness in her heart she looked up at James thinking, *Do you love me, James Scott? How can I know?*

Instead, she simply said, "I really do miss my mother and father. It was difficult saying goodbye to them, as I may never see them again."

In a sense, she was trying to tell him just how much he had come to mean to her—how much she needed him now—but it was awkward. She was only eighteen and had never opened her heart to a man, and this man was more of a stranger than even a friend. So she evaded the subject, hoping that somehow James might come to realize how she felt.

But James had a world of other thoughts on his mind. Could they make it to Ireland before the flax molded, or was ravaged by disease? Would the weather cooperate? How much time would they have when they did reach Ireland, and could they make it back to America before the cold of winter set in? He knew Mary would be secure living with his mother as long as they found favor with each other, but what would happen if Mary decided she didn't fit in, if she became unhappy and wanted to leave? Well, all he could do now was pray that wouldn't happen. Of course, having all these concerns to ponder, to plan, pushed any emotional thoughts he may have had of her from his mind.

"James, if I were to write a letter to my parents, could you find a way to deliver it when you return to Ireland?"

"Of course I will try, but our time will be limited Mary, but even if it is, there are always people going through Billikell who can deliver a letter. I will find a way Mary. I promise you. And when I come back, I will be here for a while, as we won't sail again until March or maybe even later. We'll have more time then to spend together, to really get to know each other. So while I'm gone, if it pleases you, think about plans for a church wedding." He was thinking that perhaps planning a real church wedding might keep her busy, and help her get through the next couple of months until he returned.

However, he did not realize what was really on her mind—for she was not thinking about a wedding, but how she might tell him, before he left, that she would be counting every minute, and that every minute would seem like hours, days, years, until she saw him again . . . and it would be.

The next morning, fog took over South Street Port, bringing with it a cold, damp chill—an ominous sign, yet no one recognized it as such—when the *Nancy Grace*, preparing for what would be her final voyage, pulled out of the New York port. Though the fog delayed their departure, it was not long before the sun came out, lifting the mist, making way for the *Nancy Grace* to set sail again. But just as the boat was pulling out of the quay Mary came running, yelling as she ran.

"James, James, here, I want to give you something. Put it in your pocket, and whenever you see it, let it remind you of me." Mary stretched up the side of the ship, while James leaned over as far as he could, to take the shining gold locket from her hand.

"Oh, Mary, are you sure you want me to have it?" James yelled. "I'll keep it beside me always, Mary, and don't worry, I'll see you soon. God keep you, my. . . ."

Mary couldn't hear his last words, as the *Nancy Grace* had left the wharf and was turning into the brackish waters of the East River, heading out toward the bay and the sea beyond…

Chapter 5

It was Tuesday, October 15, 1822; they had been at sea for two weeks. When the sun came up that day, casting its light on the world, it promised to not only be a beautiful day but an exceptional one. It was one of those mornings that captured the imagination, turning thoughts into dreams, desires into prayers. The sun, spreading its warmth, seemed to move effortlessly over the clouds. It swept the horizon, leaving streaks of yellow, gold, and orange. Soon the clouds disappeared like a canopy opening on a stage, exposing an azure sky, which reached down to touch the water below, becoming one with the sea, as if making a statement: "All is well with the world; sail on my brothers, sail on."

One could almost hear music in the wind. It was coming directly from the west hitting the rigging, flipping the sails, beating out a tune that kept in time with the waves as they whipped the sides of the ship, helping to push the *Nancy Grace* forward toward her destination.

The view of the sea and the sounds of the wind were so beautiful that it spread a soothing peace across the tired faces of the seamen who, more often than not, experienced harsh conditions; a sailor's world was anything but easy.

As James watched the tranquil scene now displayed before his eyes, a calmness filled his heart—a serenity which, in turn, produced thoughts of Mary. James had to come to grips now with his feelings. Yes, he did love her! He loved her laugh, her turned-up little nose, the strawberry blond hair that fluffed her face with ringlets of curls dancing across her forehead, her beautiful, lucid, blue-green eyes. He even loved the pain he saw in those eyes as she remembered her mother and father, missing them so. He loved her small body, her tiny, narrow waist that curved in from her hips, producing in him feelings, desires he had never felt before. Mary, how sweet she was, all five-foot-two of her. His only hope now was to make it to Europe and back as fast as he could to be with her again. Even as he entertained those thoughts, an ache went through his heart, as he sensed her needing him. Yet here he was in the middle of an ocean, miles from her, and sailing farther and farther away.

Though the pain of missing her tugged at his heart, still the beauty of the day, which was now displayed before him, brought with it a peace—and with that, a promise that all would go well and that soon he would return to be with her again.

But later that day everything began to change. The afternoon sun, as if touched by magic, suddenly left the sky covered by clouds that grew larger and darker causing the azure sky to turn an indigo hue, and then to black. Soon the wind, changing direction, picked up dramatically, pushing the clouds away only to reveal clouds more menacing than the ones before.

Just another afternoon shower? James wondered.

Still the sky seemed different somehow, as the air current, which started out as a gentle blow, had gained velocity and was now coming out of the northeast. It was blocking the ship's progress, pushing against the sails, making it impossible to move forward at any speed.

The *Nancy Grace*, having grown older, began to creak and strain under the force of the wind, giving a reminder that nature, not the seafaring skills of the sailors, was now in control.

The boatswain, standing watch, attempted to secure the ropes, rigging, and cables while Captain John, with the ship's wheel in hand, tried to steady the *Nancy Grace*. She was a large ship, nearly one hundred and fifty feet from stem to stern, which made controlling her a major feat in such a ferocious wind.

They were fifteen days out to sea. It was three o'clock in the afternoon. The captain had calculated them to be about forty-two degrees latitude and approximately fifty-five degrees longitude west when they saw the storm coming.

"It looks like a pretty bad storm coming up from the tropics," James heard his father say, as he observed the clouds that were now forming over their heads. Surmising what it could be, he looked up wondering, when suddenly his father shouted:

"Oh no, dear God, please don't let it be. . . . Quick, James, tell the sailors to strike the royal, the topgallant, all the gallants, and reel the mainsail. This could be a hurricane!"

They had never experienced a hurricane, for such storms were found mostly in the Caribbean, certainly not in the North Atlantic Ocean. So when James returned from giving the seamen their orders, he looked at his father, wondering what in the world would they do now. The harsh, determined winds had continued to relentlessly whip around them when he heard his father say:

"We have to make a fast decision, James. Whatever this storm is, it won't be long before it'll be upon us. Since the winds have turned and are now coming out of the northeast, it will be impossible to move the ship forward. We have to decide: Do we turn the ship around and proceed southwest or not? If we do, we might be able to evade the storm. Perhaps, if all goes well, we can make the crossing south from Bermuda over to the Canary Islands, and then proceed up the coast to Ireland."

As they tried to sail around the storm, the wind picked up and became so violent that it made standing on the deck an impossible feat. And trying to hear the commands of the captain was almost impossible too, leaving each man on his own. James was thankful that the boatswain, the petty officers, and other crewmen knew and did their jobs well, but trying to perform them now, in such a dramatic situation, was a real challenge.

As they sailed, trying to fight their way around the storm, James became aware that they were being pulled deeper and deeper into the heart of it. However, they did seem to be making progress, even though the catastrophic force of nature that now surrounded them was unleashing a deadly fury he had not counted on. It put an overwhelming fear not only in his heart, but in the hearts of all who were aboard the *Nancy Grace*—she was being tossed about as though she was a toy in the hands of a destructive child. Her sails were being ripped from her; those that survived being hurled into the water were now wrapped around the spars and masts like rags on a mop. With most of the sails gone, there was nothing they could do to guide the ship. The crew struggled, each trying to do his job, but even attempting to maneuver the *Nancy Grace* became hopeless, as the rain came down from the sky like a river spreading its waters into the air. The sea, a mad fury, raged about them, so much so that it seemed to cause the very heavens to cry out, as clouds swelled over their heads. Suddenly, James realized that the worst of all possible things had happened, when he heard one of the seaman yell,

"She's sprung a leak!"

It seemed as though every joint of the ship was in trouble, as she was spewing out her oakum and had begun to take on water.

"We need to free her of her cargo," James told the men. "Make your way to the hold where the flax is stored, form a line, and pass the bundles of flax to the person beside you, up through the hatch to the men on deck!"

The job was tedious, as many were now standing knee-deep in water which swept across the main deck. James, with compassion, watched the men struggle, trying to keep their stance as they threw the bundles of flax, as many as they could, over the side of the ship. He knew it was a burdensome job, as the flax was heavy, saturated with water coming from the steerage.

Suddenly, James heard the men from the lower level yell, "The leaks are down here in the hold of the ship, where the flax is! The bundles have soaked up the water. We can patch the leaks!"

Still the crew, what men were left, continued to bail and pump water until they were completely exhausted and then, out of pure desperation, continued in their labor. James, his father, and the men all worked diligently for the rest of the night, until James saw what he thought was the sun coming up. Perhaps the worst of the storm was over.

However, it wasn't the sun he saw, but a strange golden radiance in the sky, bringing with it an unrealistic stillness, as the winds had died down, producing an eerie feel. *Have we sailed into heaven, or is it hell?*

Lacking understanding, James did not realize they were in the eye of the storm, and soon would be facing the horrible winds again, as the hurricane once more raged about them.

Late into the night the winds began again to show their mighty fury, having no mercy on man or sea. The *Nancy Grace* was listing now to the larboard, which made reducing her weight an immediate urgency. James yelled, "Throw everything not fastened to the ship overboard! Crates, trunks, chests . . . everything has to go!" In a last desperate attempt to save her, they would cut the foremast, but before they did James heard his father yell, "Pray, like you've never prayed before! If God doesn't help us and we have to cut that mast, there's a good possibility we'll lose the ship!"

"Merciful Father in heaven, help us!"

Can it be that God is testing our faith now, or maybe we're being punished for sins we've committed? James could only surmise how God might be using the situation, when suddenly someone yelled, "Land ho!" Off the larboard side was an island.

It would seem God had heard their prayers. Even as the winds raged about them, hope manifested itself in his heart. Still he knew they were far from being out of danger.

"We must be in the friendly waters of the Bermuda Islands," James heard his father say. "With any luck at all, we might be able to get help, repair what's damaged, and make it back to New York within a month or two. I think God may have heard our prayers."

The next day, the wind did become manageable. The *Nancy Grace* would survive, but she still needed their labor, so every man aboard continued in his efforts, applying strength and endurance beyond his ability to do so. They bailed, patched, and secured the ship as much as they could, given the circumstances. Late that night, they finally rested.

When the sun came up the next day, Captain John—with chronometer, sextant, and other navigational instruments in hand—determined their approximant location and reported his shocking conclusion to James: "We're much further south than the Bermuda chain. We were hit by the storm at around thirty-seven degrees latitude, but it's carried us south between twenty-three and twenty-five degrees latitude, and seventy-six degrees longitude west—the exact location of the Bahamas Islands."

James knew little about the Bahamas. He had heard rumors that privateers—naval men who had offered their services to the United States during the War of 1812, but were now no longer needed and therefore had no chance of finding a meaningful job on the high seas—had turned to seizing ships, and were now the desperados of the seas. "Pirates," they called them, and they sought refuge in and around the seven hundred islands of the Caribbean.

Later, much later, James was to learn that there were as many as two thousand pirates attacking ships in the West Indies. They were reported to have operated out of Cuban ports. Sailing the Caribbean, they sold slaves or anybody or anything they could get their hands on. They were notorious for capturing merchant ships, plundering and sinking them, with their crews locked below deck. More often than not, they took ships just for the pure joy of taking them, often slaughtering their prey simply for the shirts on their backs. He heard that many of the pirates were English, yet most of them were Latin American.

"I don't like the position we're in, James. Have the men make the needed repairs quickly, so we can set sail as soon as possible and get out of here!" his father said.

"I'm glad we kept the canvas, when everything else was thrown overboard," James said. "I'll get the men to mend the sails. They won't be perfect, but they'll do, till we can get better ones."

"Hopefully, we'll be able to leave the islands in a day or two," John said, as he brushed the sweat off his forehead, "and head for Bermuda. We can pick up some needed supplies there, the bare necessities, and make our way home."

Realizing they were dangerously near coral reefs, James yelled to the boatswain, "Take a sounding!"

As the boatswain stood on the fore chain, casting the leadline into the water, he yelled back, "It's clear! No reefs! But as he stood there, looking out across the water, he saw it—a small ship on the horizon, a Bermuda sloop, and it was coming up fast, from the southwest.

"Ahoy, off the larboard bow!" He shouted, as James and everyone on deck scrambled to take a look.

Unimaginable fear hit him, and now with his heart beating faster than ever, James looked at his father. He knew they were in trouble. He had heard about the Bermuda sloop. It was a small fore-and-aft-rigged sailing ship, which was developed in the 1700s, and known to be fast. It could easily be maneuvered, outrunning larger sailing crafts, as it could sail upwind, leaving its pursuers foundering in its wake. There had been rumors that during the War of 1812, privateers sailing the Bermuda sloop had captured as many as five hundred or more British ships. Now, most of those vessels were in the hands of pirates, men who were known to show no mercy to those they captured, as they brutally butchered, hacking off arms and legs, raping women, locking survivors below deck, and either setting their ships on fire or boring holes in the sides, leaving them to sink.

"Get the long guns," John told James. "This doesn't look good."

There was only a small amount of ordnance on board. They did have one cannon and several guns, but they had not been unlimbered in years, for there had not been a need for them. There was a time before the War of 1812, when merchant ships were being seized, that John had ordered the seamen to fire a few, just to make sure they were working properly.

James remembered his father telling the story of how the British had stopped ships during those years, on the pretense of getting sailors who had deserted the Royal Navy, but were actually taking innocent men—men who were American citizens and had the papers to prove it. "Tearing up their papers," John said, "the British were forcing those men to serve on their vessels anyway. At that time, I guess, Napoleon had become a real threat to the English, as he had conquered all of Europe and was now looking to take England. The only way the English felt they could stop him was to block the entire continent of Europe. They had the ships to do it, but they needed men to man those vessels, so they took anyone with a British accent, or who spoke English, to serve on their ships. Eventually, that action, along with other conflicts, would lead them into a war with the United States!"

Fortunately, during that time the *Nancy Grace* was never stopped, so James knew, since her weapons had not been deployed, the supply would be negligible. Nonetheless, they pulled out what weapons they could find, supplying each man with some sort of armament, and made ready for the worst.

With her skull-emblazoned flag now flying, the *Bald Hornet* pulled up broadside, fired a shot, and ordered the *Nancy Grace* to heave to. One of the seamen, taking a long gun, aimed it and fired back. Then the tide broke loose. One by one, the pirates jumped on deck, showing no mercy. With their pistols cocked or long knives in their hands, they struck anyone who stood in their way, severely wounding many. The sailors tried to fight back, but were defenseless.

The pirates wanted money. With broken English, they made their request known. They would spare lives if they would show them where the money was.

John did have a small amount of silver he was keeping to pay the crew, help with repairs, or anything else they might need on their voyage to Ireland. It was in the master's cabin below the quarterdeck, and the cabin doors were opened. James watched his father lead the pirates down the steps. He had just let the last one in, when James caught a glimpse of a cutlass being drawn, and saw his father step aside just in time for the blade to find the side of a wooden door.

"Have mercy on us!" James heard him cry. "We'll show you the silver, but you've got to realize, we've just come through Hades and experienced the devil himself!" referring to the hurricane they had survived. "If God can see us through that hell, he can deliver us now."

"Ho, Ho, Ho." That remark not only struck them as humorous, but seemed to produce a strange sense of respect. *If a ship could survive a hurricane, was it worthy of their veneration?* James wondered, as he heard the pirates talking now among themselves, in a language he did not understand. He assumed they were trying to put in perspective how a ship could have managed such a feat.

James calculated, with some certainty, that the pirates would take the silver, plunder the ship, and then kill all aboard. Fearing now for his life and his father's, he started shaking, shivering, as if in the middle of an ice storm; yet, at the same time, perspiration cascaded down his face. *It won't be long till they'll find out the ship is stripped of her goods—there isn't anything to take—and when they do, that will be the end us!*

Soon, though, he and his father and the sailors who had survived the attack found themselves being pushed onto a boat and taken to the pirate sloop. James, now completely confused, looked back at the *Nancy Grace,* wondering about the men who the pirates had left on the ship, either dead or injured. Even though he had not been killed, still, a sadness he had never experienced now seemed to consume him. Sitting on the deck of the *Bald Hornet* under the guard of one of the men, he watched as some of the pirates made their way back to the *Nancy Grace*.

What will they do next? James wondered. *They'll probably search the ship for any booty, plunder it, take whatever they can find, which won't be much, then set the ship on fire.*

As he watched the scene now set before his eye, that is exactly what happened. James saw the smoke bellowing from the bow of the ship, knowing full well it would be the last time he would see the *Nancy Grace*. This was worse than the storm they had gone through, worse than the attack, and certainly worse than anything he thought could possibly happen to them now or in the future. As James watched the flames consume the ship, memories flashed through his mind—memories of when he was a young lad and his father had taking him on board the *Nancy Grace* for the first time. His mother thought he was too young to go. Still she relented, knowing he wanted to, but also because his father had strongly insisted.

James looked at his father, wondering what he was thinking. *He's probably thinking about his uncle, for he loved that old man. How sad his uncle would be, if he was still living, to know he lost the* Nancy Grace *like this.*

Helplessness consumed James now, as there was nothing he could do but watch the *Nancy Grace* disappear before his eyes, consumed by the fiery flames, its sad remains slipping away as it sunk to the bottom of the sea,

Soon the pirates were back on board the *Bald Hornet* talking, but in their native tongue, and looking at their prey as if trying to decide what to do with them. James knew not what they were saying. He could only surmise that whatever it was, it wasn't good.

The sloop was full of men. There must have been fifty or sixty pirates aboard the *Bald Hornet,* while there were only six of them left from the *Nancy Grace.* The boatswain and several of the other seamen, who had perished in the brutal attack, were now on the burning ship. That thought only added to his anguish. *Those young men were barely out of their twenties, only starting to live, and now to die. What a shame.*

The day lingered into night, with James and the others still on deck—tied, tired, and hungry. *The* Bald Hornet *had sailed away from the burning ship, but to where?* He wondered.

All the next day James, his father, and the other men had been given little to eat and drink. Since the days had grown warmer now, James could only surmise that they had sailed further south.

Late into the night they heard noise. It sounded like laughter coming from the steerage. There was loud talking and singing. James could hear women screaming, and then more laughter. Soon two of the men came on deck. One was carrying a bottle filled with some sort of a liquid. As he slung it over his shoulder to take a drink, the other man came alongside and took it from him. This started a fight, and ended with one of the men lying on deck in a pool of blood.

The screams and laughter continued until the sun peeked its head above the horizon, and then as suddenly as it started there was silence, a deathly silence.

With no one to man the helm, the *Bald Hornet* seemed to be drifting.

One of the seamen had managed to loosen the ropes from around his arms, but did not completely free himself from them until now. With no one watching, it was easy to slip his arms from the noose, and then one by one untie James, John, and the other men. Now loose, they gingerly searched the deck.

"Look around—see if there is anyone!" John said.

Minutes later James reported, "There's no one on deck. It looks like the helm has been left unattended. Unless the ship is anchored, and I feel almost certain it isn't, we are drifting, and could hit a coral reef."

"Since I don't know where we are or where we're going, all I can do is keep the *Bald Hornet* away from there." John pointed toward an island. "I feel certain there are reefs, many of them surrounding that place."

The morning drifted into noon and then afternoon. By four o'clock James saw the clouds forming in the southeast. They grew dark and then darker. It was a tropical storm, and was approaching fast.

Some of the pirates were on deck now, alarmed that James and the others were free, but soon realized that they were not armed and therefore did not pose a threat, but had actually saved the *Bald Hornet*. With the fast-approaching storm, the pirates would need all the hands they could get.

As the storm advanced, it gave a good resemblance to what James and the others had already gone through, with one exception: With the last storm, they were in the middle of the Atlantic Ocean, free from any islands. Now there were hundreds of islands, with thousands of coral reefs spreading their treacherous, jagged teeth everywhere.

As the rain battered the ship, seawater flooded the hold. There were so many men and women on the *Bald Hornet* that it made saving her an impossible feat. They needed to reduce the weight in the ship. James heard his father tell the pirates to throw everything overboard, but the pirates were not about to do that.

John yelled above the horrific sound of the wind, "Lighten the ship or we're doomed!"

Someone yelled, "Throw the women overboard!" With that order came a riot, and a fight broke out. The pirates were in a free-for-all, each thinking of his own pleasures and needs, and willing to defend them to the death.

There was little chance now they would make it, so James, his father, and the other crewmen from the *Nancy Grace* resigned themselves to the inevitable. The pirate sloop was doomed. It would perish. When and where? James did not know, but most certainly it would happen.

Chapter 6

"I don't want you to go, Mary, but I do understand." Margaret Scott said, as she watched Mary put the last garment into her satchel. She was saddened, as Mary was in the process of getting an annulment and soon would no longer be her daughter-in-law.

"What makes it so distressing for me, Margaret, is I don't think he loved me. He was a gentleman, a kind gentleman, and he knew how very much I wanted to come to America. He saw the tears in my eyes, my heart breaking as I watched Ann and Will boarding the *Jupiter*, and being the gentleman he was, he couldn't just stand there and not do anything about it. But loving me? No! I don't believe he ever really did."

Margaret and Mary were now living in the Kellys boarding house. Margaret's dad had passed away; and her mother, growing feeble, was no longer able to handle the work. Margaret needed the income, so made the decision to sell her home and, with Mary by her side, moved into the boarding house to take over managing it. It did bring in some income, at least, enough to put food on the table and to pay for a few of the other necessities. And Mary was a great help, a companion, and had become more like a daughter to Margaret than a daughter-in-law. It was distressing to her that Mary was leaving, but Mary's sister Rachel and her husband Will were going to Pennsylvania to the Cumberland Valley to find family. They wanted Mary to go as well, and Mary wanted to go.

"What will I do without you, Mary? I've lost a husband and a son, and now you!"

Hugging Margaret with tears forming in her eyes, Mary made her regret known, "Oh, Margaret, I am so sorry. I don't want to leave you, but staying here keeps his memory alive for me, and I must forget him. It's been almost two years since we've heard anything about them, where they are, or what happened. And when I'm with you, I think about him, how much I loved him, and how much I miss him, but he's gone, and he'll never return. I have to accept that. It's the most difficult thing I've ever had to do, even more difficult than leaving my mother and father. Perhaps, if I still had them, it would help, and I do realize what you must be suffering. You've not only lost your John, but James too. In some ways it's a reminder of Ireland and how much we had to endure there. But Margaret, I pray that someday you can come to Pennsylvania, and we can be together again. You have family there, too. Surely they would want you to be near them now, now that you're by yourself."

"As long as mother is alive, I must stay here. She could never make such a long journey." Margaret said, as she looked sadly at Mary. "But Mary, if the Lord is merciful, maybe, just maybe, I will see them again one day, if not walking up the front walk to the Kellys' Boarding House, then surely on the road to glory. I still pray to God, that wherever they are, He will keep them safe, and that we will all be together again one day, if not here on earth, then certainly in heaven. I haven't that much time on this earth, myself, so I can only trust that heaven will bring its own reward. But for now, I must stay in New York, or until I have news of their passing. Don't fret yourself about me. Mother and I will do just fine. She has her knitting, and I have my hands full with running this place. I'm just sad, because I probably will never see you again. The trip to Pennsylvania can be hard, and crossing the mountains into the Cumberland Valley is dangerous, or so I'm told. I can only pray you make it there safely."

It was a difficult separation, for losing her husband John and her son James was a sadness Margaret never thought, in her wildest imagination, would happen. And now the one person she could turn to, who shared in her grief, was also leaving. But Margaret understood, for it had been almost a year and a half since anyone had heard anything about them. Margaret's heart was broken, but Mary had stayed by her side, always optimistic that one day they would see them again . . . always, that is, until now. Now she was getting an annulment and would soon be Mary White again. She was young, and needed to get on with her life. Margaret felt certain that one day Mary would find someone to fill the void. As for herself, she had nothing left— nothing, that is, but to wait, hope, and pray that someday she might see her husband and her son again.

James had been on the island for many months. He had experienced all the seasons, with little change in any. The only way he could tell summer from winter was by the length of the days and the position of the sun in the sky. Perhaps winter was a bit cooler, but only a bit.

As the days stretched into weeks, and then months, James spent a good part of that time exploring the island. It was a small island. He guessed it to be not more than twenty miles long and perhaps ten miles wide. It was uninhabited, and he doubted if anyone had ever set foot on its shores. Coral reefs, which gave a unique color to the water, could be seen extending to the north as far as the eye could see. They circled the island, but to the south lay in more shallow water, and that was where James found fish in abundance. He had constructed a spear with his pocketknife, which he tied to the end of a long pole, securing it with fiber-like material he pulled from the outer layers. Using it, he was able to obtain a substantial amount of food; not only did he catch fish, but could lance smaller animals as well.

Every sort of sea creature was at his disposal: stingray, which he very carefully avoided, but there was also snapper, mullet, crayfish, grouper, and even shark. On a good day he saw oysters, crab, and giant sea turtles, which shuffled onto the beach in early February to lay eggs, eggs he found to be delicious. "Surely," he thought, "there could be no island in the world with a better supply of fish." The biggest problem was trying to avoid stepping on the sharp, razor-like edges of the coral, which was a natural part of their habitat.

Storms hit the island more often than not, especially in the summer. There seemed to be dark ominous clouds billowing somewhere in the sky almost every day, but with the storms came water—lots of water, fresh water, water to drink and to wash with. James did find a small freshwater stream in the middle of the island, but quite insufficient to sustain his life, so he continued to capture rainwater in the kegs, bottles, and barrels he found on the sand.

A rather large carpenter's chest washed ashore. In it were tools, enough to help him construct a shelter, sufficient and comfortable. It was home. It took weeks to complete, but it gave him something to do, keeping his lonely mind occupied. He built it as close to the coast as he deemed safe, making it easier to watch for passing ships. With that assumption in mind, he piled wood from the leftover trash that washed ashore, along with tree limbs that could be set ablaze to alert a passing vessel, if and when there were any.

After a while, he began to grow fond of the island and to refer to it as *his* island, with its swaying palms, dancing dolphins, and glorious sunsets. And when the sun came up in the morning, he praised his Father in heaven that he had made it through yet another night.

On a hillside he erected a small cross overlooking the sea. Here he carved his father's name and the names of the other seamen who were lost, either dying aboard the *Nancy Grace* or drowned when the pirate sloop hit the rocky reef. Looking at it helped him to remember God's redemptive power, and that thought enabled him to keep the faith even in the darkest of times, producing order in his life rather than fear.

Along with the many things he found on the beach from the pirate sloop was a logbook. The pages, having been soaked throughout with water, were unsuitable for use. Leaving them to dry, he hoped he would be able to eventually record thoughts and feelings he desperately wanted to write—to tell someone, or anyone who might read them. When the pages were dry, he took a small pencil from his box and began to write. Doing so helped him fill the lonely hours.

February 12, 1823

I have been here more than three months now, and have found this island to be deserted, void of any people. I find myself wondering how it might be possible to survive without human company! But as the sun comes up each day I gain hope, realizing more and more that our glorious Creator is in control, for I could not find a more beautiful place in the world to live should I be here for the remainder of my life.

February 23, 1823

This is a small island, but quite sufficient to support life, as there are plants and animals, fish of every kind. I have searched the forest for fruit, and fished the sea. I have built a house, not perfect, but perfect for me; and thatched it over my head with leaves from strange-looking plants which grow here to keep the rain from entering. And I have given God praise for defending me against any wickedness of nature that might seek to triumph, for God has oft reminded me of His redemptive power, and for me to keep faith even in these darkest of times.

March 16, 1823

As the days stretch into weeks and then months, I have remained healthy for the most part. My back, which was first injured upon reaching this island, has since healed, causing me to, again, give God the praise, for He is teaching me through that still small voice that speaks to my heart, "James, I will never leave you nor forsake you, for I have plans for you. Like a living stone, you are being built into a spiritual house to be a spiritual offering, acceptable to me."

If God, and I do not doubt Him, has plans for me, then I have to believe He will one day bring them to fruition, and thus deliver me from this place, for should that happen, I will surely dedicate my life to be used by Him.

August 2, 1823

Today I saw a passing vessel, so far from my sight that I need not hope of any rescue, but it caused me to remember my father's fate, and how sad life can be upon this earth. There are so many unanswered questions about life and death that I am now struggling to understand; questions, which cause me to ponder: Does God have the answers, and if He does, will He reveal them to me?

September 30, 1823

Regularly there are storms hitting this island. Even though many are violent, lashing out with thunder and lightning, they pass quickly, leaving damage that can be repaired with little effort. Always with these storms, memories fill my mind of the frightful days spent aboard the Nancy Grace, and how we hung on and endured, only to watch her burn to ashes, set ablaze by godless men, proving how the wicked nature and savagery of man can triumph over godliness and civility.

October 10, 1823

Today it is my twenty-third birthday.

I was thinking of my mother today, and praying that she is well, and has found the courage she needs to face life without father or myself, and that she finds the means to support herself. Perhaps she will go to Pennsylvania to be near brother John, and thus have family around her. I pray it can be so.

January 28, 1824

Today I have felt the hand of God, as I remember the cruelty of man, for God has reminded me: "In the world ye shall have tribulation, but be of good cheer; I have overcome the world."

If this be so, and I believe it to be, then God in his mercy must be preparing me for that world, for here I have suffered much! Oh, how this world needs to hear about the God of all Creation.

June 12, 1824

I think of Mary often, and deeply regret we did not have more time together. I left without letting her know that I loved her. How sad, to remember that now! But I can and do continue to pray for her, that she will find a good life in America with someone who can give her the love she so rightly deserves. As for me, could it be that, if God has purpose for my life, I must live it apart from Mary? I find myself now feeling void of any certainty that she and I could ever be reunited, and those thoughts cause me great pain.

September 28, 1824

I ofttimes think of Ireland, especially Ulster and County Down, for it was in that county that Saint Patrick lived and died, and it is there in which he lay. It's the very place where my father dwelled, and it was there I first saw Mary, my wife to be.

Did God have His hand on Saint Patrick, and does He now have His hand on me? Could it be in God's plan, that I should be alone on this island, just as Patrick was alone on that mountainside in Ireland, after he had been shipped there as a slave, before God sent him back to tell the people about Christ? Perhaps it was the only way God had of gaining Saint Patrick's attention, and now, it seems He is gaining mine. For He certainly had His hand on Saint Patrick, not because he was such a Godly man, though I feel he was, but because he believed God, and was willing to be used. Could I do the same, if I would so dedicate myself, and, if so, will God then deliver me from this place? A scripture now comes to my mind that the minister at the Scotch Presbyterian Church in New York must have read one Sunday. . . .

"For what does it profit a man if he gains the whole world, but loses his soul?"

I can testify that it certainly does profit a man to lose the whole world, and gain his soul! For that is exactly what has happened to me! I did gain my soul, and now I am dedicating it to be used by God!

"Oh, God and Savior of my soul . . . deliver me from this place, and I promise You, I will serve You for the rest of my days upon this earth!"

Chapter 7

"Good morning, Captain. It looks like it's going be another beautiful day," Ensign Aiken noted as he mounted the steps to the quarterdeck where Lieutenant Commander Lawrence Kearny was standing. The commander was observing the fresh-scrubbed look of his ship, as the bell of the *USS Decoy* rang four times. It was 6:00 am and the sun, poking its head above the horizon, was just beginning to spread its light over the New York City harbor. Soon the *USS Decoy* would be sailing again, but this time it would go south to carry much-needed supplies to the fleet in Key West—a fleet that had been ordered by the United States Government to suppress piracy.

Commander Kearny hoped the American public, as well as the angry shipowners, were aware that good men were now risking their lives to stop those hijackers, marauders who traveled the high seas looking for anything or anyone to plunder. He did sympathize with the public's anger, though, for over the past two years America had lost more than twenty-seven ships to piracy. Now, because of public pressure, President Monroe had authorized the establishment of the fleet. It was considered an anti-pirate squadron, known as the "Mosquito Fleet," mainly because of the small, shallow-drafted vessels that made up the convoy.

"But unlike mosquitoes, we aren't looking for blood," Kearny said, as he stood on the foredeck the day before with

Robert Peterson, captain of one of the two-mask schooners. "Our ships are scouring the islands of the Caribbean and the Gulf of Mexico, looking for renegades . . . pirates."

Peterson had been talking with Kearny, telling him about the brigs, sloops, barges, larger frigates, and schooners like his that made up the convoy.

"And there is one merchant ship with hidden guns that can be used as a decoy," he said. "However, most of them are shallow-drafted, for, as you know, being shallow-drafted they can maneuver more easily over areas where larger ships can't go, and, of course, would less likely be detected. And they need to be able to sail close to those islands, since it's mainly there where those pirates are hiding."

Peterson and Kearny took their orders from Captain David Porter, the commanding officer and admiral of the fleet. In April of 1823 the United States Government had established a base in Key West for the seventeen ships and eleven hundred men who would be deployed aboard those vessels—all of which were under the authority of Captain Porter. Scouring the islands of the West Indies, their hopes were not only to capture pirates, but to help escort American ships to safety, putting an end to this deadly plague.

James had grown used to hearing "the voice." It had spoken to him many times. It was not an audible voice, nothing that required his hearing, but a voice which seemed to speak within his mind, touching his heart, and teaching him with its profound messages. It became more and more distinct the longer he paid heed; and had he not been alone on an island for many days, weeks, months, and now years, he supposed he would not have been aware of it at all. Now, though, it had become his companion, his friend—a trusted friend, one he would not want to lose.

On more occasions than not the voice spoke Scripture, and when it did, it would leave him marveling at its profound messages, causing him to wonder, *How could I have known that?* Soon the answer came:

"James, while you are abiding in Me, I have spoken these things to you. My peace I give to you; do not let your heart be troubled, nor let it be afraid. The Holy Spirit, whom the Father has sent in my name will teach you all things, and bring to your mind what I have told you."

He had been on the island for nearly two years when, one evening, he heard the voice again. It seemed to be telling him to go to the cross on the hillside. It was now late October, and the days had grown shorter. He knew it would take twenty minutes or more to climb the hill where the cross stood, and it was already beginning to grow dark, as the sun, fading from the sky, had caused the stars to appear.

Many times he had climbed that cliff to offer prayers to God, prayers to thank Him and to place before Him the many hurts that plagued his heart. Always at that cross, he felt closer to his father, remembering the times they had spent together aboard the *Nancy Grace*. His routine had been to go in the glow of the early morning sunrise, but now the voice seemed to be telling him to go at night.

It was a beautiful night, as the moon had never been so full. Spreading its light everywhere, it now became easy for him to see the path winding up the side of the hill to where the cross stood. Stars filled the heavens and sparkled like diamonds in the sky. Never had he seen so many.

As he reached the pinnacle of the cliff, he looked back at the beach he had just left. The glow of the campfire was burning brightly; and the waves, breaking over the reefs, reflecting in the moonlight, were so beautiful that it filled his heart with serenity, a peace he had not expected.

He would kneel at the cross, offering up a prayer, but felt compelled, first, to just stand there for a moment, taking in the view that now seemed to mesmerize him.

As he stood on the cliff, looking out across the water, he suddenly saw it. Silhouetted on the horizon was a small boat, a two-masked schooner obviously anchored, as it wasn't moving. It was standing at the edge of the coral reef not far away, and had he not been on the hill he supposed he would not have seen it at all.

"Oh, dear God, please let it be. . . ." he heard himself saying, but soon after his initial reaction, fear captured his mind, as he rushed down the hill to the beach, never taking his eyes from the silhouetted vision. Within minutes of reaching the campsite he saw a longboat full of men rowing toward the shore. "Pirates!" flashed through his mind. They would kill him! He felt certain of that, and he had no way of defending himself, but he stood there anyway, watching. Whether pirates or not, they were human beings—something he had not experienced for a very long time. Perhaps, if they were pirates, he could talk his way out of a confrontation and beseech them for help.

The small boat soon touched the beach as men, perhaps as many as six or eight, jumped out to pull it further onto the sand. A second look convinced him that they were not renegades, as they were all dressed alike in a uniform of sorts. They carried guns, but upon seeing that James was unarmed, they lowered them and greeted him.

"Ahoy there, mate. Are you alone on this island?"

"Yes . . . sir, I am. I've . . . been here . . . two years," Amazed, James stammered, trying to get the right words out, as the whole situation was beyond his ability to grasp. "I'm . . . by myself. There's no one else here."

The captain reached out his arm toward James, taking his hand, he said. "Well, well, it's good we found you. Just sorry we have to meet this way. I'm Robert Peterson, captain of the Savoy. You've been here for two years, by yourself?"

"Yes sir, my ship was hijacked by a pirate sloop, the *Bald Hornet,* in late October 1822. I've been on this island ever since."

"Well," Lieutenant Peterson said, "I want to hear more, but we need to get you off this island first. When will you be able to go?"

"Now, sir, right now, the sooner the better!"

James was dressed in rags. The clothes he was wearing were the clothes he had on when he first reached the island two years before; other than that, there wasn't anything he needed or wanted. His only desire was to make it to civilization as fast as he could, and that is what he focused on.

"We saw your fire and knew there had to be someone on this island. Do you mind if we scout around for a few minutes?"

"You won't find anything, but help yourselves," James said.

They didn't stay there long; as they could easily see that James was telling them the truth; there wasn't any reason for concern.

So the men—along with James—climbed back into the boat and pushed off to leave the island. Disoriented, yet excited, James sat in the boat, anxious now to leave that lonely, deserted place which had been his home for more than two years.

On the schooner, James told them his story—how the *Nancy Grace* was caught in a hurricane of sorts and blown off course, only to be over taken by the pirate's sloop.

"You're fortunate you weren't killed. Pirates are notorious for not taking captives. We've been scouring these islands now for more than a year, and we've met some pretty craggy-looking characters. Hopefully, we will soon be rid of them for good.

"By the way, we're part of a squadron of ships, seventeen altogether, paid for by the government to stop these pirates. We're called the Mosquito Fleet, and Captain David Porter is our commanding officer. The United States Government has had so many complaints about ships being taken by pirates they decided to do something about it, and it wasn't any too soon in my judgment."

"Yes, those men can be pretty brutal," James said, "and I have often wondered, what would cause a man to turn to piracy in the first place?"

"Well, it's my understanding that part of the reason had to do with Napoleon. It seems he has weakened Spain's control over the Spanish Main."

"Those are the countries around the Gulf of Mexico, aren't they?" James said.

"Yes, and after Napoleon came to power, many of those countries decided they wanted to be free from Spain, so they hired what we call privateers to help them; but after those men did what they were hired to do, they found themselves without a job. They had no money, and the only thing they knew was how to capture ships, so they turned to piracy. Of course, the United States has to take some of the responsibility as well, for it's my understanding that the War of 1812 also contributed to the problem."

"We had no way of knowing that that was happening. Certainly, if we had known, we would have been more prepared to defend ourselves," James said.

"You were fortunate you had that campfire burning. We saw it, since we've been watching for any signs of life on these islands for some time now, realizing that it could be pirates."

"You can't know how thankful I am you saw it," James said. "There were times when I thought I would be on that island for the rest of my life."

"Well, you better get some rest now. We'll be headed back to Key West in a day or two. That's where we're headquartered. There will be a ship there that can take you to New York. You'll probably be back home by mid-March, I would think," Lieutenant Peterson assured him.

James slept that night like he had not slept in a very long time. Security covered him like a warm, wooly blanket on a cold December night. But before he drifted off into deep slumber, he remembered his Heavenly Father, giving him his very grateful thanks, knowing for certain, *God truly does work in the affairs of men*, certainly in his affairs, as he now remembered the voice that would not let him rest until he climbed that hill—the hill that led to his rescue.

Chapter 8

The white organdy curtains bellowed out, pushed by an early April breeze that swept by the window. The horse-drawn hackneys were passing on the street below, making a "rat-a-tat" sound as they moved over the cobblestones. It was spring, and New York City was coming alive. Tulips and daffodils that had been planted along the palings which surrounded the boarding-house yard were now poking their heads above ground, as if to say "hello" to the few buds that were beginning to appear on some of the trees, which lined John Street. After a harsh winter, it promised to be a beautiful spring day in the city.

Margaret sat at her mahogany desk in an upstairs bedroom, sorting through the monthly bills, trying to decide which ones needed her immediate attention. She would pay those, with the hope the others would find a payment source soon.

Weary of the task, she stretched for a moment, then got up from her chair and moved over to look out the window. *Perhaps*, she decided, *the fresh air might help clear my mind.* She could smell the aroma of coffee coming from the dining room below.

Claire is up and at it early this morning.

Looking at the scene beneath her, she saw people passing on the street, some, she thought, out just taking a walk in the freshness of the early morning air.

They certainly are enjoying a nice day of spring weather.

As she stood there looking down John Street, a young man came walking toward the boarding house. He was thin and rather peaked-looking, but still had a spring to his gait and was moving along the street at a rapid pace. He soon approached the boarding house and stopped at the gate, as if unsure whether to open it or not. Margaret stared at him for a moment. Who was this young man, and what did he want? His having paused gave her a chance to see his face clearly. Suddenly, as if waking from a dream, she realized that not only did she know that face, but she knew it well. It was James!

Tears swelled in her eyes, as she grabbed her mouth with her hand and the hanky she held in it to hinder the scream that was forcing its way to the surface. Her body was shaking; she could feel a cold chill prickling up her spine. Suddenly finding her voice, she heard herself saying, "James! James! James! Oh, dear God, it's James!" as she ran down the stairs to the front door.

Throwing the outer door open, she crashed it against the side of the porch as she ran down the front steps and into his arms. She could not believe what was happening was real. It had to be a dream, but the most wonderful dream she would ever experience.

"Oh James," she said, "It's really you!"

"Hi Mumsy," was all he said, and she fell into his arms sobbing.

After a moment they walked, with their arms around each other, back into the living room of the boarding house in complete silence. She still couldn't believe it, but it really was James.

"James, you've come back from the dead! What happened? How did you . . . what happened, son? You've been gone so long. We hadn't heard from anyone that you were alive."

"Mum, I want to tell you the whole story, but I will tell you this much: Father was drowned." James closed his eyes then opened them again, only to look down at the floor, as if to hide the tear that formed in the rim. Margaret saw it spill out and cascade down his cheek.

"Oh no, James, how did it happen?"

When he looked up again, he said, "Do you have anything to eat? I'm hungry. I haven't eaten a thing since noon yesterday, and then it wasn't much."

"Oh, of course, son," Margaret assured him, as she turned to Claire. "Claire, would you please fix. . . ." That was all she needed to say, as Claire, standing in the foyer of the house, had observed the whole scene and was now turning to go into the kitchen to fix the best things she could find to feed this long-lost son she had heard so much about.

"Yes, will do. I'll have it ready in no time at all," Claire responded as she walked through the hall leading to the kitchen door.

When Margaret turned to put in her request to Claire, she suddenly became aware that she and James were not alone. Many of the people who resided at the boarding house were now either standing on the stairway or by the door leading to the sitting-room where she and James were now. She introduced them one by one, as they reached out a hand to James, making sure he knew how very happy they were to finally meet him. However, they didn't leave after the introduction was over, but stayed where they were, as each and every one wanted to hear the story of this son who was dead, yet was now alive.

As Margaret set watching James eat, it was difficult for her to talk; a hundred questions filled her mind. What happened to her darling John? Why did he drown? Why was James so thin?

Where had he been that he could not have contacted her, and what would cause him to look so sad, so solemn? This was not the James she knew. Yet how grateful she was to see him, sitting here, beside her, eating.

Between the bites of food that James filled his mouth with, he tried to talk, but it wasn't until he took his last sip of tea that he began to tell her clearly what had happened.

"I want to start at the beginning," he said, as he relayed the whole sordid story of the hurricane, the pirates taking the ship, and then setting it on fire. How his father had died urging him to save his own life, the days he spent on the island, and his timely rescue. He didn't leave anything out—especially the part when God had spoken to him, how much he had learned from that voice, and how real God had become.

Later, when Margaret and James were alone, they talked about Mary. Margaret told him how Mary had stayed, becoming a wonderful companion to her through those dark, lonely days.

"Mary always believed you would return, James. She never quit believing, no, not until a few months ago. I guess there comes a time when we just give up, and have to accept what life throws at us, and that's what Mary did, but I have to tell you, son, she didn't think you loved her."

"Oh, but she was wrong. I did love her. I *do* love her! I was brokenhearted when I first hit that island and found her locket in my box that washed upon the beach, but what could I do? I was alone, Father was gone, I had no one to turn to. The strain of it all, and the sadness, was just too much for me. I was a broken man. I didn't care if I lived or died. I honestly believed that I would be on that island for the rest of my life." James now fought back tears that were again forming. "But where is Mary now? Where did she go?"

"Prepare yourself, son; I have some sad news to tell you. Mary left last September with Ann and Will to travel to Shippensburg in the Cumberland Valley, but before she left she had your marriage annulled. She just didn't believe she would ever see you again, and even more than that she wanted to forget you, as it hurt her knowing how much she loved you, and feeling for certain you never loved her."

"Well, she was wrong on two counts. I wasn't dead, but alive; and I loved her, though the thought of her did lessen in my mind, as hopelessness filled it. But I never forgot her. Have you heard anything about them since they left? Is she okay?"

"No, I haven't heard a thing."

"I am so sorry, so very sorry this all had to happen, but you know, Mum, Jesus told us that in this world we will have trouble, but He also said for us to fear not, for He has overcome the world. We will have hardships and disappointments while we are on this earth, especially those of us who believe, and hold His words close to our hearts, but some day that will all be over when we are, at last, with Him in glory. Is it worth the suffering while we wait? Yes, I believe it is.

"By the way, where is the family Bible? I would really like to read it."

Margaret looked at her son. His body showed signs of weakness due to the stress he had been under, but his eyes were the same. Those same deep, penetrating blue-gray eyes he had inherited from his English grandfather seemed now to be searching, needing to find answers to "why," yet, at the same time, appeared to already have an understanding of it all.

That night, James fell asleep with the Bible in his arms. He had read it until he could no longer keep his eyes opened, for soon it slipped from his grasp, as he drifted off into deep slumber.

The next morning, James and Margaret walked to the cemetery to visit the grave of Margaret's parents, Douglas and Ann Kelly. Knowing his grandparents had died, and that he would never see them again, was just one more hurt piled on top of all the others. As he remembered his grandfather, he could not help but appreciate the knowledge Douglas Kelly had about history, especially of Ireland, and its church. Though they were Catholic, the old man knew much about the Presbyterian Church as well. He had loved Ireland and had lived there through some of the worst times that country had ever experienced. Now he, along with his wife, had been laid to rest in America, but in a Catholic cemetery near Saint Patrick's Church on Mulberry Street, not far from the place where George Washington had given his inaugural address thirty-five years before.

Walking to the cemetery and back gave them time to talk, and that is when James told his mother he had felt the call of God upon his life. What exactly God intended to do, he was not sure. He would continue to pray, and see what purpose he was to fulfill, for he felt certain there was a reason why he had been rescued from that island.

"Last evening, Mum, I read this scripture. I'm not certain I am saying it exactly as I read it, but this is what it had to say to me. . . . It was in the book of Acts, after Jesus had left the earth. The apostle Paul was accused of inciting a riot against the Jews, of which he declared his innocence. He was brought before King Agrippa, and there, before the king, he told the story of how he used to persecute the saints, those who believed in Christ. He was on his way to Damascus when he, along with the men who were with him, saw a light, brighter than the sun, blazing all around. He fell to the ground and then heard a voice speak, and this is what that voice said to him, but now, Mum, it seems to be saying it to me: '*Arise, James! Stand on your feet; for this purpose I have appeared to you, to appoint you a minister, a witness not only to the things which you have seen, but also to the things I will show you. I am sending you to open the eyes of others so that they may turn from darkness to light, and from the power of Satan to God, so that they may receive forgiveness of their sins and inherit a place along with those who have been sanctified by faith in Me.*'"

"How and when do you think this will happen, James?"

"I don't know. But I do know the One who is in charge of our lives. Though He gives us the freedom to choose what we will do with those lives, oh, how it must please Him when we choose to live our lives for Him. My deepest desire now is to please Him, to do whatever He has called me to do. How or when it will happen? I do not know. But I know the One who has called me, and because I do, I have to believe it *will* happen."

Chapter 9

On Sunday morning Margaret insisted James go with her to the Scotch Presbyterian Church on Cedar Street. The thought of going was painful, for he knew the church would remind him of Mary, since it was there he had hoped they could be married again. Reluctantly, though, James told his mother he would go.

As they approached the church building, the sight, its two Gothic towers faced with brownstone, along with the cast-iron and wooden ornamental fence that surrounded the churchyard, brought back memories of times gone by, when as a young child he had gone there with his father.

Entering the building, he remembered there were no arches to obstruct the view. It had always been possible to see the podium from wherever they sat. Those seats were pews carved from black walnut wood, which he supposed had come from trees that still grew wild in parts of the island that were uninhabited. The ceiling, with its ribbed arches, displayed beautiful hanging lamps. An impressive sight indeed, especially to a man who had spent nearly two years with nature, void of any human contact, let alone the beautiful artwork which was now displayed before him.

As they settled themselves in one of the pews at the back of the large room, James watched the people who were now coming into the building. He wondered how many had serious needs, and, perhaps, were hoping for an answered prayer or two. He certainly could relate, for he had many of his own!

In the somberness of the moment, his eyes fell upon the altar, and he thought of Mary. It was there he had hoped to make her his wife again; how long ago that was, and how sad, now, the memories. As he was recalling the few special moments they spent together, he heard music playing softly, coming from somewhere in the building, its lilting melody penetrating the room as it drifted over the heads of people, seeming now to soothe the very soul. Though the memories of Mary hurt, still listening to the lilting music caused James to reflect; *it's all in God's hands, and I must leave it there. If Mary and I are to be together again, God will make it happen.*

Suddenly, being pulled from his thoughts, he saw the minister rise from a pew at the front of the church and climbed the steps to the podium. The pastor closed his eyes, and bowed his head for a brief moment, as though in prayer, and then started to speak. His rich baritone voice having little trouble being heard across the building, he read verses from a Bible he held in his hands:

> Be not deceived; God is not mocked: for whatsoever a man soweth, that shall he also reap. For he that soweth to his flesh shall of the flesh reap corruption; but he that soweth to the Spirit shall of the Spirit reap life everlasting (Gal. 6:7–8).

> Another parable put He forth unto them, saying, The kingdom of heaven is likened unto a man which sowed good seed in his field: But while the man slept, his enemy came and sowed tares among the wheat, and went his way.

But when blade was sprung up, and brought forth fruit, then appeared the tares also.

So the servants of the householder came and said unto him, Sir, didst not thou sow good seed in thy field? From whence then hath it tares?

He said unto them, An enemy hath done this. The servant said unto him, Wilt thou then that we go and gather them up?

But he said, Nay; lest while ye gather up the tares, ye root up also the wheat with them. Let both grow together until the harvest: and in the time of harvest, I will say to the reapers, Gather ye together first the tares, and bind them in bundles to burn them; but gather the wheat into my [heavenly] barn (Matt. 13:24–30).

When the minister finished reading the scripture, he sat down. The church was quiet now, reflecting on what they had just heard.

In the stillness of the moment James found himself consumed with thought, but this time the mental images making their way into his mind were of his father's tragic death and the death of so many others, even the drowning of all those men and women on the pirate sloop. Yes, he knew about "tares," as he had experience, struggling with so many in his own life. The evil in the world was overwhelming.

He marveled at the scripture the minister read. But what really amazed him was how God, through these many years, had preserved those words, so that now he, James, had access to them. Yet, what was even more amazing was how profound the truth of those words was and how it still applied. As James reflected on what he had just heard, he thought of the men, down through the ages, who had risked their lives so that he, today, could read those words and profit from them. *It took faith, lots of faith, for those men to live and die as they did, in order to preserve those written words, passing them on, so that I can now know them.*

As he was reflecting on those thoughts, his mind wandered back in time, recalling some of the many history lessons he had learned from his father. "The Presbyterian Church in Northern Ireland was brought there from Scotland and has remained mostly in Ulster," his father had told him. "It was taken there by the men and women who fled the lowlands of Scotland during the time of the 'Plantation of Ulster' after the British Crown had driven the Irish Catholics out of that Province.

"The church was first established in Scotland by a Scottish Reformer, John Knox. They say that Knox, after having suffered his share of persecution, became one of the most powerful preachers of his day.

"Before they knew anything about Christ or Christianity, I heard that the Lowland Scotch were a semi-barbarous and brutal people, people who plundered the sheepfolds and cattle yards of their neighbors, but after their conversion, a dramatic change came over their lives. Now, understanding justice in light of the Christian faith, they became a peace-loving people, and those people were our ancestors—men and women who left Scotland to settle in Northern Ireland, bringing with them the Presbyterian Church," his father said.

Yes, I can certainly identify with "tares!" The world is full of them! James reasoned, when suddenly, being pulled from his thoughts, the minister started speaking again.

Then Jesus sent the multitude away, and went into the house; and his disciples came unto him, saying, Declare unto us the parable of the tares of the field.

[And] He answered and said unto them, He that soweth the good seed is the Son of man; The field is the world; the good seed are the children of the kingdom; but the tares are the children of the wicked one; The enemy that sowed them is the devil; the harvest is the end of the world; and the reapers are the angels. As therefore the tares are gathered and burned in the fire; so shall it be in the end of this world. The Son of man shall send forth his angels, and they shall gather out of his kingdom all things that offend, and them which do iniquity; and shall cast them into a furnace of fire: there shall be wailing and gnashing of teeth. Then shall the righteous shine forth as the sun in the kingdom of their Father (Matt. 13:36–43).

The minister continued his sermon, backing up scripture with scripture:

Out of the same mouth proceeded blessing and cursing. My brethren, these things ought not so to be. Doth a fountain send forth at the same place sweet water and bitter? Can the fig tree, my brethren, bear olive berries, or a vine, figs? So can no fountain both yield salt water and fresh? Who is a wise man and endued with knowledge among you? Let him shew out of a good conversation his works with meekness of wisdom. But if ye have bitter envying and strife in your hearts, glory not, and lie not against the truth. This wisdom descendeth not from above, but is earthly, sensual, and devilish. For where envying and strife is, there is confusion and every evil work. But the wisdom that is from above is first pure, then peaceable, gentle and easy to be entreated, full of mercy and good fruits, without partiality, and without hypocrisy. And the fruit of righteousness is sown in peace of them that make peace (James 3:10–18).

He who hath ears to hear, let him hear (Matt 13:43).

"Amen!"

James, marveling at the words he had just heard, suddenly remembered a prayer he prayed while on the island—a prayer pleading with God to deliver him from that forlorn place. Well, he had been delivered, and that in itself was a miracle, but now what?

Oh God, I feel You allowed me to survive the wrecking of that ship and the years I spent on that island for a reason, but for what reason? Please help me understand.

⌒

That evening, as James placed his head on a pillow, he thought about his future. What lay ahead? It seemed to him, he was, from every conceivable source, being guided, encouraged to give himself over to be used by God, but he had no idea what that meant, or how it might happen. And, of course, there was Mary. Was she to be a part of his life or not? Thinking those thoughts, he suddenly had a strange premonition that she might not be the one who would go with him into that future. As he slowly drifted off into deep slumber, he wondered; *If not Mary, then who?*

Chapter 10

She was walking the bluff, high above the river, when she saw him. It was a chilly morning, and the mist rising from the water seemed to be adding its coolness to the air. Although the moon, faintly seen now, was still visible, it was fading fast as the sun climbed higher in the eastern sky. The forest, even near the water's edge, was dense, and the tangled roots from the old sycamore, elm, and oak trees, which were now blanketed by fallen leaves, were spreading everywhere, hindering her footsteps.

He was lying beside the riverbank. At first he seemed to be struggling, trying to get up, but soon fell back onto the ground as if resigning himself to the inevitable, for now he wasn't moving at all, so she couldn't tell if he was alive—or worse, perhaps dead.

The trail leading to the river was a half mile behind her. It would take time to retrace her tracks, go down the treacherous path to the water's edge, and find the place where he was lying. Still, she felt compelled to at least try, and so turning she made her way back across the rough terrain, moved slowly down the hazardous hillside, edged her way along the riverbank, and cautiously approached the place where she had seen him.

When she bent over to take a look, she could see his eyes were closed; however, he was breathing, as strange sounds were coming from his mouth, and he was shaking. Was it "fire water"? Or perhaps the fever? Feeling his forehead would tell her. If it was hot, then it had to be the fever; so she knelt beside him, and carefully lifting her hand, laid it across his brow.

Suddenly he opened his eyes, and stared straight into hers. She pulled her arm back quickly, waiting to see what he might do next. What was he thinking? She wondered, but not for long, for just as suddenly as he had opened his eyes, she saw them close again, taking him into the abyss of unconsciousness.

Shinguaconse, "Little Pine," was an Indian, a Shawnee. Her father, along with the other members of the tribe, were leaving, having been forced out by the paleface and the great-grandfather in the East. Soon they would be going west to cross the big river. It truly would be "a trail of tears," for they were leaving a land that had been home now for many, many years—a land which possessed the remains of their loved ones, ancestors whose spirits had gone on to be with the Maker of Life.

Sadness filled Little Pine's heart, for it hurt her to see her father suffering so. He was a strong, mighty warrior and a handsome brave, and now to see him cut down so low, humbled beyond belief. . . . He had told her, with a tear forming in his eye, that soon they would be placed on the big "fire" canoe and shuttled down the great river, to resettle in a land far away.

As Little Pine stood looking out across the river, thinking about how her father was suffering, she pondered the fate of this paleface. Yes, he had been set on fire by "the fever," and he needed her help. Should she help him, or let him die? What would her father think if she brought him to the Shawnee camp to be nursed back to life? Was he not a part of the problem her father and the other men were now facing—the very reason for their hardship? No, she could not take him back to the Shawnee camp.

Yet the pale-skin people had found a very special place in Shinguaconse's heart, and they were as sad as she that the Indians were leaving. They had befriended her, telling her of a God who loved her and who gave His life for her. Many times she had turned to them for help, and they had always been there. Perhaps they would help this time; after all he was one of theirs. No, she could not let this paleface die! Somehow she had to try to save him. Perhaps, if she could get him into the canoe that was there on the riverbank, she could take him to the home of her paleface friend, Lavonia, who lived not far away. Certainly Lavonia and her family would help.

It would be a struggle getting him into the boat, as he was a big man, but with all the strength she could muster she would try. He needed help, and he needed it soon, or certainly he would die.

James woke with a start and sat straight up in bed. *What was I dreaming? It seemed so real. I was there, beside the river, dying . . . or I thought I was dying, but someone was there, sitting beside me. Who was she? An Indian, a Shawnee . . . and they called her "Little Pine." She was* **beautiful!**

As suddenly as James had awakened recalling the dream, it began to fade, leaving him wondering: *What was **that** all about?*

Little Pine! He would remember the name.

It was early, but he needed to be up early as he had work to do. His mother wanted him to paint the porch, and he knew it would take at least an hour or two to complete the job. The sooner he could get started the sooner it would get done, and the more time he could spend at the city dock.

James had stayed in New York throughout the summer doing numerous jobs for his mother, treasuring the time he spent with her reminiscing, hearing stories of Ireland. However, the East River Port on South Street was never far from his mind, for there he felt most at home, even though the sights and the sounds brought back memories of his father and the *Nancy Grace*. Those memories hurt, but the friends he and his father had made during the years helped sustain him. They wanted to hear his story, and the telling of it seemed to help heal the sadness he felt. Many he talked with were amazed at how such a thing could happen; but more than that, they wanted to help, so offered him numerous jobs, which he was happy to have, and they paid him well.

"Summer is about over, James; do you have any idea yet of what you might do?" Margaret asked.

"I've been thinking more and more about going west. Perhaps find Sister Ruth and John, my long-lost brother, of whom, as you know, I have really never known. How old was I when we left Pennsylvania?"

"You were still a baby when we came east to New York, so you never really got to know them. Ruth was married, had just gotten married, and John was older, too. He did not like the idea of living in a city, so they both stayed in Pennsylvania."

"Do they still live west of the Cumberland Valley?"

"As far as I know. I haven't heard from them for a long, long time," Margaret said, expressing concern. She had thought about them often, wondering how they were doing.

"I did get an offer from an old friend. You may remember him—Captain Jennings?"

"Oh yes, didn't he captain a ship that transported goods from New York to Baltimore on the Chesapeake?"

"Yes, Captain Jennings was an old cohort of father's. I remember he and father spent a lot of time together visiting when we were in port. They seem to have had a lot in common, and spent many a day together comparing notes and telling stories about their adventures at sea.

"Captain Jennings expressed a desire to help, so offered me a job aboard his boat, the *Cutty Sue,* as a coxswain. He said I could go with them to Baltimore. He told me that from there

I wouldn't have a problem finding my way north into the Cumberland Valley."

"Oh, James, I don't want you to go, but if you do, you can let Ruth and John know about father."

"Oh Mumsy, I was hoping I could convince you to sell this boarding house and go with me."

"No, James, I need to stay here. This is my home, I'm comfortable here, and the people who live here are like family; but also, I feel closer to your father in New York. So son, you go, but be sure you to stay in touch. Hopefully you'll be able to find a way to send a letter back so I will know you're safe and that all is well. And do let me know how Ruth and John are; that is, if you find them. I haven't heard anything from them for such a long time. If you find them, be sure to let them know how much they are missed and that they are always on my mind.

"Will you look for Mary?"

"Yes! I must find Mary, for though I try, it seems I cannot release her memory from my mind. I pray constantly that she is well, and that she is still Mary White. Yes Mum, I will find Mary!"

The day came when they would part again, this time perhaps forever. He knew the parting would be difficult for his mother. She had lost him once, not knowing whether he was dead or alive. But now, he was alive and he certainly would try to keep in touch with her, so he made a promise to send word back to her as soon as he could.

"If I can get a letter to Captain Jennings, he said he would bring my letters to New York and give them to you personally."

The week before their departure, Jennings, whose wife had died the year before, offered to visit Margaret from time to time, if that was acceptable to James.

When James told Margaret about Jennings' offer, Margaret did not remember Jennings that well, but was delighted that he was willing to help and began to think of him as a friend when James told her, "He promised me, Mum, he would take care of you, and see to it that you receive word from me, as he can get my letters to you, and deliver yours when he is in Baltimore."

"Oh Jimmy, that makes me feel much better about your leaving."

"I wish I could convince you to go with me; however, I know, too, how you feel about staying. But with Captain Jennings here to help you, it does take the worry away for me."

"Thank you, son, and tell Captain Jennings 'thank you' as well," Margaret told him with a relieved mind.

The day finally came when James would leave New York forever. As he stood on the deck of the *Cutty Sue,* watching the city disappear behind him, sadness gripped his heart. So many memories he was leaving; sights and sounds he would never see or hear again. It was another reminder of how sad life could be, but he had found hope—and that hope would sustain him, taking him into the future with a promise of things yet to be fulfilled. He had given his life to his Heavenly Father, and now with that life in God's hands, to be guided by Him, the future promised to be exciting, as he watched, waiting to see how the doors would open.

The trip down the coast was uneventful, but the forty-six thousand square miles of the Chesapeake Bay was an exciting experience to James. "The Algonquin Indians, who lived around the bay when the first settlers arrived in America, named the bay the *Chesepiooc*, which means "Great Shellfish Bay," Captain Jennings said.

On that day in 1825, the bay was full of boats, but the newly invented ones powered by steam fascinated James. Having been aware of them on the rivers that framed the city of New York, he had always been excited on the rare occasion when he saw one, but here, on the Chesapeake, they seemed to be numerous. Their ability to navigate the twisty, narrow channels of tidewater rivers was a wonder to behold. Flying by, going ten to twelve miles an hour, with their paddlewheels pushed by steam, wiping the brackish waters of the bay, was a marvel to see. On the other hand, the *Cutty Sue,* a two-mast schooner, having to depend on the whims of the wind, wasn't going nearly that fast. The steamboats were an impressive sight indeed, for James had never experienced anything like them.

As they continued sailing up the Chesapeake to the Patapsco River on their way to Baltimore, James could see the wooden siding of the clapboard houses as they became more and more apparent, their pitched roofs outstanding against the sapphire sky. They seemed to shine now under the rays of the afternoon sun.

When Fort McHenry, which was strategically placed, came into view, Jennings began to talk, recapturing images of the War of 1812 when the city of Washington was set ablaze by the British, who then moved further up the bay to take the city of Baltimore.

"That fort was built during the Revolution," Jennings told James, as he pointed toward the garrison. James found it interesting to now see the fort, as he remembered Jennings talking about it while they were on the waterfront in New York City.

"The people of Baltimore were afraid of a British attack back then, and so used the peninsula as a fort, but recently, during the last war, the British tried to attack Baltimore from there. When the bombing began, the *Cutty Sue* was anchored in the harbor over there, not far from Fells Point," Jennings turned his head and looked toward the west. "We were frightened beyond belief, because we really didn't know what was happening. We could hear the bombing, and it seemed like it went on for hours. We thought it would never stop, but, thank goodness, the artillery in the fort was able to keep the British at bay.

"They say there were a thousand soldiers there that day. Some were federal soldiers who were stationed at the fort, but many more were just volunteers from the city. I heard the British had powerful weapons, but I guess they weren't very accurate, which to them was alright, because they really weren't all that interested in a war with America. They did it more as a punishment because of their defeat in the Revolution. The British felt they could fight that war and it would cost them precious little; so as far as they were concerned, the war could go on forever."

"I remember talking with you about that on the waterfront, how the British were worried about Napoleon and didn't feel they could take on another fight—that is, until he went into exile. After that, it freed them up so they could then concentrate on their war with America," James said.

"Yes; however, I don't think the British realize how resourceful we Americans are," Jennings said, "for we had that huge instrument of defense, called 'privateers' or legalized piracy."

"I remember those men, who rescued me from that island, talking about those privateers," James said.

"Well, it was too bad that we were forced to use them, but our navy was so small. We only had ten ships, and were going up against a British force of nine hundred or more, so our government, in order to reward those privateers for their help, let them keep and sell any of the British ships they captured. I heard it was possible for a well-trained, well-captained ship to take as many as two or three a week."

"Yes, and unfortunately, after that war, those men turned to piracy," James said, as he looked toward the fort, amazed that such a thing could happen.

As Jennings talked, images of the *Bald Hornet* filled James' mind again, causing him to wonder, *Could the* Bald Hornet *have been one of those vessels fighting the British, defending America during that war?*

"Baltimore, I guess, became the major port for a lot of those privateers," Jennings continued. "Sailing from here, they captured more than five hundred British vessels, as those privateers went everywhere. They even went to the ports in the United Kingdom. The British tried to stop them, and that's when they attempted to penetrate Fort McHenry but were unable to do so, as the entrance to the Baltimore Harbor is strewn with their sunken ships, numbering as many as twenty-two, or so they say. I guess the British had to bomb the fort from a pretty far distance away.

"I remember the bombing. All through the night, missiles and bombs burst, exploding everywhere. Though they were at a distance, they seemed to be bursting over our heads, and it continued for hours. We thought it would never stop, but then just as suddenly as it started it came to a screeching halt, as it began to rain, and the rainfall was heavy. We couldn't tell who was winning, but in the faint glow of the early morning sunrise, someone yelled, 'I see it, our flag, it's still there; it's flying!' I remember it like yesterday. I couldn't believe it, but it was true! Actually, there was little damage done on either side, when the British stopped their attack. It was September the

14th, 1814, almost eleven years ago. I will always remember that day."

As Baltimore Harbor came into view, James could see more clapboard houses and so many ships that it was impossible for him to count them. They covered the waterfront, either loading or dispatching numerous products.

James spent several days on the waterfront, helping Captain Jennings and talking to anyone along the port who could advise him on how he might find a way north into the Cumberland Valley.

"Those wagons were built by Mennonite Germans in the Conestoga near Lancaster, Pennsylvania," one of the drivers said.

James struck up a conversation with the fellow, as he stood looking out across the waterfront where numerous wagons were either being loaded or unloaded. That day, the driver told him tobacco was being exported, coming from Maryland and other surrounding states. "It's bound for England," he said.

"Those wagons look like boats."

"Yes, they're shaped that way because it makes it easier for them to float across rivers and streams. They're heavy, too. They weigh up to six tons, but they'll be even heavier after we load those bags of sugar on them," the driver said.

"Where did that sugar come from?"

"It's imported from the Caribbean, and it's slow travel, as you'll find out," the driver said. "We have to walk most of the way guiding those horses, and there's at least a dozen of them pulling each wagon. We're lucky if we can make fifteen miles a day, but if you want, you're more than welcome to join us. We can always use help."

"It's worth a try, and I can certainly use the pay," James said, "and I am going your way, as I want to get to Shippensburg in the Cumberland Valley. How close to there will you be going?"

"We'll be traveling that way, as we're headed to Hagerstown. We'll be taking the Frederick-town Turnpike to Boonsboro. In Boonsboro the turnpike goes to Hagerstown. I'm sure in Hagerstown you can find a way north to Shippensburg."

As James listened to the fellow, he suddenly thought of Mary; *I might find her before crossing the mountains to look for my brother and sister.*

It was nearing October, and the need to encounter the mountains before the harsh winds of winter hit the rugged peaks was paramount.

James spent his last night on the *Cutty Sue*. By the morning light, he made ready to depart the ship, saying his goodbyes to Captain Jennings and the crew. It was a difficult thing to do, for he was leaving behind another world, another life that would never again be a part of his. Now, daring to discover a new one, and with his Heavenly Father as his guide, he left the schooner to join the wagons departing the river port.

The travel was slow, just like the driver said it would be, and it was uneventful, but they did eventually reach their destination. James helped unload the bags of sugar, received his pay, and said his farewells as he headed toward the streets of Hagerstown.

Making his way along the dirt roads of the town, he stopped at an old inn to inquire how he might go north, hoping to gain information on the time and length of a trip to Shippensburg.

"The major route north is a road that follows an old Indian trail the pioneers called the Virginia Path," the innkeeper told him. "It connects the Potomac River with the Susquehanna, and runs through the center of the Cumberland Valley. It's about thirty miles, or perhaps a little more, up that path to Shippensburg."

With a good night's rest James felt, with some certainty, he might make it in a day or two, and the thought of finding Mary kept him going.

Chapter 11

It was daylight, but the Cumberland Valley was dark, covered by a dense forest which hid the sun. Occasionally the trees parted, and when they did James could see spots of amber, crimson, and ginger on a distant hillside, shining among the massive green leaves. Preparing for the winter ahead, the summer trees were beginning to display their autumn beauty as James walked along the old Indian path, taking in the view. Pleased to see a break in the trees, he looked up. A flock of migrating birds was circling, but soon turned, crossed over the mountains, and headed south. He would see an owl on a branch of a tree, a raccoon, a fox, or some other animal occasionally peek its head out of the thick underbrush, as if curious, wondering who he was and why he was there.

Even though the forest was dark, James could sense a glorious day spread out before him. The vision of it now captured his attention, bringing with it stories he had heard about Pennsylvania.

"Most of southwestern Pennsylvania was settled by our people, men and women who came here from Northern Ireland throughout the 1700s," he remembered his father saying. "There were many reasons why they came, my son, but the failure of the United Irishmen brought a new wave of immigrants to the area in the late 1700s."

As James walked the dark forest, he recalled a conversation he had one Sunday with Cyrus Mason, pastor of the

Cedar Street Presbyterian Church in New York. He remembered him saying how much the Scotch-Irish had influenced America.

"Second to the British, they were the most prominent English-speaking group in the colonies, and certainly held a strong influence in establishing our representative government. Many of them were leaders who advanced the idea of liberty, especially the right to be left alone, since they had experienced much suffering and hardship in their own country."

James learned that many of the Scotch-Irish had left or were leaving their homes along the Eastern seaboard. They were coming west through the Cumberland Gap, to settle in the backcountry of Pennsylvania.

"Because they left their churches behind, life has been difficult, for many have given up the faith, or so I've heard. They've turned to bad living, certainly not the kind of life they were taught when they attended church, or lived where there was a strong Christian influence," the pastor had said.

As James walked the old Indian trail, he prayed that if God was not already doing so, that He would send men willing to trudge that wilderness to reach those people with His Word. Yet, even as he prayed, he had a strange premonition that he, James Scott, was being called to do that very thing. It seemed as though God was placing within his heart an awareness that the only way the nation could continue to be free was not just from knowing the Bible, but believing it . . . putting its very words into action!

It would take faith—lots of faith—and much courage. He wondered if he had enough of both.

It was Sunday morning when James finally approached Shippensburg, the dense forest disappearing behind him. He could now see houses scattered across a hillside, surrounded by cleared fields. To his right was a spring where water was surging to the surface from an unknown source, making a rather loud lapping sound. He would continue on his path toward the town, which he supposed was not more than a mile or two away, but before he did he stopped at the spring to get a drink and wash his face and hands. As he stood there, relaxing in the early morning sunlight, he suddenly heard singing coming from somewhere in the woods.

What is that? James wondered.

With an aroused curiosity, he found himself walking toward the sound. Cutting through the forest, he saw men standing beside the stream, which seemed to wind itself around a hillside. There were other men sitting on logs—trees they had cut down and split in two for that purpose. As he approached the group, a man turned to him, stretched out his arm, and took his hand. Soon others did the same.

"Welcome, my brother," was their greeting. They motioned for him to have a seat on one of the logs, which he most graciously accepted, for he was tired from having walked several miles that morning and all day the day before.

As soon as the singing stopped, a man climbed upon a tree stump and began talking.

"Brethren, we are all under a law. No, it's not a law made by man, and governed by force, but one of love. For the Lord told them, 'if you love Me you will keep my commandments, and this is the greatest commandment: that you love the Lord, your God, with all your heart and all your soul, and love your neighbor as yourself.'

"Love is the fulfilling of that law . . . now there is faith, hope, and love, but the greatest of these is love.

"The Scripture says, 'Bless those who curse you, do good to those who despitefully use you . . . love your enemy. For who knows, that man may be an angel in disguise. . . .'

". . . and the Good Samaritan that day, on the dusty road to Jerusalem, took in the fallen man after he had been stripped and left to die by others. The priest and the Levite past him by, but the Samaritan stopped, bound up the stranger's wounds, and carried him into the village. Did he check to see if he was a Presbyterian or a horse thief? No! He was just a man needing his love and care.

"And Jesus said, 'Go and do likewise.'

"Remember the woman caught in adultery? They were ready to stone her to death when Jesus bent down and wrote on the ground, and then told them, 'Let him who is without sin cast the first stone.' Ashamed, they each went away, and Jesus said to her? "Woman where are your accusers? Has no one condemned you? Then neither do I; go and sin no more.' Was that not an example of God's love, teaching us to love one another, to forgive as He has forgiven us?

"Remember when Jesus fed the multitude? With only two fish and five loaves of bread, He fed the five thousand. There on that hillside, away from the city Jesus fed them and instructed them. He healed the sick, made the lame to walk again, and the blind to see. It was God's love teaching us, by example, to love one another.

"And did He not die for us, and is that not the greatest love of all?

"Brethren, we all have needs, and we must help one another. Is there a stranger among us? Does he have cares? Let us reach out in love to those we do not know, telling them of Jesus and His love for all. It matters not if the stranger is a horse thief, a liar, or a murderer—all the more, for if we love, if we really care, we will take the time to help him get on his feet, to make amends, and above all, to know the love the God of all creation has for him—and brethren, the only means God has of doing this is through our hands, our feet, and our mouths—and through our love one for another.

"And Paul, while he, himself was suffering and in prison wrote: 'Therefore I, the prisoner of the Lord, beseech you that ye walk worthy of the vocation wherewith ye are called, with all lowliness and meekness, with longsuffering, forbearing one another in love; endeavoring to keep the unity of the Spirit in the bond of peace' (Eph. 4:1–3).

"Overcome evil with good. Amen."

When the man stopped talking, he bowed his head for a brief moment.

Remembering the prayer he had prayed, James thought, *Well, it seems God is sending men into the backcountry to proclaim His Word.* Suddenly, being pulled from his thoughts, he heard a man from somewhere in the crowd singing, and it wasn't long before others joined in as well.

> A mighty fortress is our God,
> a bulwark never failing;
> our helper he amid the flood
> of mortal ills prevailing.
> For still our ancient foe
> doth seek to work us woe;
> his craft and power are great,

and armed with cruel hate,
on earth is not his equal.

Did we in our own strength confide,
our striving would be losing,
were not the right man on our side,
the man of God's own choosing.
Dost ask who that may be?
Christ Jesus, it is he;
Lord Sabaoth, is his name,
from age to age the same,
and he must win the battle.

And though this world, with devils filled,
should threaten to undo us,
we will not fear, for God hath willed
his truth to triumph through us.
The Prince of Darkness grim,
we tremble not for him;
his rage we can endure,
for lo, his doom is sure;
one little word shall fell him

That word above all earthly powers,
no thanks to them, abideth;
the Spirit and the gifts are ours,
thru him who with us sideth.
Let goods and kindred go,
this mortal life also;

the body they may kill;
God's truth abideth still;
his kingdom is forever.

When the singing was over, the man sat down. Almost immediately, someone else got up to continuing the discourse, which went on for another hour or more, captivating James. He took in every word, which was mostly scriptural, and marveled at their knowledge. It was as if he had met Jesus in the wilderness, hearing Him speak.

When one man finished talking, another man began. Hours passed. Soon the morning sun slipped well beyond the ridge of the hill. Then just as suddenly as it started, it stopped. James wondered why, when suddenly he saw women in the distance, coming over the hillside carrying baskets filled with food. He assumed or perhaps hoped it was food, as he was hungry. And there were children following along beside the women, as well.

The men lowered their heads and began to pray, asking for God's guidance, His mercy, and His blessings. The women joined the men, displaying an impressive array of food. James couldn't remember when he had seen so much in one place. There was corn and potatoes, and he could smell roasted pork. It was harvest time, and food was plentiful. Some of the women carried pies as well—peach and cherry, and his favorite, apple.

The men invited him to eat, for which he was most grateful, and then they introduced themselves one by one. Seeming pleased he had come, they wanted to know more about him: who he was, and why he was there.

"I walked here from Hagerstown in search of family," James told them. "My father and mother lived for a short time in Pennsylvania. I was born, at the turn of the century, on the other side of the mountains along the Valley View Road, but my parents moved back to New York City when I was a baby, as my father was a shipper. I have not been back to Pennsylvania since. I came here, to the Valley, to look for my wife."

Realizing he had a captive audience, James continued, and soon he found himself telling the story of his short yet spellbinding life.

After he finished talking, one of the men stood up and said, "That's fascinating, James. I wonder if you would like to come to our church this coming Wednesday evening to tell it again? Our church is the Middle Springs Presbyterian. It's the old stone building on Middle Springs Road. You can't miss it. We feel the folks there would love to hear your story. We'll check with our pastor, to see if he would be agreeable."

"I certainly appreciate your wanting me to do that," James said, dumbfounded they had asked him. "I will consider it, that is, if it is acceptable to your minister. But, for now I would like to know about you, and why you are holding a church service in these woods." He could tell they had been there for several days, as there were tents at the edge of the woods.

"You're witnessing a camp meeting," one of the men said.

"Amen!" said another.

"We're here because the Lord has asked us to. He has directed us to care for the souls of men. We have criss-crossed this land teaching and preaching His Word. We've set up these camp meetings, praying that God will not bring down His judgment upon our land, for He has made us aware of how easy it is for men to drift away from His truth. It's out of a love and concern for this country and its future that we are having these meetings." The man speaking seemed to be the leader of the group.

"Amen!" someone else shouted.

"Have you heard of the Great Awakening? It was a revival that took place in the early 1700s in New England. They say it stirred the hearts of men so much so that it caused more than twenty-five thousand people to turn to God and to seek His face," the leader continued. "We certainly don't want to lose that, for just as Jesus taught the five thousand on a hillside that overlooked the Sea of Galilee, and so we, feeling His calling, are now His voice, here in this wilderness, these virgin forests of Pennsylvania. It is our prayer that His words will make a difference in the lives of men—and with that knowledge, we will be able to keep this great nation free."

"I find that most interesting," James said, as he reflected on what the man said. "I have often wondered if He is not asking me if I would be willing to do the same."

As James continued listening to the men talk, while enjoying his meal, a rather tall, lanky fellow approached him. With his long beard hanging, swaying in the breeze, he bent over and reached down to offer his hand to James.

"How'dee, it's good to make your acquaintance. I'm thinking we're family. My name is Samuel—Samuel Willis. You can call me Sam; ever' one else does. I believe your grandma and my Great Aunt Viney was sisters. Anyway, I've heard of the *Nancy Grace* and about your dad being a shipper. She used to talk about him all the time 'fore she died."

James reached up to take the fellow's hand, but when he heard the word "family," he sprang to his feet.

Sam Willis continued, "Not much family here in the Valley now, nor over on them mountains. They've moved to Ohio! Didn't you have a brother over them hills? Well, I heard tell they moved, too. He's a'livin' in an area called Jackson in one of those new states, Ohio. They moved about two year' or so ago."

"You don't say?" James now gave Sam his complete attention. Desiring to learn more, he wondered if that could be the reason his mother had not heard from his brother and sister for such a long time.

"I don't know much more than that. Guess they just got tired of livin' on them hills. They wanted flat land to plow, or so I'm told."

James offered Sam a seat beside him as Sam continued to talk, for James wanted to hear all Sam had to say about his family. In the end, Sam invited James to his house to meet his wife and 'kinfolk,' and offered for him to stay the night, but James decided to spend what time he had left in Shippensburg at the village inn, as he was hoping he might gain some knowledge as to the whereabouts of Mary.

That evening, at the village inn, James was able to talk to a few people, but he was disappointed that none knew Mary. He found out that most of the inn people were passing through, and were as much of a stranger to the area as he.

On Wednesday evening James entered the quaint little stone building that housed the Middle Springs Presbyterian Church. The thirty-five-square-foot structure, with its dirt floor, held several slab benches on which the people sat, and they were full, with many standing at the back of the room. The building wasn't heated, and on that late September evening, a chill went through the air.

James remembered the men, at the camp meeting, saying that the church always gathered on Wednesday evenings for a prayer meeting. That Wednesday evening, before the people prayed, the minister stood at the foot of the platform and introduced James, telling them that James had agreed to come and relay a short but exciting story of his life—and that he had been asked to do so by members of the church, for they had found his story fascinating.

With the pulpit high above the heads of the people, James could feel a cool draft as he reluctantly climbed the steps to the platform. Sensing a fear of the unknown, he stood before the congregation with an uneasy feeling; yet his nervousness did not hinder the excitement that seemed to fill him as he began to tell his story. As he talked, he looked out across the faces of the people who were now seated before him. They seemed mesmerized by what they were hearing, for not a person moved.

"As you can see, I felt that God, through the Holy Spirit, was directing me time and time again while I was on that island," James told them. "Then one evening the voice seemed to be telling me to go to the cross on the hill. It was late, and I knew not why I was to go there. I had always gone to the cross in the morning, but now the voice was telling me to go at night. However, the moon was full, and it was spreading its light everywhere, so I could easily see my way up the hillside to where the cross stood. As I was standing there looking out across the water, I saw it, a small boat anchored at the edge of the coral reef not far away. . . ." James continued, leaving nothing out, trying to tell his now-captive audience what he had experienced, without showing the sadness and the sorrow he still felt in his heart.

When he finished his rather lengthy narrative, he told them about Mary. "Please, if you know anything about her, or have heard her name, Mary White, please do let me know. I would deeply appreciate it," James said, as he stepped down from the podium, praying that someone might come forward with knowledge of her whereabouts.

The minister, having been moved by James' story, approached him as he stepped down from the pulpit. Putting his hands upon his shoulders, he asked if he might say a prayer specifically for him.

Later, after the service was over, they talked.

"My brother, I believe the Lord has his hand on you. Perhaps He has predestined you to be in His service. Where and how, only our Heavenly Father knows, but I do believe it might happen. I will certainly remember you when I pray, James, and I wanted you to know too, that Mary, Rachel, and Will came to church here a few times before they left Shippensburg. Yes, they left a month or so ago. I'm not quite certain where they were headed when they left, but they did talk about Washington County. They were hoping to look for family who had moved there not long ago. Sorry, James, but that's all I can tell you. You might inquire at the inn. Perhaps the innkeeper would know more. God bless you in your search, my brother. My prayers go with you, for I do pray you find her."

Well that's that, thought James. *It seems Mary and her sister might be living somewhere in Washington County, and my family left Pennsylvania some years ago for Jackson, Ohio! No need for me to stay here! Guess I'll be moving on.*

Chapter 12

Dear Mums,

As I write this letter, I am praying all is well with you. I miss you more than I can say. My journey to the Cumberland Valley proved to be disappointing. I did not find Mary. I did, however, meet a fellow, Samuel Willis, who said he was my second or third cousin. Do you remember him? I was happy to make Sam's acquaintance, as he knew the whereabouts of David and Ruth. It seems they moved west to one of the new states, Ohio, and are living somewhere in an area they call Jackson. I'm on my way there now, but first my plans are to stop by Washington, Pennsylvania to look for Mary. The minister of a church in Shippensburg told me that he believes that is where she and her sister and brother-in-law went. He wasn't certain about it, so I may not find her. I pray I will, as thinking of her fills my mind more and more, for it seems I cannot release the memory of her from it.

Did Captain Jennings meet with you? I'm anxious to know if he was any help. I enjoyed being with him on my trip down the coast. In many ways he reminds me of Father!

I don't know much else at this time. I will try to get this letter to you by way of Captain Jennings and will write more when I find Mary, as I am determined now to find her.

God be with you, Mums.

Your loving son,
James

James made his way back to Hagerstown, Maryland, where the Conestoga wagons stopped. He was eager to see if anyone there could deliver a letter, for he had heard that getting mail sent by the newly established postal service was next to impossible.

"A person might be able to send a letter, but the chances of it getting delivered is uncertain, as the service lacks experience, and transportation is poor," he remembered the innkeeper saying.

If I could get one of the Conestoga drivers to take it to Baltimore, perhaps they could get it to Captain Jennings. He was hoping, too, that he might find someone who knew the way to Washington County; and after conversation with numerous people, he soon found himself on a turnpike leading to Cumberland, Maryland. From there, he was told, he could take the newly developed Cumberland Road that went right through the town of Washington. Walking, it would take him several days, as it was about one hundred and fifty miles from Hagerstown to Washington. Calculating the cost, he decided to take what they called a "coach and six"—it was a coach drawn by six horses—and soon found himself crowded on the stagecoach with five other people. The ride was anything but relaxing as they flew down the highway swinging back and forth, sitting on seats that were much too narrow for comfort. But the newly built Cumberland Road, which James found exciting, was reliable and he learned that the fastest way west was by stagecoach. So James settled back, resigning himself to the inevitable, while observing the other people traveling with him. He wondered if they, too, found their state of affairs as unpleasant as he.

The Cumberland Road was wide. He estimated it to be at least sixty feet across, with a surface of stones and gravel. It made a solid track for the numerous wagons and stagecoaches traveling its route, and the traffic seemed as dense to James as any street in New York City.

Crossing over the mountains, he soon realized why the stage had six horses instead of the usual four: The hills and valleys, with their elevations and depressions, seemed to require it. On many occasions a postillion—an extra driver—was needed to assist them up the steep slopes, with the crest at Negro Mountain being the highest point, reaching an elevation of more than three thousand feet.

Although the task of getting use to the stagecoach was difficult, listening to the driver blow a horn—which made an ear-piercing sound each time it came to a stop—was unnerving to James. And the stage stopped every ten to fifteen miles either to water or change horses, pick up mail, get new passengers, or let someone off. James soon realized that if he left the coach for even a few minutes to stretch his legs, there was never enough time before the stagecoach was off and running again.

But the hours went quickly by, as James' attention was captured by the many heavily laden canvas-covered wagons they passed. He wondered where they were going and what they might be carrying, and never far from sight were numerous horses and buggies as well. But what really excited James were the iron posts he saw along the way, which marked the distance from point to point. Reading them, he could easily calculate how far they had traveled.

As they were flying down the highway, suddenly the weather made a turn for the worse, as a heavy storm brewing in the west soon made its appearance on the mountainous roadway. The rain pelted down in sheets, eventually turning into a torrential downpour. With the rain coming down hard now, bright flashes of lightning boomed in the air, frightening the horses and causing them to run faster than usual. After a while, though, they seemed to settle down into a slower, steadier pace—realizing, James assumed, that they had had similar experiences in the past, and all had gone well. The canvas-covered wagons, however, did not fare as well; many were stopping by the roadside waiting for the storm to pass.

The situation certainly wasn't producing an environment for conversation, so James and the other passengers traveled along in silence for several miles before the rain finally came to an end.

"Boy that was some rainfall!" James said, attempting to start a conversation with the fellow seated next to him.

"Yep!" the stranger said.

"Are you from around here?" James asked, trying his best to be friendly.

"Nope!"

"Oh? Well, I'm hoping to get to the town of Washington. This highway is a marvel, isn't it?"

"Yep."

"How far are you going?"

"Grantsville."

"How far is that?" James was now becoming a little exasperated with the one-sided conversation.

"Fifteen mile."

"Is that where you live?"

"Yep."

"Well, I'll be going a little farther than that, I guess. Do you know how far it is from there to Washington, Pennsylvania?"

"Sixty mile."

With that little bit of information, the conversation seemed to come to an end, so James and the stranger sat in complete silence, listening to the clip-clop of the horses' hoofs as they moved over the stone-paved highway.

As they continued their journey on the Cumberland Road, James would occasionally see an inn, tavern, or other businesses which were either being built or already established along its route. But most of the countryside was wilderness. A thick forest dominated the landscape, blotting out the afternoon sun. He could hear the sound of bleating sheep or saw herds of cattle, either being driven to markets in the east or new pastures in the west, and both were never far from sight.

As they approached Grantsville a huge bridge came into view. It must have had an expanse, James calculated, of at least seventy-five or eighty feet. It was made of stone, the like of which he had not seen before, even in the city of New York. Later he learned the river was named after an Indian. They called it the Little Youghiogheny, and that night he considered camping along its bank. However, the ground had been saturated by the rain, and the autumn air which now penetrated the mountains was anything but warm, so he made the choice to stay at a newly constructed inn, which sat on a hillside in Grantsville.

The next morning James ate a light meal at the inn before picking up his pack and heading out onto the highway again. He would walk the rest of the way, soon realizing the benevolence of his fellow travelers, as he didn't go far before securing a ride, which turned out to be the first of several, shortening the two-day journey.

Reading the markers, he guessed he was nearing Washington when a man in a two-wheel carriage with its calash (top) folded back, drawn by a single horse, stopped and asked if he would care to join him. The body of the carriage hung on leather straps and moved slightly, as James placed his foot on the step to climb into the seat beside the stranger.

"Hello, thanks for the lift," James spoke first, desiring his benefactor to know how much he appreciated the ride. "We must be getting pretty close to Washington."

"It's not far now. Is that where you're headed?" the gentleman inquired. He was dressed in a black suit, with a white and black cravat tied loosely about his neck. His tousled reddish-brown hair and long Roman shaped nose revealed a dignity that immediately demanded respect. James guessed the man to be about forty.

"Yes. How far, exactly, is it?" James said.

"Oh, maybe five miles. Where are you from?" the stranger asked.

"I'm from nowhere now, but I lived in New York City for a number of years. My father was a shipper, and I was his first mate. We made many trips to Northern Ireland and the British Isles shipping flax."

"Oh, you're from Ulster then?" the stranger asked with some curiosity.

"Well no, I'm not, but my father was born there, in County Down, near Newry. He came to America in '98. I was born here, in this country."

"Your father was a shipper? How interesting. And he lived near Newry? My father lived in Newry for a while when he was a lad, and I have two uncles, my dad's brothers, who started a school there. I attended their school for a couple of years when I was ten, and then taught there myself later. It was an interesting place for a lad of ten, as I remember the wharf and all the ships that sailed to and from. When I was nineteen, I went back to Newry to teach for one of my uncles, who was no longer living, but soon after that, we sailed for America.

"By the way, I'm Alexander Campbell." The stranger now reached out his hand in a friendly gesture towards James.

"Nice to meet you, Mr. Campbell; I'm James Scott."

"Please, call me Alexander."

"That is interesting, Alexander," James responded. "My father lived out in the country on a farm. It was closer to Bellikiel, but I had other family who lived in Newry. He and my mum came here after the siege by the Britons, when the English government proclaimed martial law. I guess there were some pretty bad things going on then," James noted.

"Oh, how right you are, James. My father has told the story many, many times of preaching in the country at a rural church, not far from Newry, when someone came running into the church yelling, 'The Welsh horses are coming!' Not too long after that, troops, dressed for battle, surrounded the building and were ready to assault any and all as soon as they left the premises. The captain of those troops thought the men inside were rebels, since they were meeting out in the country, and soon came marching into the church making threats. He was looking for anyone who might be a member of the United Irishmen. My father, a pious man, started to pray, and when he did the captain bowed his head, too. After the prayer ended, the captain left. It was a frightening experience, as my father was aware that several of the men who were there were a part of that group."

"But, tell me more about your experiences at sea, James. I find that fascinating. My experience with ships has not been a good one, especially since I was shipwrecked once on my way here to America. Even though it was bad, yet it turned out perhaps to be ordained by God, as I was able to spend a year at the University of Glasgow, which was very rewarding, but that's another story. Tell me about your experiences," Alexander said.

James went into the whole account again, leaving nothing out, and his story totally fascinated Alexander.

"I believe the Lord has his hand on you, James. How much do you know about the faith?"

"Not as much as I would like to know," James confessed.

"Perhaps I can teach you. I would consider it a privilege. How long will you be in Washington?" Alexander asked.

"I'm not certain. I'm going there to look for my wife. Well, she isn't my wife any longer, but we were married once, before I was shipwrecked and on that island for two years," James said, as he continued telling Alexander his long, sad story. "I've traveled a long way to find her, as I've been told she is living somewhere in Washington County. I'm not absolutely certain about it, as a minister at a church in Shippensburg said that's where she and her sister and brother-in-law were going, but he wasn't sure. I may not find her." James lowered his head, as he felt a pain going through his heart, but the rays from the afternoon sun, brushing the side of his face, replaced the feeling with hope.

"I'm a part of a group of Christians who are now meeting in the town of Wellsburg, about twenty miles west of Washington, but I know many people who live in Washington. Someone may know her. I can ask them. What's her name?"

"Mary White." James' hope was now getting a boost.

Growing more interested, James asked Alexander, "What do you know about the town of Washington? How many people live there?"

"Well, there are over a thousand people who reside there now, mostly Scotch-Irish. It's the county seat of Washington County and an important trade center. It seems to be a rapidly growing town, and has several different churches. I was an elder in a church not far from there called Brush Run; that is, until a new church was started in Wellsburg. The town does have a weekly newspaper, so perhaps you could put a request in the paper to see if anyone might know Mary White."

"That's a great idea! Yes, I will do that," James said, as he considered the possibility.

"Do you live in Washington, Alexander?"

"No! I live on a farm twenty miles west of the town, along Buffalo Creek. It's across the county line in the Virginia panhandle. I would be happy to have you come and visit while you are in the area, perhaps stay a night or two at our home. I could teach you about the faith, and how we came to know what we now believe. James, have you been baptized?"

"Yes, I was sprinkled as a baby," James said, curious now as the question seemed to come out of nowhere, but Alexander's inquiry held a passion that demanded an answer.

"Remember Paul in the New Testament?"

"Oh, yes. I read the Bible a lot."

"Well, he tells us in the book of Romans: 'Know ye not that so many of us as were baptized into Jesus Christ were baptized into his death. Therefore, we are buried with him by baptism into death; that like as Christ was raised up from the dead by the glory of the Father, even so we also should walk in newness of life' (Rom. 6:3).

"A man, James, isn't buried in water if only a few drops are sprinkled on him. To be a believer, you've got to be immersed; that's scriptural baptism and it's the only way. I was sprinkled myself once," Alexander continued, "and I believed, at the time, that, that was the correct way, as I was told by the church it was right; but later as I read Scripture, I found no authority for infant baptism. Baptism isn't a matter of someone's opinion, or for men in the church to decide. It shouldn't be a preference because it's always been done that way. Baptism is a divine command and is written in Scripture. Faith is the reason why we become a child of God's, but it is in baptism that we display that faith and become united with Him.

"*Baptizo* is a Greek word which means 'baptize,' or to plunge, dip, or immerse. And it is for believers only. An infant can't believe. But should he die before he is old enough to be immersed, he would go straight to God. For Jesus said. 'Suffer little children to come unto me for such is the Kingdom of Heaven.'"

"Where," James said, "did the idea of infant baptism come from then?"

"Tradition! Perhaps in the early church when it was under enormous persecution, a persecution which, we, today, living in complete freedom, cannot begin to comprehend; when killing a Christian was like slaying a wild animal. The church, during those dreadful years, may have sprinkled their young out of fear that they would soon die, and an open baptism in a river would certainly have meant death." Alexander Campbell looked at his young prodigy, as if wondering if he fully understood the impact of what he was saying. And then he continued.

"Sprinkling would have been the only way, James. But now, in this country, where the church is freer than it has ever been, freer than even when Christ was on earth, we have the privilege, and the preservation of Scripture, thanks to all those Christians who sacrificed their lives to pass the Word of God down to us, to go forward with it baptizing, immersing the believer in the name of the Father, Son, and Holy Ghost."

"So, you are telling me," James said, "that instead of looking to Scripture in understanding the faith, the church, by long tradition, has, in sprinkling babies, continued doing what the church has always done since that second century, when it was under persecution?"

"Exactly, and I do understand how difficult it is giving up those traditions, for I have had to do that. But I now believe, in this land of freedom, we not only have the privilege of breaking those traditions, but are being called to do so. We must return to the 'simple' gospel of those first-century Christians who walked and talked with Jesus, and I have felt the call to encourage all churches to do that very thing—to teach the Bible and the Bible only." Alexander slapped the reins over the back of the young mare, as if putting emphasis to what he was saying.

"One of the things I noticed," he continued, "was when we landed in Philadelphia and traveled across the Allegheny Mountains to our new home here in Washington County, a journey of about five hundred miles, that every door of every inn and tavern we stopped at along the way opened with merely a latch. There weren't any locks. My, in Ireland they barred the doors, especially at night, for fear of the unknown, and many times during the day as well.

"James, this country was founded by Christians, and because it was, we, here in the rich virgin forest of Pennsylvania, Virginia, Kentucky, Ohio, and beyond, have the privilege of being in a land abounding in freedom. I believe God is calling his people now to loosen the ties of man's 'creeds, opinions, commands and traditions' and to return to the 'simple gospel.' We need to look at our 'orthodoxy' through the lens of Scripture, and where it differs, we need to declare the Scriptures as truth. I cannot emphasize that enough." Alexander, sitting high in his seat, with his long legs stretched out before him, was expressing a passion, the knowledge of which had taken years of study and experience to acquire.

James, quietly pondering what he had just heard, thought, *Perhaps I should be immersed. I would like to be, but how?*

"James, I can give you directions to my home. It would be an honor to have you go to church with us in Wellsburg on Sunday. After church, if you desire, I will bring you back to my house and baptize you in Buffalo Creek. This time of year it will be cool, even cold, but we can do it fast in order to get you out of the water as quickly as possible; but you need not waste time, as the days are not getting any warmer."

"Yes, I think I would like that, if what you are saying is true, and I now believe it is. I have one problem: Mary. I must find her. I'll put a notice in the Washington newspaper to see if anyone knows of her whereabouts, and if I don't find her, then I will come to your home. If I do find her, perhaps she could come with me and we could be baptized together."

Gaining a feeling of optimism, James set back in the carriage, relaxing. He looked out over the rolling hills of the countryside. The blue sky, with its few fleecy white clouds, reflected the afternoon sun, while the thick forest which previously dominated the landscape had disappeared behind them. He could now see cleared land, dotted with goldenrod and persimmon, ripened by autumn's first frost. They hugged miles of log fencing that criss-crossed over farms where grazing cattle and sheep were claiming the last bit of nourishment from the fields before the cold winds of winter hardened the fertile soil. There were rows of shucked corn, which had recently felt the farmer's scythe, and fodder placed in long furrows, having been prepared for the cold winter months ahead.

It was not long before farmhouses came into view, their orchards bare and their gardens plowed under, having given their summer's best and deserving a rest. Sparkling streamlets flowed through the valleys connecting, he assumed, with miles of small rivers that would eventually feed larger ones. In the distance James could still see the ancient forest on a steeper hillside, where virgin timber of ash, oak, and hickory were no longer green but now displayed a multitude of autumn's finest colors.

As they entered Washington, Alexander said to James, "I know your desire is to be near the town, so I suggest you stay in the newly built Washington Tavern, across from the two-story brick courthouse at the center of the village."

Stopping in front of the courthouse for the horse to drink at a ten-foot watering trough gave James a chance to see down the street. A row of general merchandise stores lined the block, with a newly built post office in the middle. Across the street was a blacksmith shop, and at the far corner a log building stood with a sign identifying it as the Washington *Reporter*. The newspaper had been established sixteen years prior. Seeing it, James was anxious now to go inside, to see if he could find out what could be done to locate Mary.

Alexander and James stood on the street, saying their farewells. First they shook hands, and then, like the Christian brothers they were, embraced each other.

"Remember, James, you are always welcome at my home, whether you find Mary or not. I pray you do, my brother, but if you don't, please come and we will look for her together. I love you. God bless you, James." Alexander climbed back into the carriage, anxious to get home before the darkness fell about him.

That night, as James closed his eyes, his thoughts were of Mary. He had not known her well. Only blurred images came to his mind now, but where his memory lacked substance, the imagination took over. She was beautiful, and he needed her. Those were the only thoughts that filled his mind as he drifted off into slumber, praying he would somehow locate her, and soon.

Chapter 13

James did put a small notice in *The Reporter,* requesting that if anyone knew the whereabouts of Mary White that they please contact him at the Washington Tavern.

A few days had gone by, and James was growing weary. His money—the small amount he had earned from the trip down the coast, along with what he had acquired working on the waterfront during the summer and the small pay he received from the Conestoga drivers—was almost gone. He would have to find a job if he stayed in Washington much longer. But around ten o'clock the next morning James, somewhat bored, yawned then stretched and walked over to look out a window in the inn. As he stood there, he saw a man on a gray mare come riding up the street, guiding another horse behind him. Throwing the reins over the horses' heads, the fellow slid from his saddle as if in a hurry, and then tossed the leather straps around a hitching post. He quickly stepped upon the brick pavements leading to the entrance of the Washington Tavern.

Curiosity got the best of James; he had to know why the man was in such a hurry, so he ran down the stairs just as the fellow was approaching the front desk. At first, James did not recognize him, but on a second look, he realized it was Will, Mary's brother-in-law.

"Will! Hello! My, it's good to see you. How are you?" James shouted with excitement as he reached the bottom step.

Will looked haggard and had a somberness about him that alarmed James, and for a quick moment James wondered if he had made a mistake. Perhaps the gentleman was not Will? Certainly not the Will he remembered. The Will he remembered had always been energetic, with an effervescence that made him stand out in a crowd. He could never forget, on the voyage coming over from Ireland, the funny stories Will told. The fact was he joked with everyone and always had a positive attitude—which, as James now recalled, was very much needed and appreciated on that stressful voyage.

Will reached out his hand to James, "Good to see you too, James. How are you? My, I can't believe I'm actually shaking your hand. We thought you were no longer living, since no one's heard from you for such a long time. We read in the *Weekly News* that someone with your name was looking for Mary, and wondered if it wasn't you. What happened, James? Are you alright?"

"Oh, Will, I'd love to tell you the whole story. Do you have time for a cup of tea?"

"No, James, I don't. I need to get you to Mary as soon as possible. She's ill, James, very ill!"

James could feel his heart beating. "Where is she, Will?"

"On my uncle's farm, not far from here. Do you have a horse?"

"No Will, I don't. How far is it?"

"Well, it isn't far, and I brought a horse just in case you didn't have one. Mandy isn't a fast horse, but we can make it there in less than an hour; however, we need to leave right away." Will seemed to have an urgency to his voice that was unmistakable and alarming.

"Let me get my coat, Will. I'll be down in a minute."

For the first mile, they rode along in silence. When they finally reached the edge of the town and headed out into the country, James spoke.

"Will, what's wrong with Mary?"

"The doctor isn't sure, but he thinks she has the 'fever.' We thought she was getting better, and seemed to be doing fine, but then suddenly she took a turn for the worse, and began vomiting blood, and well, it's just terrible. She's hardly breathing at all now."

James didn't say another word. He just sat on Mandy's back, unable to speak.

Eventually they turned off the main road, and traveled up a winding lane. Leaves from the October trees were beginning to fall, covering the path before them. The pungent odor of apple butter steaming in iron pots penetrated the air, and in the not-too-far distance James could hear the sound of the sickle and scythe at work in the fields. Soon a log house came into view as they rode through a gate. The horses, as if by habit, turned toward the lean-to, ready for a rest and a drink at the watering trough.

Seconds later they reached the cabin. Mary's sister stood in the doorway and motioned for James to follow her to a back room. Rachel opened the door as James entered, then she quickly closed the door behind him.

The room was dark and quiet. Mary lay on a bed in the corner, with her hair in ringlets about her head, wet now from perspiration. The loss of fluid and days of nausea had taken its toll. She was frail and barely breathing. It was difficult for James to believe that it was Mary. Certainly not the Mary he once knew.

"Mary, Mary, can you hear me?" James spoke softly, as he knelt beside her bed. "It's James. I'm here, Mary. Yes, I'm here.

I'm not dead. The *Nancy Grace* was taken over by a pirate's sloop. Everyone was killed but me. I was on an island by myself for two years, in the middle of the ocean. Someone found me, Mary. Can you hear me? Oh, Mary, I love you. . . . I love you, Mary. . . . I think I loved you from the first time I saw you in Bellikiel, in County Down. I'm so sorry you never knew that, how thoughtless of me. . . . Oh Mary, can you hear me?" James, desperate, now, spoke the words a little more loudly.

Mary opened her eyes just long enough to see his face. A smile formed on her lips, as a tiny tear appeared at the edge of her eye and rolled down the side of her cheek onto the pillow where she lay. Seconds later she gave a sigh, releasing the remaining air from her lungs, and she was gone.

"No, Mary, don't leave me! I love you. . . . Please, oh please, dear God, don't let her go! I need her! Mary, come back, come back. . . . *Come back!* Oh, Mary!"

Realizing she was truly gone and there was nothing he could do about it, James laid his head down on the bed beside her and sobbed, caring not who heard it. Nothing mattered now, nor ever would again. Mary was gone. What would he do without her?

They called it the 'fever.' They thought it might be yellow fever, but no one knew for certain. An outbreak had occurred in Philadelphia several years before, and more than a thousand people died then, but there had been only a few cases since, and most of those were in the southern states. Where or how she could have gotten it no one seemed to know, yet she had all the signs and systems of yellow fever.

When at last James opened the door, it was to tell them that Mary had died.

"I am so glad you got here when you did," Rachel said. "I truly believe she held on until you came. We told her about the notice in the newspaper. We weren't sure she understood or even heard us, but evidently she did. Oh, I am so sorry, James. I know you loved her. This must be a terrible thing for you. I wish there was something I could say or do to help ease the sadness you must be feeling."

"I have to leave! I'm sorry, but I just can't stay here." James started towards the door.

"I understand, James," Will said.

James ran out of the door. He would walk back to Washington. He needed to walk and think. This was a hurt piled on top of all the other hurts; only it was the worst. Perhaps he should stay, at least until she was buried, but he just couldn't do it; there was too much pain. It would be impossible for him to see Mary's frail little body being placed into a grave . . . to see his future suddenly disappear before his eyes, all he had dreamed about, planned for! No, it was better that he leave.

"James." Will ran after him. "Let me take you back. I'll harness ol' Jim. We can take the buggy. It will only be a few minutes. I'll have it ready in no time."

"No Will, I need to walk. Thank you for all you've done, and thank Rachel, too. I'll write you, and explain everything. You can get my letter the next time you're in Washington. The innkeeper will have it. The Lord keep you, my friend."

When Will went back into the house, he found Rachel standing in the middle of Mary's room with a curious look on her face. Softly—as though she might still somehow wake Mary—she said to him, "Look, I found it beside Mary, on the bed." In her hand was the gold locket.

As James walked the road back to Washington, his thoughts were focused on finding his new friend, Alexander. He needed him. He had a hundred questions to ask, but the most prominent was "Why?" Why did this have to happen? Was he to be used by God or not? If so, how could he ever do it without Mary by his side?

Throughout the evening James felt as much alone in the world as he did when he was on the island in the middle of nowhere, and it seemed those feelings would not go away. Somehow he had to put those feelings to rest, so the next day he decided to walk back to the cabin where Will and Rachel lived, where Mary had died. Perhaps being there, seeing her being placed in the ground, would help. And so he stayed as long as it took to bury her, to make his condolences known to Mary's sister, and to meet the rest of Will's family, and then he left.

The following morning James packed up his belongings and paid the innkeeper, giving him a letter he had written to Rachel and Will thanking them for all they had done for Mary and for him. He then took one to the post office for his mother, with a prayer that she would receive it, and then made his way out of town.

Following Alexander's directions, James soon found himself on the Washington Pike. The Campbells' home was along Buffalo Creek in the Virginia panhandle, which was west—but James was going west into Ohio to look for his family, so it was not out of his way.

The early morning air hung heavy with dew, unusual for an autumn day, as he walked along the winding, leaf-covered road. He had gone only a few miles when he secured a ride with a man who sat upon a wagon loaded with hay. The ride shortened the twenty-five-mile journey from Washington to the Campbells' home; however, the last ten miles found James alone again, sauntering down the road. The trip at last ended, as he reached a fork in the road and turned north off of the Washington Pike, just as Alexander had directed. The road led up a sloping hill. Climbing it, he could see in the distance a two-story white-framed house, with glass windows reflecting light from the afternoon sun.

James—weary now not so much from the long walk but from a grief which still tugged at his heart and would not release itself—sat down beside the road on a fallen moss-covered tree to rest. There were sheep grazing in a field not far away, and the scene brought a scripture to his mind. Now, attempting to remember it, he bowed his head, softly repeating the words to himself: *The Lord is my Shepherd; I shall not want. He maketh me to lie down in green pastures: he leadeth me beside the still waters . . . though I walk through the valley of the shadow of death, I will fear no evil; for Thou art with me; Thy rod and Thy staff they comfort me. Thou preparest a table before me in the presence of mine enemies. . . . Surely goodness and mercy shall follow me all the days of my life: and I shall dwell in the house of the Lord forever. Amen.*

Since he had made the journey in about five hours, he felt the need to refresh himself before appearing at Alexander's front door. Repeating the scripture seemed to help, yet the impressive-looking house caused James some apprehension, as he came nearer. *Perhaps I shouldn't have come*, he thought, yet the need to talk to Alexander was overwhelming. So, gaining some courage, he cautiously approached the house and pulled at the wooden knocker.

A black-faced woman appeared at the door. *Was she a slave?* James wondered. He had not encountered a Negro before and was surprised to see one.

"Is this the home of Alexander Campbell?"

"Yessir, but the massa's in de printen' house down by de creek." Pulling a hand out of the pocket of her checkered apron, she pointed toward the place.

James turned to walk down the path to where she had pointed, when a lady wearing a blue flowered calico dress came to the door.

"Hello, may I help you?"

"Oh, hello, well, I came to see Alexander Campbell. I'm James Scott. I met him on the Cumberland Pike going to Washington a week ago."

"James Scott—my, it's good to meet you. I'm Margaret, Alexander's wife. He told me about you. Come in and make yourself at home. Holly, will you get Mr. Campbell, please? Tell him that James Scott is here," she said, as she turned toward the black woman to put in her request.

"Yes'um," Holly said, as she slipped out the door and headed for the printing office.

James could see Alexander's eyes radiate excitement when he saw him, but his voice seemed to reflect some distress.

"It is a delight to see you, James. How wonderful to have you visit, and I would love for you to stay as long as you feel the need; however, I just decided last week to tour some churches in the Kentucky and Tennessee area, so I will be leaving within the week, and my wife Margaret is going too, so unfortunately we won't be here for long."

"Oh, that is not a problem, as I have no thoughts of staying but for a few days. I want to get to the Jackson territory in Ohio before the cold of winter sets in. Once there, even though the weather might be bad, maybe I can find my family. If I do, I will at last be home, or rather that's my hope."

"Tell me, James, did you find Mary?"

James lowered his head and briefly closed his eyes. Opening them again, he told Alexander what had happened.

"Oh, James, I am so sorry." Alexander put his arm around his new friend's shoulders. "What happened? How did she die?"

"They're not sure, but they think it was yellow fever. I just don't understand how a loving God could permit these things to happen." James, feeling alone in the world, was confessing a sadness that was incomprehensible, and yet he *did* know why. Yes, the voice on the island had told him why: *"James in this world ye shall have tribulation, but be of good cheer; for I have overcome the world."* But now he needed a human voice, a man of God's own choosing, to tell it all to him again.

Alexander, releasing his hand from James' shoulders, suggested they sit for a while in the cane-bottomed ladder-backed rockers which had not been stored yet for the winter and were on the porch. The air was cool, but after the long walk it felt good to James.

"James, God never said it would be easy for us on this earth. It wasn't easy for Him, but He didn't leave us without hope. We have a place, far greater, more wonderful than we can ever imagine, to go to someday, that is, for those of us who remain faithfully in His arms. What a glorious hope that is, and all because of what Christ did for us on the cross. Think of the people who have given their lives, passing down those ancient words, so that now we, here in this land of freedom, can read them and have that hope. Mary is in a far better place, James, and someday you'll see her again." James looked at Alexander, as he leaned forward in his rocker. James could see his face fully now, for not only were Alexander's words a comfort, but his expression seemed to add an assurance to what he was saying.

But James was still not totally convinced, so he said to him, "I'm not sure of that, as she wasn't baptized, certainly not in the way you say we should be. Do you think she will be in heaven then?" James was desperate now to know.

"That is a difficult question, James. Only God knows the answer. He sees our hearts. He knows the depth of our belief, and the circumstances that surrounds us. Remember the thief on the cross? When Jesus was crucified, His cross was placed between two thieves. One of the thieves believed, asking Jesus to remember him when He came into His kingdom, and Jesus told him that he would be, that day, in paradise with Him. *He* hadn't been baptized! No, but Jesus knew his heart. He knew that He truly believed and took him up into heaven anyway.

"There is much, James, we do not know, nor can understand on this earth. The Bible tells us that for now we see through a glass, darkly, but then (someday we will see) face to face (1 Cor. 13:12). Although we lack knowledge in this life, some day we shall know fully.

"The Bible is full of mysteries we humbly try to read and understand, but a god we could completely understand, a god who holds no mystery would be a god that man, in his own mind, has made up; he certainly would not be the God of the Bible."

James understood what he was saying, and had some of the same thoughts, but Alexander's words reinforced what he was thinking, and that was truly a blessing. Even though the pain was still there, he could cling to that knowledge, and the hope that was in it.

In the evening after dinner, Alexander and James talked more about the faith, as James had a deep desire to learn as much from Alexander Campbell as he could before he left.

"We preach the gospel only," Alexander told him, "the gospel that was proclaimed by the apostles. As you well know, men will not, nor do, think alike. But it isn't the job of the church to make them think alike on any human opinion; however, it is of optimal importance that they hold Christ as the head of the church and keep His commandments as is written in the Gospels.

"In other words, James, faith in Jesus as the true Messiah, and obedience to Him as our Lawgiver and King, is the only test of a sincere Christian character, and the only bond of Christian union, communion, and cooperation—regardless of all creeds, opinions, commandments, and traditions of men. We may read what men have written and consider their thoughts, but where they differ from Scripture, we must stand firmly on the Bible, and the Bible alone. For Christianity, in its purity, is not to reform the world by a system of legal restraints, no matter how admirable that may be, but its primary objective should be and must always be to touch the hearts of men, implanting there a principle of love. And we receive all men of every denomination, all sects and parties who will make the good confession that Jesus is the Christ, the Son of the living God, and our only Lord and Savior. And it is on that sincere confession of faith we immerse all believers."

Alexander pushed himself up from the mahogany rocker where he was sitting, walked over, and stood in front of the four-foot fireplace in the center of the east wall of the parlor. He folded his hands behind his back, as if contemplating his next words.

James looked around the room. It was an impressive one, with its hand-hewn rafters and tooled molding of polished black walnut. Large too, as the whole house showed an elegance, a grandeur, that surprised James, yet Alexander said he never took money for preaching; he didn't believe it was scriptural and would never consent to it.

"Paul was a tent-maker, he received no money; therefore, neither shall I receive any earthly compensation whatsoever for preaching," James remembered him saying.

How, then, did he get this beautiful home and acres of farm-land? James wondered. It was a question needing an answer, so he asked.

"I believe it was the providential hand of God, James. When I first came to this country, I was nineteen. My father, because of health concerns, was forced to come to America a couple of years prior. My mother, sisters, and brothers, and I came later, to join him. My father and I had a growing concern, even in Ireland, with how the church was going, and gradually realized its need to be restored as it was originally intended in the New Testament. We found, here in America, the freedom to try to influence it to do so. We had no thought of starting something new, but only to encourage the established churches to that end. We formed what we called the Christian Association of Washington, which was a group of Christians from many different denominations, and we met at a building called Brush Run for Sunday service. My father was an elder for that group, and I preached there myself, but never did a Sunday go by that I received any money.

"Eventually I met and married Margaret. She was an only child. Her father and mother loved her dearly, and they owned this farm. They encouraged me to come here and make it my home, too. I was reluctant at that time to do so, but eventually did. Margaret and I lived here for a time. I helped with the farm, and Margaret's father, a generous man and a good Christian, eventually deeded it over to me. He was getting older and felt the need to cut back on all the responsibilities a farm like this afforded. Since then I have enhanced it, thanks to a good farm manager who works for me. But, no! I do not receive any money for preaching, nor will I ever. God, I believe, has provided that, and how do we know God is able until we let Him try?

"It takes faith, James, lots of faith to let go and allow God to bring about the results of our prayers, our requests, but we can never know that He is able until we take that step of faith. There are times when He does say, 'No!' However, more often than not, He provides. But when we pray, we must pray in accordance with His will, and we can't know that will until we know the Bible. So it is essential that we study the Word of God; our very lives depend upon it. If our desires do not line themselves up with Scripture, then it isn't God's will for our lives." As Alexander talked, James gave him his complete attention; he did not want to miss a single word of what this great man of faith was saying.

"I will be praying for you James, that somehow God will touch your heart and guide you into complete understanding, for I feel, some day, He will be using you in a mighty way."

When the sun came up the next morning, it promised to be a beautiful day. Since it was sending down an unusual warmth for an October day, Alexander said to James. "Perhaps the time is right, James, for you to take that step of faith and be baptized?"

"Yes Alexander, I do believe I would like to do that, as I have felt the Spirit strongly telling me I need to be baptized."

So with the family gathered to witness the occasion, Alexander led James down a gently sloping hill to the river's edge. As James stepped into the cool waters of Buffalo Creek, the giant old oak trees which lined the banks of the river, randomly dropping their autumn leaves, seemed to be spreading their boughs out over the water like a canopy, as if to protect them from the cool air.

There, before God, James confessed his faith in Christ, as Alexander repeated the ancient ordinance: "James, upon your confession of faith, I now baptize you in the name of the Father, the Son, and the Holy Ghost for the forgiveness of your sins, and the gift of the Holy Ghost." He then immersed him in the waters of Buffalo Creek, just as John the Baptist had immersed Jesus, God's sacrificial Lamb, in the Jordan River so long ago.

Chapter 14

James, longing to know more about the Campbell family and why Alexander had chosen to come to America, was grateful to once again have the opportunity to talk with Alexander before he left on his trip to visit the churches in the Kentucky and Tennessee area.

"My father, Thomas Campbell, was a Presbyterian minister in Northern Ireland, He came to this country 1806 because of illness," Alexander said. "The doctors advised my father to take the voyage because he was overburdened, not just from the regular duties of a pastor and teacher, but from his strong dedication to the Scriptures and his conviction to encourage the church to a more Christian spirit of love and unity. Prayerfully, he wanted the strife, which for centuries had disgraced and disrupted the Lord's work, to end. He felt that professing Christians should honor their profession by being an answer to the prayer of Jesus, for the church to be one, uniting in love and in action. However, the synod, the leaders of the church, opposed him. Realizing that his constant devotion was to the Scriptures, to the exclusion of the church's creeds and disciplines, they insisted he conform to their rules. Their opposition to him, indeed, stressed him. Please understand, James, I am simplifying something that was much more complex.

"My father came here first before we, the family, came. It wasn't until two years later that I, along with the rest of my family, sailed for America. And that was quite a voyage, as we were shipwrecked, but out of that came a blessing, for I was able to spend some time studying at the University of Glasgow.

"You know, James, that my heartfelt desire, which came about from my father's dedication and influence, has always been to embrace all Christians as brothers, having a vision of the coming of *one* church.

"On many occasions I've heard my father say, 'We speak where the Bible speaks, and where it is silent, we are silent; for if we are to return to that first-century church, the church of the apostles, we must adhere to the inspiration found only in the Bible, for that and that alone is our constitution.'

"The Bible is a practical and an indispensable guide to our moral lives. It is the key to our ability to live and work together in freedom. I find it amazing that it isn't even a textbook for our schools, yet our country was founded on its truth. How will we be able to hold on to our freedoms if we know nothing of the Bible?"

Alexander, standing in the foyer of his home with the early morning sun dancing through the windows and reflecting light across the room, approached the door and then turned to look at James. With a conviction in his heart that was undeniable he said, "You know James, we are Christian only, but we are not the only Christians. God's church is spread throughout the world in many denominations, and He knows His true church, hearts directed toward Him and Him alone. Some church buildings may hold many people, but only a few who truly believe. In others, there may be a small group in attendance, with most of them true believers, but just as this country has separate states, sovereign states within themselves yet acknowledging the authority of a central government, so we, the true church, having many parts, recognize that our supreme authority is

Christ and Christ alone. We must encourage that spirit of unity, for I do believe it will grow first and foremost in this country, here in these United States, in this land we call America. God help us if we ever lose sight of why we are here, or if we ever forget the suffering and hardships that sent men of faith to this country in the first place. You and I know and understand that suffering, for in part we too have felt its pain, and because we have how much more we treasure the freedom it has spun."

It seemed that Alexander, expressing a passion that had dominated most of his life, wanted to be sure that James understood what he was saying.

"I am telling you this, James, to encourage you to read and know the Bible, and the Bible only. If you do, I can envision you, my friend, carrying the cross of Christ into America's heartland," Alexander said.

That certainly took him by surprise, yet it did confirm, in his heart and mind, all the times that events had happened in his life which seemed to be pointing him in that direction. Yes, he, James Scott, needed to stand true to the cause, dedicating his life to proclaiming the simple gospel, and the gospel only.

James had been at the Campbells' home now for several days, gaining much knowledge from Alexander. They talked, but mostly in the evening or the early morning hours; James knew Alexander needed to finish work he had started, since he would be leaving in a few days.

"I regret not having more time to spend with you, Alexander, as I do treasure your knowledge, especially knowledge about the Bible, and how to proclaim it," James said.

James stayed at the Campbells' home till the following Sunday. On Thursday evening, Alexander said, "James, I want to tell you goodbye this evening, as we will be leaving early tomorrow. We plan to take a Troy coach to Cincinnati, and from there we will be boarding a steamer for our trip to Louisville. I'm sorry to have to leave you, but I do pray that you will stay here as long as you desire, as there are still many books that would be good for you to read. Also, I want to encourage you to go with the family to church Sunday in Wellsburg. Margaret has a close friend who will be staying here with the children, and you are more than welcome to go with them."

"Thank you, yes, I would like to go to that church in Wellsburg," James said, with some sadness in his heart. Knowing his friend was leaving, he wondered if he would ever see Alexander Campbell again.

On Sunday morning James packed up his belongings, put them in the carriage, and joined the family on their trip to Wellsburg. He would go with them to church, and perhaps there he might gain some knowledge on how to travel west.

Alexander had told him that he might find a way into the Ohio territory by traveling a river called by the same name, the headwaters of which ran through the town of Wellsburg.

On Sunday mornings James learned that he might find the steamboat captain or other men who worked along the river at the Wellsburg Church, as it was the only church in town. Making contact with one of the men, he soon found a way south to Portsmouth. He learned that Portsmouth was on the Scioto Trail, which followed a river by the same name. Traveling it he could find his way north, and eventually into the Jackson County region.

As they approached Wellsburg, James could see numerous homes along the riverbank. Standing in the middle of town was a little stone courthouse, displaying a small light cupola spire. Several taverns lined the street, as well as a brick academy, but looking on further down the street he could see the one and only church building in Wellsburg.

"In all of Wellsburg, there was not a single church until a brick building was erected in 1816 at the upper end of the main street," he remembered Alexander saying. "It was there that my father and I joined the small, dedicated body of believers."

The stone building had a narrow entryway, and as James walked through the wooden doors he became aware that the entryway helped to keep the cold air from entering the main part of the structure. The building, with its high ceiling and oil lamps hanging from the rafters, had several potbellied stoves along the interior walls, which certainly felt good to James on that cold October morning.

Entering the main part of the structure, he was directed to seat himself to the right of the speaker's platform, and that platform could clearly be seen at the front of the fifteen-foot-long building. Unmarried women sat at the speaker's left, while single men were encouraged to occupy the other side. Married couples were seated in the center section. Alexander and his father Thomas had felt that seating the single men and women, boys and girls separately would improve their interest in the service.

As soon as they sat down, the people began singing and the sound resonated across the building.

When I survey the wondrous cross
On which the Prince of glory died,
My richest gain I count but loss,
And pour contempt on all my pride.

Forbid it, Lord, that I should boast,
Save in the death of Christ my God!
All the vain things that charm me most,
I sacrifice them to His blood.

See from His head, His hands, His feet,
Sorrow and love flow mingled down!
Did e'er such love and sorrow meet,
Or thorns compose so rich a crown?

Were the whole realm of nature mine,
That were a present far too small;
Love so amazing, so divine,
Demands my soul, my life, my all.

When the singing ended, Alexander's father Thomas Campbell took the platform, explaining to the church that he was prepared to speak that morning in the absence of his son who was traveling and would be back in a month or two.

As James sat down, he remembered his conversation with Alexander about his father living a good portion of his life in Northern Ireland as a minister in the Presbyterian Church.

"'Alexander,' my father would often say to me, 'remember this, my son, no man, no matter how highly trained he may be, can know the soul of another, for only God knows and sees all.

The Scripture reveals the mind of God, and it is our privilege to read it for ourselves, prayerfully letting the Holy Spirit guide us. But, can we not differ with our interpretation of it and still commune with one another, as Christians? I fear dogmatism has divided us into armed camps. We seem to fight each other with more gravity than we do the devil. The church of Christ, upon this earth, is essentially, intentionally, and constitutionally one. That is what our Savior taught, and that is what I will preach.'"

As James sat, considering all of what Alexander had said, he did not realize that those words would, one day, become a reality in his own life.

Suddenly, his attention was drawn to the words Thomas Campbell was now speaking:

> . . . and thus, in proportion as we memorize, and so become intimately acquainted with the contents of the Bible, we will be able to think and converse about them to our own and each other's edification. But what is not in the memory can neither be in the heart nor in the mouth. Therefore, the divine command given by Moses, is, "Thou shalt lay up these my words in your heart and in your soul; teach them to your children, speaking of them when thou sittest in thy house, when thou walkest by the way, when thou liest down, and when thou risest up; that your days may be multiplied, and the days of your children, as the days of heaven upon earth." Hence they were required to get them by heart, that so they might think and talk of them--that they might enjoy them. "For out of the contents of the heart the mouth speaketh," Therefore, the apostle commands Christians "to let the word of

Christ dwell in them richly," for the blissful purposes of edification, the word of the Lord is the food of the soul. David says that he loved it more than his natural food. And Jeremiah exclaims, "Thy words were found, and I did eat them; and thy words were to me the joy and rejoicing of my heart."

This, indeed, must necessarily be the case with the spiritually minded, for they hunger and thirst after righteousness. Whereas, the carnal mind is enmity against God, for it is not subject to his law, neither, indeed, can be, so, then, such characters can take no delight in it. But if we would get rid of this horrible distemper, we must have recourse to the word of God. It is the only medicine in the hand of the Spirit, divinely intended for the cure of our deadly carnality; for it is the law of the spirit of life in Christ Jesus-- that is, the blessed gospel—the provisions of which alone can make us free from the law of sin and death.

He sent his word, and healed, and delivered them from their destruction, Faith cometh by hearing the word of God, and it is by grace, through faith, that we are saved. There is no way, then, of getting out of this deadly calamity, but by believing the gospel; for "He that believeth not shall be damned." Therefore, if we would be saved, we must make the divinely prescribed use of the word, that we may truly understand, believe, and obey the gospel and law of Christ. There it is evident that those who obey the gospel are also divinely bound to observe all the teachings of the apostles. But they have taught us to search the

Scripture—to lay them up in our hearts. "That all Holy Scripture is given by inspiration of God, and is profitable for doctrine, for reproof, for correction, for instruction in righteousness; that the man of God may be perfect, thoroughly furnished for all good works." Amen.

James sat up straight in the pew, for it suddenly hit him: How could God be calling him to preach? He had no education. These learned men of God; the minister at the church in New York, the preacher at the Presbyterian Church in the Cumberland Valley; his friend Alexander, and now his father, Thomas Campbell, were all educated men. They had studied the faith under others who had significant knowledge. How then could he, who had no education, be called to preach? All he knew was shipping, sailing a boat, and of course, how to survive life on a deserted island for two years! Oh yes . . . and how to marry and lose a wife, whom he never knew!

Well, he was certain of one thing: If God had called him to preach, then he, James Scott, needed to know the Bible. If he was to carry the Word of God into the heartland of America, he must read and understand what was written there. So bowing his head, he now made an oath, not just to God but to himself, that from that day forward, he would not let an hour go by but that he would read and meditate on God's Holy Word.

Suddenly, as if hearing "the voice," a Scripture penetrated his mind: "Let us hold fast the profession of our faith without wavering; for he is faithful that promised" (Heb. 10:23). And then another Scripture entered his mind: "My soul, wait thou only upon God; for my expectation is from him. He only is my rock and my salvation; he is my defense: I shall not be moved"

(Ps. 62:5–6). It was as though God had given him those passages to set his mind free of the worry that now seem to consume him.

Yes, he thought, *God will be with me.*

Chapter 15

"Those flatboats are made in Pittsburgh forty-four miles north, up the river from Wellsburg. It's where this river connects with the Monongahela and Allegheny. The Indians call it the 'Oyo' but we say 'Ohio.' It stretches west across miles of virgin land, where it eventually meets the mighty Mississippi," the old boatman told him.

Standing on the east bank of the river, James took in the sight. From where he stood, high above the Ohio, he could easily visualize what the fellow was saying. For the river looked like coffee mixed with cream, as it mirrored the island, hills, and countryside it passed. The land on both sides of the Ohio was covered with a dense forest, for every kind of tree stood along its banks. Many looked as old as the river itself. *One day,* James thought, *those trees will provide handles for axes that will cut through their trunks to make logs for cabins, and maybe rails for fences that will eventually enclose the fields those trees leave behind.*

But of all the trees along the riverbank, none stood out to him like the gnarly, white-flecked sycamore, its branches towering high above the water, protruding out over the river, dominating the landscape.

He remembered Alexander telling him that Wellsburg had become a county seat in 1797. "When the War of 1812 came to a close, it became one of the most noted shipping centers on the Upper Ohio, with a population of almost a thousand people. Its exports could rival those of Pittsburgh, as not only does it send out numerous products, but is the beneficiary of such imports as glassware, pottery, and fine china from as far away as England."

The river seemed to be an artery of movement that day, as there was a continual progression of watercraft, and river men to man them. James saw numerous flatboats on the water, as well as keelboats, lumber, and log rafts. But the one that fascinated him the most was the steamboat.

"The *New Orleans* was the first boat propelled by steam to travel the Ohio River. They launched it from Pittsburgh," the old boatman said.

Having sailed himself, James found the river fascinating, and now desiring to learn more, made contact with men who either traveled it or actually worked on those vessels. Soon he was able to find a job on a flatboat, which would pay for his passage south to Portsmouth. From there, he would head north into the Jackson County region to look for his brother, and, hopefully, spread the Word of God.

As he talked with one of the boatmen, he learned how to navigate the flatboat, which was done by means of an oar; there were four of them, needing four people to man them.

"The boat goes in one direction, downstream with the current, which on a normal day will flow about two and a half miles in an hour. Once we arrive at our destination, we'll dismantle it and sell the lumber," the boatman said. "If you join us, beware, for there are many times when we'll have to battle the elements such as ice, fog, snags, sandbars, bank cave-ins, rapids, falls, eddies, and the like. Believe me, when a boat runs aground, it's no picnic pushing it back into the current, and we've had to do it many times in freezing water."

They told him, too, about the warring tribes of Indians. "It wasn't long ago that the Shawnee and the Miami Indians were really bad. I remember when they use to lure unsuspecting boatmen ashore and then attack them!

"Of course, after that battle at a place called Fallen Timbers and the Indians signed the Greenville Treaty, we haven't had any problems with them. They no longer seem a threat, at least not along the Ohio River. Most of them are gone now from the area, but a few still remain."

It intrigued James to listen to their stories. Whether real or made-up, it tempted his imagination, and he found the men's tales captivating. But what really perked his interest were the stories the boatmen told about the river pirates. They had become a real threat. James, however, was relieved to learn that the pirates did their pillaging further south, along the Natchez Trace.

"Even though we personally have not encountered any on the upper Ohio, we're still ever watchful," the boatmen said.

The boatmen had been a great help, giving him instructions on how to maneuver the craft, so it was not long before James found himself falling in sync with them, beating out a tune as his oars hit the muddy waters of the Ohio.

Looking down the river, with the current moving them swiftly along, James' mind began to recapture images. He was back on the *Nancy Grace*, with the waves raising the bow of the ship high above the horizon, and then down again, as he once more felt the rhythm of the water. The solitude and the splendor of the moment, with his father by his side, teaching him, taking him back, back to a childhood spent at sea. It seemed so real.

For miles and miles of the river, these solitary moments were unbroken by any signs of life, only a lone eagle soaring high in the late October sky. Occasionally they would pass a cabin tucked away in the wilderness, erected there on a tiny piece of cleared land, with moss stuffed in its chinks to keep the elements out. As they passed quickly by, he could see a thread of blue smoke curling up into the sky from its chimney.

The boatmen were transporting pork and flour to Portsmouth and Cincinnati. Corn, oats, and some animal skins were going further down the river. Along the way, they would be picking up other products and possibly some passengers as well. Depending on the weather and the navigability of the river, it would take at least two days for James to reach his destination; so as evening approached, it found them camped out in the open on the riverbank.

Gathering twigs from the woods, the men made a fire, which was now burning brightly, spreading its warmth as they ate their salt-pork and beans and listened to stories they told each other about their experiences along the river.

"There're a lot of bad things happenin' to folks at that Cave-in-the-Rock," one of the boatmen told him, "All kind of bad stories I've heared about that place!"

James, intrigued by what the boatmen were telling him, gave them his full attention.

"That cave sat high on a hill in southern Illinois, overlookin' the river. It was in a prime location, for from there anyone could easily see boats comin' down the river. It was in a secluded area, surrounded by lots of trees. There were lots of cliffs and bluffs, too, which helped hide where they were located," one of the boatmen told him.

"Yes, and I heared there was horse-thieves and counterfeiters and robbers that used that cave for a long time, and they're still there. A lot of times travelers would pass by, and wonder about it, and so they'd stop to get a closer look at the place, and when they did, those pirates would kill them, and take their boats. I've seen many a cargo leave ports on the upper Ohio and never be heared from again. I heared those pirates took those boats to New Orleans and sold them, and their cargo too . . . for cash!"

"There's a tavern there now, they say. I ain't seen it myself, but I heared it's a jumpin' place!"

As James sat listening to their stories, he couldn't help but recall, again, the words of Alexander Campbell: "Remember, James, it wasn't easy for Jesus upon this earth, and it won't be easy for us. Satan is the master of this world. He is the great deceiver, and he uses men, many times good men, to do his bidding. But we have a book, the simple gospel; passed down through the ages, with many, many men giving up their lives to preserve it so we can, today, in this land of freedom, have access to it, deciphering good from evil, right from wrong. We not only need to read this book, but study it well. It is our manual for living, and it is as relative today as when it was written. Keep it with you at all times, never letting it out of your sight. Follow what it says, and teach others to follow it, too. It will protect you from the devil's snare."

The embers of the campfire needed a prodding, and had died down a bit when suddenly, James noticed, the men seemed to have run out of words. After a while, James slowly began to talk. "I want to tell you my story about pirates," James said, as he began to unfold the long, sad story of his life and how he had been left on an island for two years in the middle of a vast ocean.

He then asked them if they knew anything about Jesus. Had they heard of Him? If so, did they know Him personally? They had heard the name, and a couple of the men had even gone to a small church in the wilderness a time or two, but they really knew little about Him.

Holding a small Bible in his hands, James began to explain just who this Jesus was, and why He was so important. "You see,

His death was a sacrifice, a gift to you, and to me, from an eternal God who doesn't want any of us to depart this life without knowing Him, for when we do, when we believe in Him and what He taught us, we will have eternal life in heaven with Him. It's all here in this book, the oldest books in the world." James lifted the Bible higher for the men to see.

The men, thankful for what they had just learned, wanted to accept this gift, and so James told them they could show a holy God that they had, indeed, accepted His gift by being buried in baptism just as Jesus was buried in the tomb, to rise again out of the water, just as He rose from the tomb, to walk now in a new life.

The next morning James led the men down the banks of a small creek that fed the Ohio and baptized them there. It was a cold morning, but soon they were all working the oars of the flatboat, breaking a mighty sweat, as they thought about what had just happened.

Later in the day, as they were nearing Portsmouth, James told the men they needed to know the Bible, and wondered if any of them knew how to read. Only one did. So James gave the fellow one of his Bibles, and told him, "Please read it to the others. This is God's instruction book. It teaches us how to live at peace with one another in this world, and how not to stumble and fall into Satan's trap! I will be praying for you, my brothers. God be with you always."

As James walked away from the men, a feeling of satisfaction embraced his heart, and he marveled at what had just happened. He actually led three men to Christ! His first! He wondered, if given the opportunity, could he preach as well? Only time, he guessed, would tell.

Columns of blue smoke could be seen now along the Ohio as they approached Portsmouth. Soon two log cabins, nestled in a densely wooded area, came into view, with their stone chimneys sending out smoke that circled up into the air. It wasn't long before the riverbank was covered with cabins, as they approached the town, which lay on the north side of the river. As James left the flatboat, saying his farewell to the men, he made his way up a hill from the water's edge to the town, which sat high above the river. He would spend the night in Portsmouth, hoping to gain some information on a journey north into the Jackson County region.

The next morning, a strong northwest wind churned the fallen leaves and blew them straight into his face as James stepped out of the inn, where he had spent the night, onto a dirt road which led from the town toward another river that fed the Ohio. It was now November, and James could feel the sting of the cold autumn air as he turned north toward his destination. He had learned, from talking with some men at the inn the night before, that he could take an old Indian trail which followed the river the Indians had called Scioto, meaning "deer eyed." The Scioto flowed south toward the Ohio; it was a long river reaching almost two hundred and thirty miles north into the middle of the Ohio territory.

"It's a very deep, fast-moving river, and very dangerous. In some spots it's twenty feet deep. Yes, the Scioto has drowned a lot of people," the men had told him.

He needed to go about twenty miles up the Indian trail, which was east along the river, before finding a place where it forked off. The town of Jackson lay another twenty miles or more beyond that point. If he could get to Jackson, he was hoping to find a way from there to locate his brother. Always in the back of his mind was the thought that he might not find him. However, James' main concern now was to look for the feeder road that turned east toward the town.

As he walked the Scioto Trail, there were signs that Indians had been there. Birch-bark frames of old wigwams partially standing, their ropes and strips of wood which had held them together, were now scattered across the fields. The houses had deteriorated to a point where it became difficult to recognize them; however, there were other items giving evidence of their presence in the area, as arrowheads, and bits and pieces of old pottery were numerous. He even saw a moccasin half-buried in the dirt, lying beside the path.

He remembered the men at the inn saying there were still some Indians in the area; however, after the War of 1812, the vast majority of them, having been forced north of the Greenville Treaty line, were now living on a reservation in Northeastern Ohio.

"I remember when Indians attacked a white hunting party along the Scioto, and another time they killed and brutally butchered a driver of a wagon near Fort Hamilton," one of the men told him. "Although we have not encountered any ourselves, we certainly have heard some gruesome tales told about them. They not only treated the white men horribly, but each other as well. It seems as though they live in constant fear and hatred, even of other tribes, and it's an ongoing struggle for them. They're masters at inflicting unimaginable pain, torturing their captives to the point of death, then backing off enough to keep them alive, letting the person rest a bit, before going at it again. I've heard it told that they actually skin the victims alive, and they did it, many times, while the person's families watched. And it didn't matter if it was a man or a woman. The fact is Indians got such a pleasure from inflecting pain it was nothing short of satanic. Now, though, it seems many have come to know Christ and it has made a big change in their lives. They no longer are the savages they once were and now seem to be fitting in well with their white neighbors. I guess that's the reason the government is leaving those Indians alone. Yes, most are gone now, but there are still a few who remain."

Thank God for the men who came to this country proclaiming Christ, for had they not come here, those Indians would have never heard about Christ. James wondered if it had not been by God's design. *Yes, those Indians are fortunate, and I pray that many more will come to hear about Him as well.*

The November air, having turned colder, stung James' face the farther north he walked, and soon he found himself moving at a slower pace. He was a big man, with a wide and steady gait, and could cover several miles in an hour; however, he was not feeling well at all and began to slow down a bit when suddenly he spotted a bear in the woods.

James did have a knife, which he had not had occasion to use. Now, considering the position he was in—walking through a wild and somewhat treacherous terrain with no civilized person in sight—caused him some concern. Keeping his eye on the bear, he slowly lifted the knife out of his shoulder pack, when suddenly he heard a dog barking in the distance. The bear, as if by instinct, darted across the path in front of him, and ran down the slope of a hill to the river's edge, with several dogs now in pursuit. James' curiosity got the best of him. He had to see what was happening, so he moved cautiously toward the river. The dogs—there were three of them standing on the riverbank—watched as the bear braved the rapidly flowing current of the Scioto, swimming toward the other side and to safety.

When James walked down the hill to the water's edge to get a better view, he made a decision to rest awhile. He guessed it to be about midday, so decided to take the opportunity to eat a bite before continuing his journey north. He wasn't feeling well at all, and even though it was a cold day, it seemed unusually warm to him.

"I am so tired," he thought.

A rather large tree had fallen, spreading its trunk across the riverbank. With its foliage gone, it left behind bare branches and stems, which were half-buried in the water. James pulled himself up beside the tree's trunk. He would rest there a while, but soon found himself feeling a bit sleepy.

Perhaps a nap might help me feel better, James thought, as he lay down beside the tree and closed his eyes. That was the last thing he remembered.

Chapter 16

"Where am I?" James wondered, as he looked up into the eyes of a woman who was now standing over him.

"Howdy! How ya' feeling'?"

"Well, I don't know. What happened? Where am I?" James, slightly baffled, tried to make some sense out of the situation he now seemed to be in.

"I'm Lavonia Foster. Ya' been terribly ill; we think ya' may have had pneumonia. A friend of ours found ya' in the woods by the river a week ago. Ya' had a bad fever. We thought ya' might die a time or two, but, ya' seem much better now. Ya're' fever broke last evenin', and ya' slept much more peaceable."

"Yes, I feel fine now," James pushed himself up on one arm, hoping he could get up, find out where he was, and be on his way; however, that was not to be the case, as the room started swirling around him. He laid his head back onto the bed, wondering what he might do next.

"Wait! Ya' can't do that now," the woman said, as she pushed him back down on the bed. "Ya' gotta take it easy for a while. Ya' just got over a terrible illness. Ya' gotta rest!"

James didn't remember a thing. *Where am I, and how did I get here? It was a complete mystery!* She said he had been there a week? That was difficult for him to believe. He couldn't imagine that a week had gone from his life, a week he didn't remember. Well, it certainly was a mystery, a mystery he hoped he could solve, and soon; but for now he had to take it easy. He closed his eyes, and it wasn't long before he drifted off into sleep again.

When he awoke, it was evening. The room had grown dark, as the sun, having left the sky, no longer sent its rays of light across the wide planks of the pine floor from the one and only window in the cabin. Although the door was closed, he could still see the glow of a fire burning through a crack in the door, and there were people talking.

Suddenly all was quiet, and then a man began to speak. As James listened more intently, he realized the man was praying. Along with the numerous requests he made, James heard him say: "Our Father, we know not who this young man might be, but Ya' do, and Ya've' told us, through Your Word, O Lord, to show hospitality to strangers, for in so a'doin' we may be entertaining angels. Let us not forget that now, now that he is much better, and ifin' it be thy will, O Lord, let this poor fellow have a good night's rest. We thank Ya' now, for all Ya've been a'doin' for him and for us, for a'hearin' our prayers, and for the many blessings Ya've bestowed upon us. We give Ya' praise. Amen!"

The next morning, James woke to find two women standing beside his bed. He recognized Lavonia; the other woman, who was much younger, seemed familiar, yet there was no way he could have known her.

"We thought ya' might like a bite to eat, so we brought ya' some oats and warm milk and a bit of honey," Lavonia said. Leaning over James, she put one arm under his to help pull him up so he could rest his back against the wall, then turned toward the other woman, took the bowl of oats from her hands, and placed it on James' lap.

"How's that? Are ya' comfortable?"

"Yes, quite."

"Ya' eat now. We'll be back later to get the dish," Lavonia told him as they made their way out of the door.

James, with his back against the wall, closed his eyes for a moment. *Where in the world am I?* he wondered, as he opened them again. Then his mind suddenly captured an image of a woman with black hair and beautiful eyes, eyes the color of hair on a doe's back. *Little Pine! Where have I heard that name?* James wondered. *That woman looks like a "Little Pine," but who is Little Pine?* It certainly was a mystery. Maybe he could sort it out later, but for now he wanted to eat, and the oats, warm milk, and honey certainly looked good.

Later that morning when Lavonia came back to get the empty bowl, she sat down in an old cane-bottom oak rocker that was beside the bed, to talk awhile with James. James had a hundred questions to ask, but didn't manage even one once she began to tell her story.

"Our friend Nancy found ya' beside the river bank. Ya'd passed out. Ya' was terribly ill, and hot. At first, she didn't know what to do with ya', but then decided to make a bed, a kind of a *travois* the Indians use, something she could put ya' on and pull ya' with. She said she took tree branches and a rope she found beside the Scioto Trail to make it. She had a devil of a time a gettin' ya' up that thar hill by the river, but finally managed to. She was afraid of a leavin' ya', as thar was bears and wolves in them woods. Our dogs was with her, and they helped keep the animals away so she was able to pull ya' to our house, which turned out to be not far from where she found ya'.

"Nancy's a Shawnee. When the Indians left ten year or so ago, she stayed behind. Her pa was killed somewhere in northwestern Ohio in a battle led by that Shawnee leader, Tecumseh, or at least we think that might be what happened to him. She and her ma waited for him to come back, but a couple of year went by and they hadn't heard nary a thing, so they figured he was dead. She doesn't know for certain, but anyway none of them Indians come back. She and her ma was a'livin in a pitiful way along the Scioto Trail, all by themselves. Her ma died last spring, and Little Pine didn't have anyone or anywhere to go, so we took her in, wanted her to stay with us. It's sad, so sad for her.

"They called her Shinguaconse, which means 'Little Pine' in English, but we give her a Christian name, and now we call her Nancy. I had a cousin named Nancy; it was the only name I could think of, and Little Pine kind of reminded me of my cousin. My cousin lives in Kentucky, across the Ohio, and that's where we're from. My pa and ma had a farm there, near a place they call Maysville. They planted tobacco, but they ain't no longer a'livin' neither.

"Nancy had two brothers, and she was married, just got married at the time, when her brothers and her husband decided to go look for their pa, but they ain't came back neither. That's been six year or so ago now.

"Do ya know the Lord? Well, Pa—that's my husband—didn't know Him years ago. He drank, I mean strong whiskey, and he was drunk most of the time. We was poor then, didn't have a thing, and Pa sat around in a drunken stupor; it was just awful. We was a'livin way out in them thar woods, far from town, but he managed to get in there to get that thar' liquor in a town they call 'Maysville on the Ohio.' He would get in fights and ever'thing, come home bleeding and bruised. I didn't know what on earth I was gonna do with him. It was just awful, but then he come to know the Lord and now is just a wonder. He's a'quit a'drinkin' and everything, and is a'livin' a clean life now, and the Lord, He's a'blessin', don't ya know? Everyone aught a know Him. We was the dregs of Kentucky till them preachers came to that clearing at Cane Ridge. They say they was thousands of people who came to that camp meetin'. They was a'camped out in hundreds of wagons, and some even had tents. They had enough food, and so stayed for days. Well, ya' know they say some people even brought whiskey, and some people was selling it. They hid the barrels in the bushes, but them preachers started a'prayin' and a'prayin' and boy it wasn't long before people was coming to the Lord.

"I met so many people thar. I liked that a lot. Never knew nobody before, but boy sure did by the time we left.

"I remember that meetin' like it was yesterday. They cut logs and made benches for us, and if you couldn't find a bench you just sat on the ground. Shucks, most people was too excited to sit anyway. Thar was a lot of people thar and they was a'standin' on them benches even. Those preachers stood on stumps or on wagons and was preachin' all at the same time, but ya' couldn't hear what they was a'sayin, unless ya' was a'standin' near one of them. Ya' could go from preacher to preacher and listen. They was all a'tellin' about the Lord. Well, it wasn't long before the Spirit fell; He come right down from Heaven, He did. Soon people was a'shoutin', "What must we do to be saved?" Others fell right on the ground, slain by the Spirit, and other people was a'doin' all sorts of things.

"And there was even some, they say, possessed by Satan. They stayed away from most of the other folks, and was a'standin' on the other side of the wagons, near the underbrush."

Lavonia paused, just long enough to catch her breath. She had been rocking back and forth, keeping rhythm with each word she spoke, when suddenly becoming aware she had a captive audience. She stopped rocking for a moment, and then continued.

"Ya' know, Satan prows around like a lion seeking who he might devour, don't ya' know, just like the Bible says? Well, he was there that day too, I tell ya! They said some people was a'doin' bad things and they tried to stop them, but then someone said, 'No, let them go, let the tares grow along with the wheat for a time, the Lord will separate them,' and He did.

"Those preachers, John McGee and his brother, was there that day. John's a Methodist preacher, don't ya' know, and his brother William's a Presbyterian, or so they say. They say William was a'cryin', exhortin' his brother. Someone heard him a'sayin' 'Jesus, Jesus!' Well, his heart was o' so full.

"People was a'layin' all over the ground, a'cryin'; others look like they was dead. I started prayin', 'Oh, Lord help us, help us all.'

"My husband was a'scoffin' at the whole thing and a'cursin' at people who was a'layin' on the ground. He even took a sharp stick and started poking a man on the back, but the man never felt a thing, or so he told us later. Then suddenly, like lightning from the sky, my husband fell to his knees, a'shoutin', 'Lord I am a sinner! I'm a sinner, Oh Lord. Forgive me. Forgive me for all the things I been a'doin' that's not a'pleasin' Ya, Lord. I promise Ya, I'll do better, if Ya'll only forgive me.'

"Well, I got to tell ya, it was a miracle! My husband not only got saved that day, but he quit a'drinkin', and hasn't touched a drop since. We moved from that farm and came here to Ohio, and I haven't been so happy in my entire life. He's a changed man.

"He's a'makin' a decent livin' now working those salt mines, don't ya' know, and farming, and well the Lord is a'blessin' us. We got us ten youngin's, but only two is home, and Nancy.

Nancy's twenty-four year now, don't ya' know, and what we gonna do about her? Lord only knows. She's a pretty gal, but there ain't no Indians around about here now.

"Well land-a'Goshen, I reckon I've a talked ya' leg off." Lavonia slapped her thigh and started laughing. "Hee, hee, hee . . . that's just the way I am. Pa, that's my husband, always says I don't know what a stranger is. Hee, hee, hee, and I'm a'belivin' he's right, I reckon. Well, now you just rest, and I'll be back an' talk at ya' again."

Lavonia pushed herself up out of the rocker and picked up the bowl. Turning her back on James, and with her full linen skirt sweeping the cabin floor as she walked, she made her way out the door.

James swung his feet over the side of the bed and sat up. He put his face in his hands for a moment, and then, slowly pulling them down, he grabbed the edge of the bed. With his eyes still closed, he sat there for several minutes pondering what he had just heard. He did remember the men in the Cumberland Valley talking about a great revival that had taken place, but to actually know someone who not only was there, but who *had their lives transformed because of it*, was almost more than he could take in.

James laid his head back onto the soft feather pillow. Closing his eyes again, he tried to put into perspective all Lavonia had told him. As he drifted off into deep slumber, his thoughts cried out, *Oh, how I wish I could have been there.*

In the days ahead, James desired to know more about the circumstances that brought on that great revival, and had numerous conversations with Lavonia and her husband William.

"We came to Kentucky from Virginia," William said. "'cause in Virginia there wasn't much land available. What there was had been passed down through the family from the men who originally own it, but that land was wearing out. We heared tales of the richness of the Kentucky soil, and so I tried to convince Lavonia to leave Virginia, but she didn't want to go. I told her that I heared that the corn grows as high as fourteen feet tall, and the soil is as black as the ace of spades, and the those hills, those beautiful rolling hills, where the green, green grass spreads everywhere, sort of lured me like a bear to honey."

"Yes, it surely did that," Lavonia said, "and so we left Virginia, but we sure didn't travel a road leading to heaven; oh no, we traveled a weary road. We had never been more than a few miles from home our entire lives. So it was a struggle, 'cause we found ourselves alone now in a wilderness, since we left all our family back in Virginia and our church family, too. Here in Kentucky there weren't any churches, or at least none we knew about. It was a lonely time, and there were Indian attacks! Oh my, our lives certainly became difficult, especially for William. I guess it was more than he could handle, 'cause it wasn't very long before he started a'drinkin'.

"Ya' know, the one thing we needed, but we didn't have, was our church. We could always count on those people back home, 'cause they were like family, no matter what happen, they were always there, but when we come to Kentucky, there was no church family. It was like we lost our faith in the Lord, for we oftentimes wondered if we didn't step into hell, or someplace like it," Lavonia said.

"Well, Lavonia, ya' know those prayers of the saints are powerful," William said. "They upheld us, 'cause it seems God wasn't gonna let us live our lives without Him. After some bad years, James, we heard tell of some preacher men who came into this dark, godless wilderness, and were we ever thankful. They say, those preachers had it ruff, though, as there was threats against their lives; and also those Indians did savage things, too bad to talk about now, but since they come to know the Lord, it's amazing to see how that changed those Indians' lives, and ours too."

"Yes, I knew about the great revival that took place in Cane Ridge," James said, "but never had the privilege of knowing anybody who witnessed it, that is, until I met Lavonia. What she told me was amazing, and I guess William, it changed your life too." James leaned forward in the old wooden rocker where he was sitting, as he didn't want to miss any part of what the Fosters were saying.

"Indeed it did! It changed our lives, and how grateful I am. You know, they say there was' only a few, tiny churches scattered across Kentucky at that time, but later, I learned, those churches had all signed a covenant, agreeing to pray and fast, so as to plead with God to cause a great awakening. Someone told me later that it seemed as if God wasn't hearin' their prayers, though, 'cause nothing happened. If anything, the situation got worse, as they kept on hearin' reports about murders, horse thieves, and highwaymen. There was every sort of bad things going on. But, I gotta give them churches credit, 'cause they kept on a prayin.' It took a while, as if the Lord was testing them, but revival came. You know the Bible tells us that God does hear the prayers of a righteous man, and I reckon those churches wanted to be, first and foremost, righteous in His sight, so they fasted and kept' a'prayin,' and I reckon the Lord heared them, 'cause it wasn't long after that, during one of those communion services, that some of the most wretched men on earth came in that building, got on their knees, covered their faces with their hands and wept, beggin' the Lord to forgive them. And soon I heared other stories, of other churches across Kentucky where that happened. Course I didn't believe it, no, not until it happened to me.

"My, they say, that summer, I believe it was in 1801, there was something like five hundred people, some comin' as far as a hundred miles away or more, showin' up at those churches all across Kentucky, and, I heard, that time and time again those congregations were reduced to tears, as God poured out his Spirit on their lives. Those people came from everywhere—some from Tennessee, the Carolinas, Ohio and beyond, thousands of people."

James was totally fascinated by what he was hearing. *It seems that overwhelming fear of the unknown was now giving way to a Christ like love, a sacrificial love, and that love does change lives— and it changed the country, too!*

"It's amazin' what that revival did. People's lives were so changed, you could see it. It gave people a reason to live, meaning to their lives, and they, instead of fear and loneliness, robbin' and shootin' each other, they started gathering together, helping one another. We all worked, helping building barns, clearing fields, and the women cared for the sick and homeless, like Nancy, and all because of the love of our Lord and Savior Jesus Christ," William said, as he bowed his head and closed his eyes.

James leaned back in the old rocker where he was sitting and closed his eyes, but his mind was anything but closed as thoughts continued to penetrate it. *It wasn't force that solved their problems, oh no, force would only cause it to get worse; no, it was love, the love of Christ and the freedom that love brings that cause them now to live as brothers, giving purpose and meaning to their lives. Of course the shadow of the tempter is ever present, but that darkness will begin to fade, and it fades fast, when we allow God's glorious light to shine in and through us.*

As James pondered what he had just heard, he was ever-thankful for the opportunity to get to know the Fosters, realizing that their meeting may have well be by God's design. Eventually he would learn that the great gathering of people in Logan County, Kentucky, who came to know the Lord, would become known as "The Great Awakening."

Chapter 17

"It's called 'rabbit tobaccie.' The Indians use it for all kind of problems, but Nancy said it helps cure pneumonia, so we went out and picked ourselves some, and she was right, 'cause you got better."

Lavonia was trying to explain to James how Little Pine's suggestion of using the plant—which matures in the late fall, its leaves turning a silvery-green color, and is unfit to be used until they did—had helped pull him through. As Lavonia talked, thoughts swirled around in James' mind; it amazed him that God provided a plant to grow, at the proper time of year, to help cure him and other people who suffered from colds and flu in the winter.

But then he remembered Little Pine—Nancy—realizing once again that it was this little Indian woman whom he felt certain God had used to rescue him, and now had also helped cure him.

"Thank you, Nancy," James said, as he rolled his head over to look toward the door and the little woman, barely five feet tall, who was standing there. "I can't tell you how much I appreciate all that you did for me."

Nancy smiled, and then lowered her head, as if afraid to look him fully in the face.

"Are ya' a'feelin' good enough to come sit with us at supper? We're a'havin' salt pork and potatoes; how does that sound?" Lavonia looked at James.

"Well, wonderful! Yes, I think I can manage it," James said.

That evening, residing at the supper table in front of an eight-foot fireplace, James was introduced to the rest of Lavonia's family. Two of her sons—Henry, who was eleven, and Herbert, fourteen—were present, as well as Nancy and William Foster, Lavonia's husband of some thirty-plus years.

William, it seemed, had little to say, but did manage a "howdy" and a handshake before Lavonia started telling James about the rest of the Foster children. "They're all married, except for our two youngest, Henry and Herbert. The girls, there's five of them, now live on some of our neighbor's farms with their husbands and their families, but the boys—Ernest, Calvin, and Theodor—who are our oldest, live in cabins here, near us. Love for you to get to know them, James. Ifin' you stay, at least till the weekend, you can meet them all, as the family usually gets together for Sunday preachin' and dinner afterwards."

The generous hospitality of the Fosters became more and more apparent the longer James stayed, for now they wanted him to know he was more than welcome to be there for the winter or as long as he wished, or felt the need to. But James, realizing that winter was just around the corner, was anxious now to move on—for the desire to find his family, before the first snow of the season hit the rolling hills of southern Ohio, was paramount. Yes, he would stay to hear the preaching on Sunday morning, and perhaps have dinner with the family, but Monday would see him packing up his gear and being on his way.

On Sunday, James did meet most of the Fosters, at least those who came to the meeting. The family was gathered together in the one small room, which was located at the front of the cabin. With everyone talking at once, along with the children who made such a ruckus it was difficult to distinguish one voice from another, there came a loud knock at the door.

"It's Reverend Barnes!" Lavonia yelled above the noisy din. Suddenly, all was quiet. James could have heard a pin drop as William Foster opened the door. Standing there was a man, not much older than he, with deep, penetrating eyes, and a voice as equally penetrating. Entering the cabin, Reverend Barnes began to greet them, extending his hand to each and every one.

As James reached up to take his hand, he suddenly remembered what Lavonia had told him about Jacob Barnes, "He was also a convert at Cane Ridge. He drank, just about as bad as my husband, and I guess wasn't, at all, a'livin' in a decent way. But I reckon the Lord had other plans for him, 'cause he told us he came to Cane Ridge out of curiosity but left with the call upon his life. Now, he studies his Bible on his horse, as he rides through the wilderness in order to preach and teach in cabins, here on the frontier. This Sunday he will be here, with us, and we're fortunate to have him, 'cause he's only able to make it every few weeks or so."

James watched as Jacob Barnes continued his greetings. "Howdy, my children, how are you this fine Lord's day morning? Well, the Spirit of the Lord is certainly in this place. I just feel it. Have I ever told you the story of Jonah, written in the Scripture?"

Apparently, they had not heard the story of Jonah. They may have recognized the name, but it was obvious that none of them really knew anything about the man. Now, they all listened with anticipation, some sitting on the floor with their legs crossed, others standing, and the older ones claiming the few chairs in the cabin.

"Jonah was a servant of the Lord's, but he didn't want to obey what the Lord was asking," Jacob Barnes began his sermon. "But Jonah's life was about to change. His life's priorities and comforts were about to be disrupted, as the word of the Lord came to him, directing him in a new and different direction than what he was presently enjoying."

As Reverend Barnes continued talking, James looked around the room. No one was moving, no, not even the children. They sat as if mesmerized by what this young man was saying. James had to admit the fellow certainly had a gift. He wondered, if the Lord would permit it, if he might have that gift as well. Would he dare try? Perhaps time, and some patience, might present him with that opportunity. Yes, if God had a call upon his life, he, James Scott, may very well follow the example that was now being displayed before him.

Reverend Barnes ended his sermon by bringing the group back to the New Testament: "I believe Jesus is calling all of us to be His witnesses here, upon this earth. Everything we do, and everything we say, testifies to our belief in Him. Do we truly believe? Does the Spirit of the Lord live within us, and does He not convict us when we desire to go our own fleshly ways? When we judge others, as we decide to take matters in our own hands, not leaving room for God to judge? For He tells us in the book of Romans: 'Recompense no man evil for evil. Have respect for what is good in the sight of all men, and if possible, as much as it depends on you, live peacably with everyone.' Never take revenge, for the Bible tells us, 'Avenge not yourselves, but rather give place unto wrath: for it is written, Vengeance is mine; I will repay, saith the Lord. Therefore if thine enemy hunger, feed him; if he thirst, give him drink: for in so doing thou shalt heap coals of fire on his head'—making him burn with shame" (Rom. 12:17–21).

Later that day, James had a time to be alone with Jacob Barnes. It was a sunny day, warmer than usual for mid-November. The family had gathered outside the cabin, talking, when James decided to depart from the group to take a little walk. Jacob Barnes saw him leave and decided to follow.

Catching up with James, the pastor said, "I don't believe I know you." After a brief introduction, he then asked James a most surprising question. "Do you know Christ as your personal Savior?"

"Yes, I certainly do. He has become a very important part of my life," James said. He then attempted to explain how, in a small but significant way, God had become so real to him. Then he continued, "I believe He is calling me to preach the 'simple gospel' as well. I so enjoyed hearing your message today, and want to thank you for the work you're doing. I know it must not be easy riding the many miles you do throughout the week."

"You're right, James, it isn't easy, and at times I can become very weary," Jacob Barnes said. "I ride two hundred and fifty miles or more every two to six weeks to complete my circuit. Almost every day of the week I preach, both in the morning and evening, leaving very few days for rest and a time to gather knowledge, before I'm off again. But, you know, it is God's work. It's for His glory, and He provides the strength and ability to do it. I usually preach to an average of about a dozen people each place I go; however, here at the Fosters' there is always a much larger gathering. They are a great family, and I love being with them."

"How do you know the Fosters, James?"

"Well, it was either an accident or an act of God's. I believe the latter." As James started talking, Jacob Barnes turned and looked him fully in the face, as if desiring to take in every word. When James finished his story, Jacob Barnes stood amazed at what he heard.

"James, are you a Methodist?"

"No, Jacob, I'm not a Methodist. Actually, I'm not connected with any specific church, only to God. For, I have felt His call on my life to preach the 'simple gospel,' those wonderful words of the Bible. You, Jacob, are a Methodist, but I, I am just a Christian man, a simple Christian man paying no allegiance to any specific group, only to my Lord and Savior, and to those who want to follow Him."

"I can certainly understand, James, what you're saying, and I have to say, I do admire you for taking your stance. However, it would be difficult for me to leave the Methodist Episcopal Church. You see, I have dedicated myself to preach the 'plain gospel truth' as well, but I have been appointed by a presiding elder who is the district superintendent. I've traveled my circuit for more than a year, but soon I will be given a different one, as we Methodist circuit riders are encouraged to shift circuits every year or two by order of a manual called the 'Discipline.' Have you ever heard of Francis Asbury, James?"

"Yes, I've heard the name, but don't believe I know much about him."

"Well, he was the first Methodist bishop in America. When he first came to the colonies in the mid to late 1700s, there were only six hundred people claiming to be Methodist in America, but by the time he died, the denomination had grown to at least two hundred thousand. They say he too traveled on horseback, only he rode over a quarter-of-a-million miles, crossing the Appalachians sixty or more times. He wore out numerous horses, preached at least sixteen thousand sermons, and ordained thousands of ministers to preach the gospel. He traveled from Maine to Georgia and even crossed the frontier into Indiana. He never married and owned little more than a horse, but my, what an impact for Christ he made on this country. So James, yes, I am a Methodist; and, when I think of Bishop Asbury and all that he contributed, I know that I will *always* be a Methodist!"

Later that afternoon a rather large table was set, displaying an array of delectable food: potatoes, boiled onions, cornbread, and beans, even a container of apple butter and several fruit pies. A large campfire had been lit near the cabin with a roasting spit, where Lavonia and her daughters cooked a pig for the Sunday meal. The campfire also provided heat for the group, as the sun was low now in the southwestern sky. An evening breeze had picked up somewhat when Jacob Barnes, James Scott, and the Fosters sat down to enjoy some time together over a wonderful meal.

After dinner, James was pleased to hear Jacob Barnes preach again, and sat mesmerized at his message. Looking around at the faces of the Foster family, he could tell that they too were spellbound by his words. It seemed to James that Jacob preached an hour or more, but then stopped, occasionally, to ask if there were any questions or comments. Several members of the Foster family did ask him some interesting questions, which James found fascinating—but then Jacob turned to James, wondering if he would like to make a comment. James, pleased to be given the opportunity, jumped to his feet and tried to express himself in a short but concise way—however, finding it wasn't that easy, he ended up preaching a mini-sermon. When he sat down again he looked at Jacob Barnes and then the Foster family, wondering what they were thinking. It became a little puzzling to him, for their reaction was not what he had expected, which made him wonder if they were objecting to what he had to say because he was not a Methodist. If so, that hurt, as he cared deeply for the Fosters, and their opinion was important to him.

The evening had been challenging, and the rest of the day as well. When James laid his head on his pillow that night, he remembered what his friend Alexander Campbell had told him: "James we are Christian only, but we are not the only Christians. Our desire has never been to start a new church, but to encourage the existing churches to turn their eyes to the Bible and the Bible alone. Each of us is entitled to his opinion, but where those opinions differ from the Bible, we need to stay with the Bible."

Well, he, James had certainly treasured the time spent with the Fosters. His appreciation of them was beyond comprehension, but the fact that they were Methodist and he was not caused him some concern. Perhaps, in time, he might be able to explain to them that he wanted to be a preacher of the 'simple' gospel, to stand on his own, desiring not to have to answer to some higher human authority. He would pray, trusting God to open a door and give him an opportunity to make clear to them how he felt.

Then he remembered Little Pine. This sweet little Indian woman had saved his life and brought him here to be blessed.

He wanted, now, to know her better. He could not help but think about the times their eyes had met. He had to admit, he loved looking at her; but whenever he did, she always looked away. He wondered what she might be thinking, as his own thoughts seem to bewilder him now.

He remembered the first time he saw Mary, and how beguiling she was! Although they never talked, he knew he could not forget her, and later regretted that he had not spoken to her sooner, for had he done so they might have had more time together. He wondered if he was not having the same thoughts about Little Pine, for images of her pretty face filled his mind now, as he drifted off into deep slumber.

Chapter 18

"Nancy . . . Little Pine!" James was stunned to see her standing beside the stone column, near the fore-bay of the barn. He had gone there to get Shay, a gray-haired horse the Fosters generously offered him for his trip to Jackson town to look for his brother, but he certainly did not expect to see her there.

Obviously, she was surprised too, for upon hearing his voice she turned suddenly—and when she did, he could tell she had been crying.

"Nancy, why are you crying?"

"I not want you to go!" she said, as she turned around again and looked down.

"Oh, I see." She was being honest, but her response caught him by surprise; it certainly was not what he expected.

"Well, I'll be back. I don't plan to be gone long. I want to find my brother before winter sets in."

"No! You leave. I not see you again."

"No, Nancy, you're wrong, I will come back. I promise you."

He walked over and gently laid his hand on her shoulder. With her head still lowered, as if afraid to look at him, he put his other hand under her chin and lifted it so he could see her face clearly, hoping to look into her eyes; however, she continued looking down.

"Look at me, Nancy." Slowly she looked up. "I will come back. I promise you. Do you believe me?"

She nodded her head in an affirmative way, but he could tell she still did not believe him.

"Catahecassa said he return but he not come back." More tears fell from her eyes and cascaded down her cheeks as she remembered the day, six years before, when her husband and her brothers left to go look for her father in northern Ohio, never to be heard from again.

James kissed her on the forehead, pulling her close to him. Embracing her, he held her for several seconds before he let her go.

"Nancy, you have come to mean so much to me. You saved my life! I will never forget that! I am indebted to you! I could never leave you, be gone, and not come back. I hope you believe me. I will return, and when I come back I will make you my wife. I love you. Do you understand what I am saying?"

"No! I Indian. I cannot be wife of white man."

"Why not, Nancy? There's no difference between us. You are a Christian, aren't you? If we love each other, God will permit this, I feel certain. Please don't worry. I will come back, and when I do we will marry. Do you want to marry me?"

She lowered her head again and looked down. He wondered what she might be thinking, for she did not answer him, yet her tears reveled she did have feelings. Still, he wondered, since she was an Indian, if she felt, because she was different than he, she was not worthy of his love.

James, not knowing what else to say or do, turned and walked into the barn to get Shay.

As he was placing the saddle on the horse's back, he thought, *What did I just do? I proposed to an Indian! Can I marry an Indian? What would the Fosters think if Little Pine and I were to marry? What would my family think?*

These were some serious questions he had not considered. His proposal to her had been spurred by the moment. Did he realize what he was doing? He did feel sorrow for her, but to propose marriage? What was he thinking? He hardly knew her. Yet, the feelings were real, and he felt helpless to do anything about them. This beautiful, delicate little Indian woman, who had saved his life, he adored. It was impossible now for him to deny it, and he knew, in the days to come, he would not be able to think of her in any other way.

But then he remembered Mary. He had proposed to Mary in exactly the same way. Perhaps that was his fate! Well, he would have to wait and see what the future held, what God had in mind, but if he had anything to say or do about his future, this little Indian woman would be a part of it.

Riding Shay, James knew it would probably not take long to reach the town of Jackson, but he had no way of knowing for certain. He was thankful to Lavonia, for she had packed some salt pork, potatoes, and a little bit of bread for him to eat on his journey.

"I wanta' be sure you have some vittles and a jar of apple cider too, just in case you might be delayed or encounter some other kind of problem," she said, treating him like one of her sons. "I'll be praying for you too, to have a safe trip, and that you find your brother."

As James rode along the Scioto Trail, looking for the "feeder road" to Jackson, he was remembering what one of the men at the inn had told him about the town: "Jackson's a new town, so it's not big at all. The people named it after Andrew Jackson or 'Old Hickory' as we like to call him. Jackson's Scotch-Irish.

He became a hero during the War of 1812, and then ran for president. But the election was too close to call, so they named his opponent, John Quincy Adams, president. They say he'll try again in the next election. . . . I hope he does, and I hope he wins. I like Ol' Hickory. Anyway, that's how that town got its name."

Turning Shay onto the feeder road to Jackson, James was amazed how the road seemed to wind, first going east, and then turning sharply south, as it encountered the rolling hills. Eventually, though, the road evened out, as it went more east than south. It was mid-morning, and as the road straightened, he saw a man riding about a quarter of a mile ahead of him. Gently prodding Shay to go faster, he soon caught up with the fellow.

"Hello, are you headed for Jackson town?"

"Near there," was his reply. He was a well-built man, and James guessed him to be in his late thirties. He was wearing a raccoon cap, a heavy hunting shirt, homemade breeches, and moccasins on his feet made from some kind of animal skin. A rifle was slipped muzzle-down into a short triangular leather sleeve that was attached to the saddle horn. Evidence that the morning hunt had been profitable hung from his saddle, as there were two rabbits and a wild turkey.

"Well, that's where I'm headed," James told him. "Mind if I ride along with you for a few miles?"

"No, be glad to have you."

"Do you know much about that town? I've never been there, so I don't know anything about it. Is it very far?"

"No, only a few miles now, but I'll be turning off soon, as I have a farm south of here. Do you know someone in Jackson?"

"No, not really, I'm going there to look for my brother. Maybe you know him. His name is John Scott."

Suddenly the fellow pulled back on the reins of his horse.

"Whoa, Charger! Who did you say you were looking for?"

"John Scott. Do you know him?"

"Well, I guess I do! I'm John Scott, and who might you be?"

James stopped Shay completely, slid from the saddle, ran around the front of the horse and extended his hand up to the stranger, who was now looking at him with a perplexed look on his face.

"You are the John Scott whose father was a shipper, shipped flax from New York?"

"Yes, but who did you say you were?" Reluctantly, John Scott held out his hand.

"I'm James, your brother."

"James? James!" John now slid from his saddle and extended his arms, and the two of them stood in middle of the road, embracing.

"My, my! The last time I saw you, you were just a baby!"

"Yes, well I sure am not one now," James said, with a big smile on his face, "and I've come a long way to find you. I have so much to tell you, but first I want you to know, Mum sends you her love. It's been such a long time since you last heard from you, or so she said, and she wanted me to be sure and give you that message."

"I still miss her, and pray she is fine and healthy. And how is father, James?"

"Father is no longer living. He died, drowned a few years ago now. It was a tragedy that I want to tell you about, but we need to find some place where we can sit awhile and talk. It's a long story; I want to be sure to tell you everything."

"I see. He drowned?"

"Yes, John," James quickly looked down, as if to hide the tears forming in his eyes. "I want to tell you all about it, John, and will as soon as we can find a good place to talk. . . . Does Ruth live near you?"

"Oh, yes. Not far away. She's married, you know, and has seven kids. Robert and Andrew, her two older sons, are about your age, well, maybe a little younger. Anyway, she seems happy now, now that she's living here in Ohio; so much easier for her and Tom, and easier for me, too. Love the land; it is so fertile. My, you can grow anything on it."

John didn't seem all that concerned about his father's death, but considering the fact that they had not been together for some twenty years, James could understand. John's life had gone on without his father in it, and that fact made James wonder if knowing what happened to him would not seem like just another good story.

James and John climbed back on their horses, and it wasn't long before they turned off the main route onto a horse path leading south. They came to a small stream and crossed over. As the dense forest parted, James could see cleared fields surrounded by log fencing. In the distance, smoke curled up into the air from the chimney of a lone log cabin that now came into view. Riding through the gate, he could hear dogs barking, as three boys ran out of the cabin, chased by two girls, whom James assumed were the boys' older sisters.

"Oh, those youngins' are at it again. My, how they like to tease each other! Do you have any kids, James?"

"No, I'm not married."

"Let's see, you would be about twenty-four or five?"

"Yes, but as providence would have it, I have not known a woman. I was married once, but in name only. I'll tell you all about it, John, but I want to start at the beginning, don't want to leave anything out."

That evening, sitting before the glow of a fire burning brightly in the stone fireplace centered in the main part of the cabin, James began his story. All of the family were gathered there, and he was delighted to meet them. Above everything else, it was a joy to know that he was an uncle, not only to John's five, but Ruth's seven as well, and that two of her sons, Robert and Andrew, were not much younger than he. What a special privilege, hearing the younger ones call him "Uncle Jim."

As they sat relaxing before the fire, James began his chronological account of the days before and following the sinking of the *Nancy Grace.*

"I will never, nor can I ever free my mind from hearing father's last words telling me, 'Go Jimmy, go, you can make it lad . . . swim, swim son, swim!'" James lowered his head.

John reached over and placed his hand on James' back. "So sorry, James, it's difficult for me to even imagine how such a thing could have ever happened . . . and you were on that island for two years, by yourself?"

"Yes. It was a beautiful island, warm the whole year round."

"What did Mums do without you and father?" Ruth asked.

"Well, she sold their home, and moved into the boarding house with grandfather and grandmother, but they died a couple of years ago, so she took the house over and has been quite successful in managing it herself. I was hoping she would come with me, but she didn't want to leave, as the boarding house has become more like home for her. She has many close friends who live there now.

"By the way, I do want to get a letter sent to her as soon as possible, to let her know that I found you all. She made me promise to do that."

"That is not so easy to do, James, living here in this wilderness," Robert said. "If you could find someone to take it to Portsmouth, they might get one of those new boats that travel by steam to take it east, up river. Maybe someone might deliver it from there."

"Yes, not only is it near to impossible to get a letter sent; it is expensive, too!" John said. "Perhaps next fall when the harvest is in, we could take it south then. I'm hoping to have a good crop of corn to take to the grainery. We'll talk more about it later this year. It would be good to send a letter and good, too, to hear from Mum."

"Well, tell me, James, what happened to Mary? Did you find her, and if you did, why didn't you marry her again?" Ruth asked.

"Mary died in my arms a few weeks ago, Ruth. It was sad, so sad, because I did love her very much. I had great hopes for us and didn't think I could live my life without her, but it had been two years since I last saw her, and well, you know, life does go on. . . . But the best thing that has come from all of this is that I have grown closer to God, and His Son, our Lord and Savior, Jesus Christ."

"You do still go to the Presbyterian church, don't you?" John asked.

"Well, I haven't gone to any church for a while, especially since I've been traveling, but I'm leaning toward being just a 'Christian.' I think I may have been rescued from that island for a reason, John, for of all people, I should be dead now, drowned along with father and all those men I sailed with, yet here I am in this physical body, alive! I believe God has given me this time and has made Himself known to me for a purpose. For I feel He is telling me to go and preach the 'simple gospel.' As I read and study the Bible, I am constantly reminded that it is our manual for living, for just as Paul said in his letter to the Romans, so I too affirm that 'I am not ashamed of the gospel, for it is the power of God for salvation to everyone who believes.' For me to proclaim it, I feel has been my calling."

"When do you think this will happen, James?" John said, growing more curious.

"I'm not certain. It's all in God's good timing. He knows when, and the circumstances under which it will happen. All I know, at this point, is, He has called me, telling me to 'Go into the world and preach the gospel, and he who has been baptized shall be saved.' I testify I will be ready when the time comes."

On Sunday morning, with all the family gathered in the main room of the cabin, James held a communion service, as John told him that none of them had had communion for a long time.

"We would have liked to meet with a church, but we have not been able to find anyone near us," John said. "It is really difficult to practice our faith here in this wilderness. I do read the Bible to the family in the evening after dinner, and we pray, but we have not been able to have communion."

James remembered how his friend and brother in Christ, Alexander Campbell, had held communion. So he talked a little more about the faith, and then taking a cup, he asked Aileen, John's wife, if she had any wine. She did, and so handed him a small bottle she took down from a top shelf. Taking the wine from her, he filled the cup and presented it to them, along with some bread, which he broke in two parts, and then he said, "This represents our Savior's death. The wine is the blood he gave for us as He hung on the cross, and the broken bread is His body, which was broken for us. He was our substitute, and as we take this, we remember that we were the ones who should have died. It should have been our blood, our bodies given to show a Holy God that we are truly sorry for all those bad things we do or have done, for no matter how hard we try, we still find ourselves a sinful people! But God has said, 'No! I will give myself for you!' but He has asked us to do this." Passing the bread and the wine, James continued, "in remembrance of what He gave, praising Him for it, giving thanks, which seems a very small word for all He did for us. Amen."

"As we go on with our lives," James continued, "let us remember what it cost Him as He hung there on that cross, and let us promise to humbly try to live our lives in accordance to His will, studying the Holy Scriptures, keeping the law, following His example, and that is to love one another as He loved and gave His life for us."

As James finished with a prayer, John put his hand on his brother's back, patting him several times.

"You are a wonder!" John told him, "Yes, a true wonder. I want to thank you for all you've said here, for ministering to the family and for being faithful. Yes, I do believe you have been given a gift, James. Go, and use it for God."

James, making the decision to stay with his brother and his family until the middle of December, was happy to spend time telling them stories about sailing and his father's ship, the *Nancy Grace.* He told how he had survived many exciting and harrowing experiences, "and there certainly were some humdrum days as well," he said, with candid look on his face.

The children were ever ready to hear his tales of the island, and especially the pirates taking the ship. He tried not to tell them too much about that experience, but many times they begged him to tell them more. When James ran out of stories, he read to them from the Bible, showing a correlation between the biblical accounts and the island where he spent two years of his life. He told them about the glorious sunsets he had experienced there, and how those sunsets reminded him of the glories of heaven, its splendid streets of gold the Bible talks about, and "oh those wonderful pearly gates." As the days grew colder, they found him with them, more often than not, sitting before the warmth of the fire.

The time seemed to pass quickly, and it was now late December. James, aware that the weather had turned decisively colder, now saw a light coating of frost most mornings covering tree limbs, the top of the rail fencing, and on the gambrel of their newly built barn.

When James wasn't with the children, he was helping his brother. The woodpile seemed to need constant attention, as did the animals, which still had to be fed, and the cows and goats milked. Winter was a slightly less stressful time, but there were, nonetheless, jobs that still had to be taken care of.

"The barn needs repairs, as well as the inside and outside of the cabin. We'll have to take the corn by wagon to the grainery for storage," John said.

It was paramount that there be enough food and other items to get them, as well as the animals, through the winter, spring, and the months of the growing season; if not, then they would starve until the next harvest. So James helped his brother kill hogs, and then cure them with salt from the nearby salt mines. They also stored potatoes, and other vegetables the ladies had canned, in a small mud cellar that John and David, Ruth's husband, dug out for that purpose.

"We are always hoping, or perhaps praying, that we can produce more than we can use, as we need to be able to sell some of our produce, so we can buy other things we will need, such as salt, sugar, coffee, and maybe, if we're fortunate, a bolt or two of linen cloth. Certainly, if we can't raise it or trade for it, then we'll just have to do without," John said.

"Now that you're here, James, the work hasn't been so hard this season. You know what they say: 'many hands make light work,'" John said.

"It has been a pleasure to help out, John, but now that winter is here, and the work is almost completed, I'm beginning to have a strong desire to return to the Fosters."

"Well, you certainly have been a blessing, not only to me, but to the entire family. Tell you what, James: When you come back in the spring, we'll build you a cabin, a home all your own, down that way." John pointed north through the woods. "But until we get it finished you know you're welcome to stay here."

"I really do need to return Shay, so I will probably go back to the Fosters and stay with them for the rest of the winter. I still feel indebted to the Fosters for all they have done for me, and I'm sure there is plenty of work there that could use an extra hand. But, I will be back in the spring, John. The Fosters' farm is only a few miles away, so if you need me, you can ride over. I'll be there. But when springtime comes, I'll be back here to help you with the new cabin."

John had given James one of his horses, which he had named Big Red. Now riding Big Red, with Shay trailing along behind, James left the cabin with a light covering of snow on the ground, and flakes the size of popped corn falling from the sky. Soon he would reach the Fosters' cabin, on a hillside not far from the Scioto Trail.

⁓

"Oh James, we are so happy to see you again! Come in and warm your frozen feet and hands. . . . Sit here, before the fire!" Lavonia said, as she took his coat and gloves.

As he sat down before the fire, warming his hands, James told them about meeting John on the feeder road leading to Jackson, how he had enjoyed the children and seeing his sister.

"When I get back in the spring, John and the family are planning on building a small cabin for me, and of course I want to be there to give them a hand."

"When that time comes, James, I'll help too, as I know spring can be a busy time. Plowin' fields and plantin' needs to get done then. It would be good if they could get it started while the ground is still frozen. Let us know, and maybe some of the boys will pitch in, too!" William Foster said, as he sat before the fire relaxing, with his long legs stretched out, an unlighted cigar cradled in the fingers of his right hand.

James stretched himself out in front of the fire as well and leaned his head back against the chair. Closing his eyes, he thanked God not only for them, but also for being able to find his family. Then he remembered Nancy. Little Pine—he wondered where she could be. He saw her for a brief moment when he entered the cabin, but then she disappeared. Lavonia was there, busy making some vittles, or so she said, for the noonday meal, but where was Nancy?

Nancy . . . he had thought of her often while he was gone, and each time she came into his mind it sent excitement racing through him, a feeling he had only felt one other time in his life. Beautiful Little Pine . . . soon James drifted off into deep sleep.

Chapter 19

With the noonday meal over, and the dishes washed and dried, Lavonia left the cabin and went out to feed the chickens and gather the eggs for the day, while William Foster searched the woodpile for logs to put on the fire. Henry and Herbert, laughingly, busied themselves playing with a "whimmydiddle" they had made. It was a magic stick, or so they said, that turned when they asked a question and rubbed it, supposedly telling them if the answer was a "yes" or "no."

As James sat relaxing before the fire, he wondered where Nancy was; aside from that brief moment when he entered the cabin, he still had not seen her. Could she be in the loft—the open area at the back of the cabin above where he was sitting? Lavonia told him that was where she stayed most of the time, especially now that the days had grown shorter and certainly a lot colder. The loft was comfortable, as the heat from the fireplace had little trouble moving up through the cracks in the pine logs and along the ceiling, filling the small, open space with its warmth. James could see in the loft and had looked up many times, but he did not see Nancy.

She had not come down for the noonday meal, which seemed unusual to him, causing him to wonder why—so he decided to climb the ladder to the loft to find out. As he placed his foot on the bottom rung, he called out her name, hoping not to startle her. She did not answer, so he continued up the ladder until he reached the top. There she sat on a straw-filled comforter in a far corner of the tiny upper room with her legs crossed. She had on a short skirt made from some kind of animal skin. Her legs were covered with leggings and on her feet, she wore moccasins. Her long dark hair hung loose about her shoulders, but had been hindered from falling into her face by a beaded headband. Her appearance took him by surprise, as she looked very much like an Indian, but a very beautiful one.

"Nancy," James spoke softly, afraid he might alarm her.

She raised her head and smiled, a smile that gave him a huge dose of confidence. So he said to her, "I've hardly seen you, Nancy. Why didn't you come down for dinner?"

She lowered her head again, as if afraid to speak. Slowly, he crawled over and touched her arm.

"Nancy, are you not happy to see me?"

She gave an affirmative nod, but still did not look up.

"Nancy, my Little Pine, I thought about you every day I was gone. I don't think a minute went by that you were not somewhere in my mind."

Now sitting on the floor in front of her, he reached over, put his hands on her arms, leaned forward, and kissed her cheek.

"Did you not think of me, at all, while I was away?"

She nodded yes. Still he wondered what she might be thinking. He remembered the day he left, how she cried because she thought he would not return. Was it joy she was feeling now, or sadness? He really could not tell, so he said to her,

"Nancy, I still love you, and I still want you to be my wife. Will you marry me?" James had to know, and he needed to know now. Yes, he was a white man and she an Indian, but his love for her seemed to change all of that! True, he did not know her well, but then he never knew Mary either. It seemed his fate to be a rescuer, yet Nancy had rescued *him*. She had saved him from the wild beast and brought him to the Fosters to be blessed. He could never forget that! *Isn't it strange*, he thought, *how love changes things?* For the only thing that seemed to matter now was certainly not that she was different than he, but did she love him—and if so, would she be his wife?

Shyly she lifted her head and looked deeply into his grey-blue eyes. "Yes, I will be wife of white man."

Relief flooded over James, causing a deep sigh, for the air he was holding in suddenly came rushing out.

"You will? Well, you had me worried. I didn't think you wanted to, and I have to say, I wouldn't have blamed you if you didn't, as I have nothing, other than my love, to give you. My brother and I will be building a small cabin on his farm in the spring. We can live there for a time, but other than that, I have only my love for you."

He reached over, and taking her hand, he kissed it.

The next day, and with some reservation, James told Lavonia and William what had happened. Lavonia was delighted to hear the news, and couldn't quit talking about it. "I'll bake a cake, a 'bridal pie' for the wedding, and Nancy will need a dress, too. Jacob Barnes will be here by the middle of January, that is if he comes at his usual time, so the wedding can take place on the Sabbath, on Saturday. That will give me enough time to help you prepare for it."

What concerned James was Nancy's last name, as she did not have one. She was a Shawnee Indian. Her family called her Shinguaconse; now of course, she had a first name, which the Fosters had given her, but she needed a last name.

As James pondered the problem, he decided to give her Mary's last name. *Why not call her Nancy White? After all, it won't be her name for long. Soon, if all goes well, she will be Nancy Scott.*

The thought of riding back to get his brother and sister to witness the affair was paramount to James, but he knew at that time of year it would not be a good idea. It was the middle of winter, and the days were growing shorter and certainly a lot colder.

"As soon as the weather breaks, Nancy, we'll go to my brother's farm, so you can meet my family and they can get to know you, perhaps in the early spring," James said, hoping, or perhaps praying, they would accept her.

Nancy had not met any of James' family. She realized that the long, cold winter weather had not presented him with the opportunity of inviting them to the Fosters' home, but it did excite her, knowing that soon she would meet them. At the same time she cautiously wondered, *Will they accept me?* She missed her own family; she knew she would always have a pain in her heart whenever she thought about them. After her father and brothers, and, eventually, her husband left, the one person she had in her life was her mother, but now her mother was no longer living. However, it was a blessing that the Fosters had taken her in. Being a part of their family made her feel, now, that she had a family of her own.

In the days ahead, she looked forward to becoming James' wife, and was amazed that he wanted her to become his wife. She had no way of knowing he would come back, let alone ask her to marry him; she had felt certain on the day he left, that, like her family, she would never see him again. Yes, she did care for him, for from the time she found him lying on the riverbank until he asked her to be his wife, she thought of nothing else but him; however, she could not imagine what it might be like being the wife of a white man. Certainly it would be a different life, not like the one she had always known.

And so they married, with Jacob Barnes arriving just in time to preside over the ceremony. "It's a delight to see you again, James, and to perform your marriage. Nancy is a beautiful bride," the pastor said.

"Yes, she is," James said, as he turned to look at Nancy again. She was wearing the dress Lavonia had made for her, a beautiful but simple gown of yellow calico lace. The gown had a high, unadorned neckline designed to modestly conceal her feminine charms. Strange, he thought, for on her head she wore a simple muslin turban. Later he learned that Lavonia had given her a bonnet for her head, but Nancy refused to wear it.

"She pointed to the hat and told me, 'No, I not wear that,'" Lavonia said. "I told her, 'Oh you must! A hat shows you are willing to be subject to your husband.' But she said, 'I wear this,' and then she picked up that turban. 'If that is what you want to wear,' I told her, 'then maybe you'll let me sew some beads on it, so then it won't look so plain.'"

As James took Nancy's hand, he glanced down at her feet. He could see that on her feet were the moccasins she wore the day he had proposed to her.

Jacob Barnes, performing the ceremony, repeated the scripture in 1 Corinthians, but changed the words of the King

James Bible in the hopes that Nancy would be able to understand better what those words were saying:

> Though I speak with the tongues of men and of angels, but have not love, I have become sounding brass or a clanging cymbal. And though I have *the gift of* prophecy, and understand all mysteries and all knowledge, and though I have all faith, so that I could remove mountains, but have not love, I am nothing. And though I bestow all my goods to feed *the poor,* and though I give my body to be burned, but have not love, it profits me nothing.

> Love suffers long *and* is kind; love does not envy; love does not parade itself, is not puffed up; does not behave rudely, does not seek its own, is not provoked, thinks no evil; does not rejoice in iniquity, but rejoices in the truth; bears all things, believes all things, hopes all things, endures all things.

> Love never fails. But whether *there are* prophecies, they will fail; whether *there are* tongues, they will cease; whether *there is* knowledge, it will vanish away. For we know in part and we prophesy in part. But when that which is perfect has come, then that which is in part will be done away.

> When I was a child, I spoke as a child, I understood as a child, I thought as a child; but when I became a man, I put away childish things. For now we see in a mirror, dimly, but then face to face. Now I know in part, but then I shall know just as I also am known.

And now abide faith, hope, love, these three; but the greatest of these *is* love (1 Cor. 13, NKJV).

After the pastor finished reading the scripture and pronounced them husband and wife, James bent over and kissed Nancy. It was their first kiss, and James could tell it surprised her. Later, when he learned she had never been kissed before, he kissed her again, and when he did, the astonishment in her eyes sent excitement rushing through him.

Little Pine was his, and from that moment on he would never be alone again.

Chapter 20

James faced a wilderness, as he envisioned his life now with his new bride; and as time passed, it became clearer and clearer to him that he was to proclaim the gospel, the "simple" gospel truth. He knew not the time or how it might take place, but he was convinced it would happen. Many families along the East Coast were still coming west into the frontier, and although the Great Awakening at the turn of the century had persuaded many toward Christ and a belief in the Bible, still he wondered how many of those people—and the new ones who were now coming into the frontier—either did not know the Bible at all or needed to be encouraged to live by what they had learned. If they did not have a faith in Christ and an understanding of Scripture, he felt certain they would continue living in fear, finding their courage in a whiskey bottle, with a gun by their side. He could not let that happen, not in a country abounding in freedom, a freedom that existed only because people had put their faith first in God's laws.

The days ahead found him puzzling over when it would happen, as he knew there were many men now crossing and crisscrossing the land, preaching an awareness of Christ. Still, he felt certain that if he made himself available, God would use him, as he recalled the promise he made on that island: *"Oh, God and Savior of my soul . . . deliver me from this place, and I promise You, I will serve You for the rest of my days upon this earth!"*

Still, his beloved friends the Fosters seemed to be objecting to his calling, because he was not a Methodist; and that did cause him some concern. Also, as he thought about Alexander Campbell and other men who had ministered to him, comparing himself to them, he knew he certainly did not have their knowledge! Although he spent many hours reading his Bible, still it held mysteries he had yet to decipher. James felt perplexed, and it did discourage him somewhat. *Well, it seems, the only thing to do is to keep on praying and making myself available. Perhaps sooner or later I'll have an answer; will God use me, or will He not?*

James and Nancy stayed with the Fosters throughout the winter months. James had been a big help to William Foster and his three sons, doing numerous jobs for them. They became great friends, laughing and sharing stories as they spent the long winter together.

As the winter progressed, James did not see much of Jacob Barnes, but on one rare visit he did have an opportunity to talk with him. Jacob, realizing James' desire to proclaim the Word, said to him, "James, I would like to encourage you, my friend, to join the Methodist Episcopal Church and become a circuit rider."

"I admire you, Jacob," James said, "and I also have a great respect for the Methodists, especially Bishop Asbury and all he has accomplished in this country, but I do not feel called to be a Methodist circuit rider. If what you are saying is true about following a manual called the 'Discipline,' I find I cannot do that. I have felt led to follow the Bible and the Bible only," James said, as he remembered the many conversations he had had with his friend Alexander Campbell.

"I can certainly understand and relate to what you are saying, James, and I have to admire you for taking your stance; however, I cannot leave the Methodist Episcopal Church. Although I have been appointed by a presiding elder, I too preach the plain gospel truth. But if, at some time in the future you should decide that you want to be a part of our church, do let me know and I will introduce you to our district superintendent," Jacob said.

It was late winter when James decided to return to his brother's home with his bride. The latter part of winter had been mild, and although it was too early for plowing and planting, still, if the warm weather held, it would not be long before the soil would demand it. He was hoping they would have enough time before the spring thaw to start the small house John had talked about building for him, and so he made the decision to return early.

As James walked, leading Big Red, with Nancy riding and their few possessions hanging from the saddle, they rounded a small hill on their way up the fork in the road, which led to his brother's farm, and there in the distance James saw a cabin with a stone chimney.

"Nancy, see that cabin up ahead? I don't remember it being there. I wonder where or how I could have missed it."

As they came closer, he realized the cabin was new. "It looks like it's in the process of being built, as there isn't a front door."

The cabin had one room and no windows. Looking inside, he could see a fireplace at one end where stone and clay had been used for the hearth and the interior portion. The inside walls were chinked with clay and cloth; and the floor, which was simply beaten earth, still held firm as the ground outside was feeling the heat from the early winter's thaw.

"Look Nancy, there's a sleeping loft along the wall opposite that fireplace, like the one you stayed in at the Fosters'. It must be the reason the roof is higher on that side."

As James and Nancy stood looking at the structure two men came riding up.

"Whoa Chancy! Hello James!" It was John, and Ruth's husband, David. "My, it's good to see you made it back. We didn't think you would be here before spring," John said, as he slid from his saddle.

"John! David! It's good to see you, too. How are you? Guess you made it through the winter okay." James, extending his arms up to take their hands, was certainly surprised to see them.

"Glad to see you made it back, James," John said. "I wondered about you, and hoped all went well with you this winter." He was now looking at the little woman standing so close to James that she was half-hidden behind him.

"Oh, by the way, fellows, I want you to meet my wife, Nancy," James said, as he put his arm around her tiny waist and pulled her out from behind him. "She and I were married shortly after I arrived back at the Fosters. She's the one I told you about, who saved my life down by the river and took me back to the Fosters to care for me there. My, if it hadn't been for her, I would be dead now." James felt the need to explain, as he could see the curious look on both of their faces.

The men reached up, took off their hats, and smiled, nodding to her.

"I'm so glad to meet you, Nancy," John extended his hand to her; David offered his as well. "Yes, and thank you for saving this lone, lost brother of ours."

Nancy looked at the two of them, smiled, and quickly stepped back again.

"I see you found the cabin. How'd you like it, James?" John wanted to know.

James, a little confused now, wondered, "John, is this mine?"

"Well yes, James. Hope you like it?"

"It's wonderful, but where did it come from? You didn't build this, did you? How'd you find the time? Wasn't it a bit too cold? This must have taken a lot of work."

"This last month was so mild that we just decided to do it. We knew we wouldn't have time in the spring. In fact, I want to start clearing more fields soon, and I'm gonna need your help to do it; so I was hoping you would return early, and if you did, wanted to make sure you had a place of your own to live in. Tom and I and the boys just got ourselves busy and got it put up in no time. Hope you'll like living here. It's about a half mile from our place. We came over today to do some more work on it, and now, since you're here, you can help!"

Well, James liked it very much, but there was still some serious work it needed, like a floor and a front door, and several other things he would like to do. But, of course, that would all take time. For now, though, it was wonderful, and to think he had a place of his own to live in with his new bride.

In the spring they cleared several fields. James soon realized that it was no easy task, as they had to dig up the stumps of numerous trees they felled, leaving the larger ones to rot. It would take time, but eventually, as the decaying took place, the remains could be plowed under along with the rest of the soil. Logs that were not used were burned, and their ash was spread over the ground as well. It took time and lots of work, for there was corn to be planted, along with wheat, and for some time Aileen had wanted John to plant a small apple orchard along with some pear and a few other fruit trees—hoping by late summer, or perhaps in a year or two, a taste of their sweet bounty would reward them for their efforts.

It was a busy time of hard work, with little relaxing, and always in the back of James' mind was the thought and prayer, *"When, Lord, when will you call me? When will I go to my neighbors' cabins to tell them about You? When will I talk to my family about being baptized by immersion? Help me to know. Give me a sign."*

Most evenings found James studying his Bible. The sun was low in the sky when the men quit working for the day. After saying their farewells, they each made it back to their own cabins before the sun had completely disappeared.

James, as usual, saw Nancy standing at the door with his Bible in her hands. "Here your Bible," Nancy said. "You want to read before we eat and before sun goes down."

After a supper of baked turkey and corn cakes, James settled himself again before the hickory bark fire, in an old pine rocker Ruth had given them. With his Bible in his hands he began to read until the last flames, which were blazing brightly now, became only burning embers. Occasionally James would read a passage or two to Nancy, explaining to her what he was reading in the hopes that she would somehow understand.

The hours ticked on, and soon it was time to climb the ladder up to the loft to put in a night of sleep, knowing the next day would be another one of hard work.

James had just drifted off into deep slumber, when suddenly there was a loud knock at the door.

"Someone's at the door. I wonder who it might be," he said to Nancy as he hustled out of bed, slipped on his moccasins, grabbed the top of the ladder, and climbed down.

"Preacher! Preacher!" James heard someone say. It sounded like a young boy.

Slowly James inched the door open. The full moon sending down a strong light enabled him to see plainly a young man standing there. His age, he guessed, was not more than fourteen or fifteen.

"Preacher, we need ya'! It's my ma, she's a-dyin'," the young man said the moment he saw James. He was tall and slim, and his voice, which was changing, cracked as he spoke. "Ya' can come, can't ya'? We live thar, over them hills, that away." He pointed toward the northeast. "It's not a far piece. Please, Preacher, she's a'need'n' ya'!"

"Well yes. I guess I can. You'll have to wait a minute. I need to get some clothes on," James said, still confused about the intrusion, wondering how this young man knew him. *Preacher," he called me! How did he know I was one or wanted to be one?* This was certainly puzzling. James scratched his head, as if doing so would help him understand it all.

When he turned to get his clothes, he saw Nancy standing there, as if waiting for an explanation, but because he was in such a hurry he did not notice the confusion written across her face, and so he said, "I need to get Big Red from the lean-to and saddle him. Will you be all right here, by yourself, Nancy? I don't know how long I will be gone, but I have to go with this young man. He sounds frantic!"

"No! I not want you to leave," Nancy said, but James was so focused on the young man he did not hear her.

Not realizing her concern, James climbed up on the back of Big Red and introduced himself to the stranger as they pulled on the rein of the horses. "I don't believe I know you."

"Clem; my name is Clem Barton. Preacher Barnes told usens' about ya', said ya' war' a good man of God, a preacher too, and since thar ain't no preachers here in Jackson country, we was happy to know you was here. My mom just delivered my baby sister, but she took a turn for the worse, and now is a'dyin'. Pa told me to ride over and get ya'. Hope ya' don't mind."

"Mind? Certainly not. I will be happy to help in any way I can," James told him, as they turned north, following an old Indian path through the dense woods.

As James followed Clem, they rode along in silence. Puzzling over the circumstances he now found himself in, James began to pray, *"Lord, make me zealous, but also give me compassion for the lost that I may bring them to You. I know this is Your will for Your church, for the advancement of Your kingdom here on earth, a kingdom not measured in human lives, but in souls, souls drawn to You by the work of the Holy Spirit. I want to be faithfully obedient to your call. Hear me now, Oh Lord!"*

Soon they came to a clearing, the forest of trees disappearing behind them. They traveled several miles farther before coming to a small village. It displayed a tavern and three cabins along a dirt road. As they were passing through it, Clem turned to James to tell him that his house was only a mile farther down the road. A few minutes later, they turned onto a lane, which led to a lone log cabin in a thicket of the woodlands.

Entering the cabin, children could be seen sleeping on cots scattered across the floor. Clem motioned for James to follow him to a back room. Slowly he opened the door and stepped inside, holding it for James to enter.

Whispering softly, Clem looked toward a man sitting beside a bed. A small-framed woman was lying there, barely breathing. She had a damp cloth covering the top of her head.

"Pa, here'ns the preacher you was a'wantin'," Clem told him.

William Barton looked up at James with sadness in his eyes, and nodded to him. He then got up and asked James to follow him outside. Once outside the cabin, he began to talk.

"She's a-dyin'!" William Barton looked up at James, and then lowered his head. James, feeling his heartache, reached over, put his arm around the man's shoulders, and hugged him, not knowing what else to say or do.

"She's had ten youngins'. Guessin' her body jest got a'teered of a'havin' babies. She's been a'bleedin', and can't geet it stopped. She's a'losin' too much blood. What'll I do, preacher?" William Barton looked at James, hoping he would have an answer.

"William," James stood with his hands on William Barton's shoulders, "more than anything else we can do now is to have faith, believing God can and will answer our prayers. Let's pray." James lowered his head, and with his heart so full of the man's agony lifted his prayer heavenward, pleading with God to stop the bleeding and let the poor woman live.

"You healed the leper, oh God," James began his prayer, "and let the woman who had been bleeding for more than twelve years be healed with just a touch of Your garment. You raised Lazarus from the dead and the little girl who was dead You found, with Your mighty power, only sleeping. You healed the blind and made the lame to walk again. Oh God, if it be in Thy will, touch this poor woman and stop the bleeding. Her family needs her, Lord. I know not what they believe, even if they know about You or have a profound belief in You, but Lord, I know in my heart that You are the One who has sent me here, and I will tell them about You. I will let them know about Your love, a love that was so deep, so intense that You were willing to lay down Your life for them and for me. Now won't You please place Your healing hand on," James stopped for a moment to ask William what his wife's name was. William softly whispered, "Abigail." "Abigail," James repeated the name, "and stop the bleeding, and let her live to minister to her family, for it is in the powerful name of our Lord and Savior, Jesus Christ that I am praying in this hour, at this time, beseeching You for help. Amen!"

When James finished the prayer, he took a hanky out of his pocket to wipe his eyes. His prayer was so intense and deeply felt he could not hold back the moisture that was now flooding to the surface, for Christ was standing there before him. In his mind's eye he could see Him. He knew to Whom he prayed, and there was not a doubt in his mind that God had heard, and would answer his prayer.

With his arm around William, they walked back into the cabin. As they entered the room where Abigail was lying, nothing had changed. If anything was different, there was not one indication. Abigail lay motionless on the bed. James wondered if she had died while they were gone, but as they came closer, they could tell she was still breathing.

It was a long, long night. Both men stayed by her bedside. James, with his head lowered, prayed most of the time. Occasionally he would look up, with moisture under his eyes, and a tiny tear reflecting in the candlelight, to see the frail body of Abigail Barton. She had not changed.

Soon a glow from the early morning sun could be seen from the window in the front of the cabin. Abigail was still breathing. Although her eyes were closed, she seemed to be sleeping more peacefully.

As the morning approached, James experienced a feeling of mild excitement when William found that his wife had quit bleeding. Even though she still seemed very weak, James could tell her breathing had become more stable, too. As he and William sat there beside her bed amazed, suddenly Abigail opened her eyes, as if coming out of a bad dream. James saw her look first at William, and then turn her eyes toward him, as if wondering who the stranger was and why he was there. But, then just as quickly as she opened her eyes, he saw them close again, as she seemed to drift off into a more peaceful slumber.

"Did you see that?" William looked at James.

"Yes, William, I think we may have had an answered prayer. God willing, she may live."

William, ever grateful, thought, *Yes, I believe she might, and if she does, how blessed we'll be, the family, and I, to have her back again. I wonder, could that have been because of James Scott's profound belief in the healing hands of his Heavenly Father?*

Later that morning James left Abigail's bedside relieved, knowing she would recover. He climbed on Big Red and made it back to his cabin before the sun was high in the sky, only to find Nancy was missing. She was not in the cabin or anywhere around it. "Where could she be?" James wondered as he searched for her inside and out, calling her name over and over, but she did not answer.

Upon entering the cabin again, he noticed something on the table he had not seen there before. As he moved closer to take a better look, he saw two spoons resting side by side, circled by a beaded headband. At the corner of the headband was a knife pointing south, toward his brother's house. *That's where she is,* James thought. Nancy could not read or write English, so the only way she had of leaving him a message, to tell him where she had gone, was to leave a sign.

Climbing back on Big Red, James made his way to his brother's cabin. John was gone, but Aileen was there. "Nancy came here, but she left. She seemed so distressed because you had not returned; she decided to go to the Fosters'. I tried to stop her. I told her you would come back, but I just couldn't make her understand, or get her to believe it. She was crying, and sounded so fearful," Aileen told him, with worried lines forming on her brow.

James jumped on Big Red. He knew the horse had to be tired and hungry after the twenty-mile trip to and from the Bartons' home, as well as having been ridden to his brother's cabin and back. And he needed rest as well. So decided to return to the cabin and wait, allowing Big Red some time to relax while indulging in a bucket of oats. An hour later he climbed back on the horse, praying he would reach the Fosters soon, and find Nancy.

Chapter 21

James rounded a small hill on his way down the Scioto Trail. The foliage from the spring trees had not fully extended their growth to the point where it hindered his view, for he could plainly see the river. Suddenly he saw Nancy! She was standing beside the riverbank. In the distance two men were riding toward her. He was at least a quarter of a mile or more away, when he saw the men. As they stopped their horses and climbed down, James had a strange premonition that they were up to no good. They had guns, Kentucky long rifles, hanging from their saddles, and the leather straps fastened around their waists, he guessed, housed knives.

Fear, like he had not experienced in a long time, consumed him. *"Oh, God, I have no way of protecting her. What do I do?"* James said, half-praying and half-pleading for help against a seemingly hopeless situation. He did not have a weapon; he was defenseless! How could he shield himself and at the same time rescue his beloved Nancy?

Suddenly "The Voice" shot through his troubled mind— *James, put on the 'armor,' the full armor of God!"*

Love flooded over him. Yes, God loves those men, and he too had been called to love them, for now with every step Big Red took, James recited the scripture he knew so well, scripture he had read again only a day or so ago;

> Put on the whole armor of God that ye may be able
> to stand against the wiles of the devil. For we wrestle

not against flesh and blood, but against principalities, against powers, against the spiritual wickedness in high places. Gird your loins with truth, having on the breastplate of righteousness; your feet shod with the gospel of peace. Take up the shield of salvation and the sword of the Spirit, which is the word of God (Eph. 6:11–17).

As soon as he reached Nancy he jumped off his horse and told her to get on, then watched to be sure she was safely in the saddle. Gently he hit Big Red on his hindquarters, sending them both to the Fosters'. Turning toward the men, he held out his hand in a friendly greeting.

"I'm James Scott. Don't believe I know you. Are you from around here?" James looked up at one of the men; a burly guy with a wicked smile, showing snagged teeth turned brown from chewing too much tobacco. The other fellow was portly, too; he glared at James, his eyes blazing through black hair which covered his face. Their faces brought images to his mind. *Pirates*!

With a deep and threatening voice, the one fellow wanted to know, "Where are you sending this In'gin' women and why?" Making a rather loud snuffing sound, he turned and spit on the ground.

"We was about to have our way with her. You know she's just an In'gin', no good for nothing, but that! The In'gins are gone now, must of left her behind."

James looked into the man's deep-set, penetrating eyes; "Yes, she's just an Indian," he said, "but she happens to be my wife."

It was apparent to James, from the look in their eyes, that they had not expected to hear that; but at the same time, he knew they were serious, very serious, and he was unarmed, so it would be easy for them to take advantage of him.

The larger of the two men put his hands on James' shoulders and pushed him, as if to convey the message, "he was not to be messed with." But then the fellow backed away. After all, James reasoned, Nancy was gone, so he must be thinking that fighting me was not worth the effort.

James displayed an attitude of forgiveness as his whole countenance changed. He realized he was not going up against flesh and blood, but spiritual wickedness in high places. *These men are being used by Satan, and they obviously have no knowledge of God and His plan for man on this earth.*

"Fellows, do you not know God loves you?"

It was obvious that his response took them by surprise! They had expected a fight—certainly not what was now reaching their ears. *Did God love them?*

James wondered if they had ever considered God or knew anything about Him. *God must be so far removed from their thinking that it's impossible for them to believe He would have the remotest interest in anything they ever said or did, let alone what I am about to tell them.*

"Yes, God loved you so much that He actually laid down His life for you."

"Lay down His life for me? No one has ever considered me important enough to even listen to, let alone 'lay down his life' for me!" one of the men said, as he gave out a hardy laugh.

James encouraged them to sit awhile and talk.

Reluctantly they sat down on a fallen log, beside the river, and soon began to tell their sad stories. As they talked, James began to picture in his mind what their lives had been like.

"I remember my old man coming home dead drunk, and he did most of the time. He hit my mom. She was always crying. Ya', I guess she felt his hard knuckles more times than I could ever count, and he hit me too!"

The other fellow had never known his mother. "My mom died the day I was born. My father remarried, but my step-mother never liked me! The fact was, she hated me!"

Both men had lived sad, desperate lives! And now James, realizing they had no conception of what it was like to be loved, sat with the men along the muddy banks of the Scioto in southern Ohio and began to tell them about a God who loved them so much He was willing to die for them. Yes, they were worthy to be loved.

Hours went by as James and the two men talked. He explained God's plan to save them, and then he said, "We have two ways in which we can go; one way is God's way, the other way is the devil's. There are no other choices. But to know the difference, we need to know the Bible. God tells us in the Bible to think of others first before ourselves, to treat them as we would want them to treat us. When we do this, God blesses, and contentment fills our hearts. Each time we are confronted with the need to love someone as we love ourselves, we find the way gets easier and easier. Soon we become "brothers" in Christ. Then wholeness and balance enters our lives, as we grow to maturity. But the choice is ours. God may confront us about the directions we are taking, but He will never, ever force His will upon us, for in making us independent from Himself, He has given us the liberty of either choosing to follow Him or going the other way, the devil's way. It's our decision. It's up to us."

The men wanted to hear more, but the day was slipping away. The sun was low in the sky now, so James suggested another meeting on Sunday, in the afternoon at the same place along the Scioto.

James said farewell, hugging each man, and then turned to walk the trail to the Fosters' home. *There would now be a counterforce of Light in those men's lives,* he thought, *a Light to offset the darkness that once held an upper hand.* He felt blessed, having been the man God used for that purpose. Contentment filled him.

But, it was not long before those feelings would pass, for as James approached the Fosters' cabin, he saw Big Red fastened to the hitching post. *Why hadn't they put him in the barn?* James wondered. It was a concern, for the horse needed rest and certainly food. *Where is Nancy? She must have made it back here, but is she alright?* Suddenly realizing he had not given her a thought from the time she left until now filled him with remorse, and he began to run toward the house.

When James entered the Fosters' cabin, a terrible scene met his eyes. Nancy was there, but she was crying desperately, frantically pulling her hair and screaming. When she saw him, she turned away. She obviously didn't want to see him or be near him.

"Nancy, Nancy, Nancy!" James called her name over and over again as he ran, putting his arms around her. He held her close to him for several seconds, before releasing her a little, but still held on to her. He could not let go of her.

Though Nancy had quit crying, still her sobs came intermittently. James apologized to the Fosters, as he walked Nancy outside the cabin. They needed to talk.

"Nancy, I love you. Do you understand me? I am so sorry all this had to happen to you today, and last night, too. How foolish of me not to think of you and what you must have gone through. Please Nancy, let's go home now, back to our own cabin where we can be together again." James bent over and kissed her cheek, as he held her once more.

He earnestly wanted to stay a while and talk with the Fosters, for he had much to tell them, but the need to return to his home was paramount. So lifting Nancy, he placed her on Big Red and turned to tell the Fosters, who were now standing outside of the cabin, that he would be back to talk with them soon.

Not a word was uttered as they followed the trail under the full moon. Nancy sat quietly on the back of Big Red. The fear that had consumed her seemed to have vanished. James wondered what she might be thinking as he walked along the path beside her, leading the horse.

The next morning was the start of another day of hard work. Leaving the cabin before the sun came up, James made his way to the field his brother was clearing. He put in a solid day of work, since he had not been there the day before.

All day James thought of nothing else but Nancy, and what he wanted to tell her. Could he say it in a way that she would understand?

Nancy was inside the cabin when James returned, standing in front of the fireplace, stirring something in the bulbous iron kettle that was hanging from the log-pole. He walked over, took her arm, and led her to the table, motioning for her to sit awhile. He wanted to talk.

James was very tired, for he had gone a complete night without sleep, and the following day, although rewarding in many ways, was still harrowing; and now he was exhausted from a long day of toil. But he and Nancy needed this time together, and so he sat down across the table from her. Taking her hands in his, he looked into her eyes.

"Nancy, I love you." He repeated the words again in Shawnee, "Nancy, *Yu-now-mole*, my Little Pine, I love you. I don't want you to go away from me again. Do you understand? You have to stay here, in our cabin. You must never leave here without me. I am a preacher, a messenger of God's, and I must be gone, for I cannot deliver His words if I am to stay here. But, I need to know that you are safe while I am away. Please, please understand what I am saying. If you don't understand me, let me know and I will try to explain it better to you. *Nancy, you must stay here!*" James was now emphatic with his demand.

Nancy looked down at her lap. James reached over and lifted her chin so he could see her eyes again. A tiny tear appeared at the corner of one of them. He stretched across the table and kissed it. Oh, how he loved her.

Now bowing his head, but still holding her hands, he started to pray.

Chapter 22

A feeling of despair consumed Nancy as she watched James walk out the door every day. She saw him leave the cabin every morning to go help his brother in the fields, knowing he would not return until late evening. Sunday was the longest day of all, for he left before the sun came up and did not return until it was well below the horizon.

"I'm so sorry, Nancy, that I have to be gone so much, but the few families that I feel led to be with live several miles from here. It takes time to get to their homes, to minister to them; and then by the time I return, the day is gone," James said.

Nancy tried not to complain because she was left by herself so much, but there were times when she felt very discouraged. Yet, when she saw James walk back through the door, a feeling of hope consumed her, a hope that he would not be leaving again, at least not for a while.

The responsibilities of the day weighed heavy on her shoulders, as she thought in English *"I have much to do."* But then. considering her situation through the eyes of a Shawnee, she realized she had to split the kindling for the fire; carry gallons of water from the river; drive the skunks, raccoons, and other animals away from the cabin; and even kill poisonous snakes, which found their way from a nearby stream. She planted a garden in the summer, harvested it in the fall, then stored the food for the winter; putting the turnips and rutabagas, along with the Irish potatoes under a hill of sand, sand she carried from the riverbed. She even killed game for their meals, and then stood over a hot fire to cook it. She scraped ice off the cabin walls in the winter, and chiseled ice from the river, melting it on the fire for drinking and cooking.

She remembered James saying, "Nancy, I will dig a well for you soon, so you won't have to carry all that water from the river; however, it will take time, much time, time that I just don't have right now."

Late one summer day, while they were making one of their rare visits to his brother's home, Aileen asked Nancy, "Why don't you come over and learn how to spin? You can use the 'big wheel.'" Nancy, delighted with the invitation, realized it would give her an opportunity to get to know the women better, but also she could use the wool she had gathered from the sheep James had received from William Barton.

"William Barton gave me the lambs," she remember James saying, "even though I told him that I wanted no compensation for my preaching, but he insisted."

"I'm not giving you the sheep as compensation, but only as a friend to a friend, a true and faithful friend, which you have been to me and to my family, so I sincerely want to do this, and I pray you will accept them."

"So, what could I do? I had to take them," James said, grateful to have the lambs.

It wasn't long before the lambs were fully grown, producing offspring, and much-needed wool—wool which she now held, as it became her job to shear the sheep, gathering the wool, and at the same time she learned, with her nimble fingers, how to card it. But now, under Aileen's able instructions, she could spin it as well. So the weeks ahead found them, along with Ruth, and Ruth's daughters-in-law, in the cabin of a local neighbor using a loom to produce the much needed material for clothing, the fabric of which was soon turned into a shirt for James.

"It's too bad we have to make our own clothes. Wouldn't it be nice if we could buy them already made, as I've heard there are people living in large towns who can do that. Hopefully, one day it will be possible, but for now there's no other way; we have to make our own, or else do without. I'm just thankful we have plenty of wool. Of course we also have flax, but to break the bark takes a lot of strength, so we'll just have to wait until the men have the time to do that for us," Aileen said.

"Too bad cotton doesn't grow here; and leather is difficult to preserve, for in time it can rot," Ruth said.

"Nancy, we'll show you how to comb the fibers and spin them, and we can teach you how to make it into cloth, but then you will have to learn how to sew it—that is, if you want to make a dress for yourself," Aileen said.

It took time, lots of time, but it kept her busy, and the occasions she spent with the other ladies not only helped her get through the lonely days, months, and years, but gave her an opportunity to get to know the ladies better, and to understand the culture in which she now found herself.

James knew he would be busy throughout the spring, summer, and fall helping his brother doing numerous tasks, and that the opportunity to help Nancy would be rare. The days of toil were long and hard, but always in the back of his mind were the people he now found under his guidance; although there were only a few, it seemed like their needs were many. It became his heartfelt mission to teach them, and it took many hours of his time—for first, through much prayer and study time, reading his Bible, he needed to search for and understand the answers. .

The men he had rescued along the riverbank looked forward to his teaching, and in time came to an understanding that they could not, nor did they want to, live their lives any longer without Christ and the biblical truths they were learning. Eventually James baptized them in the small creek near his cabin; and it was not long, James was pleased to learn, before their lives began to change. Both were able to secure jobs—one working for a local blacksmith, the other for a farmer, doing numerous tasks for him. In time, each would buy a place of his own. It pleased James to watch their transformation, and he was always there to encourage—teaching, preaching, and praying with them, and for them, as they walked their Christian walk.

It was a cold December in 1826. The days were much shorter now, and it wasn't unusual to see a spattering of snow in the air. Since the sun was disappearing earlier from the sky, the evenings found James at home; and many times, because of the cold weather, he was there during the days as well. It was a blessing to Nancy, as she had become aware that she was with child, and the days of nausea, which now seemed to be taking control, found her in bed more often than not.

James, elated to hear the news, put his arms around Nancy and held for a moment. His sweet Little Pine was having his baby.

"When, Nancy? When will you have it?"

"By late summer."

It delighted him heart and soul, knowing that soon he would have a son or daughter of his own.

"As soon as the spring thaw comes, I promise you I will dig a well, for I cannot let you carry any more water from the river. It's just too much for you to do while you are with child."

And so throughout the winter, he did much of the work, chopped the logs for the fire and carried buckets of ice from the river. James was now the one who shot the wild turkeys, rabbits, and other animals, and prepared them for the fire.

Although there was much to do in and around the cabin, creating endless hours of toil, still the evenings found him with his Bible in his hands, sitting before the fire, reading.

Early the following fall Nancy presented James with a little girl, and he was more than pleased to hold his new daughter in his arms. They would call her Sophia, after his aunt—his grandmother's sister who married the English man, the master of the *Nancy Grace*. James knew his father would have been pleased with the name.

Chapter 23

The fall of 1828 was once again a busy time for James, helping his brother and doing numerous jobs on the farm. But this year they had talked about a trip to Portsmouth, to deliver wheat and corn to the newly built waterwheel, where it could be ground into flour.

"It sounds like a great idea, John, as I've been thinking for some time about the possibility of getting some letters sent," James said. "One to mother, of course, but was also hoping I might send one to Alexander Campbell. Oh, what a treasure it would be to see that man again. Just to be able to sit with him for a while, in one of those cane-bottomed, ladder-back rockers on his front porch and have a long chat. I have so much I would like to tell him; but more than that, there is certainly a lot I would like to know, and I feel he would have the answers."

A week later, as they were approaching Portsmouth, there in the distance was the little inn where James had stayed four years earlier.

"Perhaps the innkeeper might know of a way to send letters. If we have the time, I'll stop there and find out," James said, as he spent the day with his brother lifting wheat and corn and the heavy bags of flour, plus doing numerous other jobs. Soon, though, he was able to leave for a time. So he made his way through the streets of the town to the inn, hoping he would find the innkeeper.

"We have been successful in sending letters by way of the steamers, up the river to Wellsburg," the innkeeper told him, "and from Wellsburg the mail can be taken to the town of Washington, in Pennsylvania. They seem to find little trouble being delivered from there, as the post office in Washington is pretty reliable.

"By the way, James, I have some mail for you, which I received last spring. I hated to throw it away, as I thought you might be in town at some point in time."

The innkeeper handed James a paper along with two letters, wrapped and held together by a piece of twine. James thanked the innkeeper, and then settled himself in one of the comfortable willow rocking chairs on the porch to read them. The first one was from Alexander Campbell, expressing the desire that the second letter be delivered to him as quickly as possible.

> I received this letter, realizing it was for you, so I am sending it to Portsmouth with one of the boatmen in the hopes he can deliver it to the innkeeper there. Perhaps you will be in Portsmouth at some point and can get it. I am also sending a copy of *The Christian Baptist*. Next Spring I will be in Cincinnati. I do not know if you can come to this meeting, but it would be good to see you again, if you can.
>
> Your good friend and faithful servant of our Lord,
>
> Alexander Campbell

The second letter James was thrilled to have. It was from his mother. She received the letter he had written to her about Mary, and was so distraught hearing of Mary's death. However,

James was surprised to learn his mother had married Captain Jennings and sold the boarding house. Although she seemed to be expressing a feeling of gratitude for having done so, still she was sad because she missed him and longed to see him again.

As James put down the letters, he closed his eyes for a brief moment. There was still a little tug at his heart when he read the part about Mary, but he was more than thrilled to learn his mother had married again and would not be alone. Captain Jennings was a good man, and she certainly could not have done any better. Yes, he missed her too, but saw no way they could ever be together again.

~

The paper was the April issue of *The Christian Baptist*, which Alexander had written, and in it was some pretty exciting news. It seems Alexander was meeting with a man, a Robert Owen, in a public debate in Cincinati the following spring.

Robert Owen, who is Robert Owen? James reflected, as he read further.

It seems Robert Owen, a wealthy manufacturer from New Lanark, England, was an atheist and had established a socialistic colony at a place in the Indiana wilderness called New Harmony, where he had barred all forms of religion, claiming that only the "goddess of reason" was there enthroned. Now, he was challenging any clergyman to a public debate of his system of moral and religious philosophy, and Alexander Campbell had accepted the challenge. It would take place on April 13, 1829, in Cincinati at the Old Stone Church of the Methodists on East Fifth Street. It was the largest church building in the city. James would have loved to have gone, but spring was the worst time of the year for him to be away, as there was so much work needing his attention. How would he ever find the time? Perhaps, if he prayed, God would work a miracle. *It would take a miracle, for there is no other way,* James thought, as he puzzled over who this Robert Owen was and why he had initiated a debate.

James, deep in thought, did not realize he was not alone, for when he looked up from the paper he was reading, he saw him—a rather distinguished gentleman who was also sitting in one of the willow rockers on the porch.

After their initial greeting and commenting on the beautiful day they were having, James, with a puzzled looked on his face, said, "Have you ever heard of a man called Robert Owen?" I just received this paper called *The Christian Baptist*, from a friend of mine. In it he talks about a Robert Owen. I don't know the gentleman, and wondered if you had ever heard of him." Suddenly realizing he had not introduced himself, James reached out his hand in a friendly gesture, and said, "By the way, I'm James Scott."

"Nice to meet you Mr. Scott, I'm Walter Scott. Don't suppose we're related, as there are a lot of people by that name, but to answer your question, 'Have I ever heard of the man called Robert Owen?' yes, I do know who you are referring to, and I'm well acquainted with Alexander Campbell, the man who wrote that article. I almost always get a copy of his paper *The Christian Baptist.*"

Not expecting that kind of an answer, James gave the man his complete attention, wondering now who Walter Scott was as well.

Later, he learned Walter Scott was himself an evangelist. Coming to America from Dumfrieshire, Scotland, he too had been brought up in the Presbyterian Church. He met Alexander Campbell in the winter of 1821, and after much discussion, realized their religious views were similar; that meeting formalized the beginning of a cooperative movement in restoring the "Simple Gospel" to the churches in America.

"Robert Owen is an interesting man," Walter Scott said. "It seems, at some period in his life he lost all belief, if ever he had any, in religion and is now a preponderant of socialism, and has come up with a creed—and that is, that man's character is not made by him but for him. It's my understanding that he believes man's nature is formed by circumstances over which he has little to no control; therefore, he feels man should not be held accountable for what he does. According to Robert Owen, the greatest secret to the right formation of man's character is to place him, from his earliest years, in an environment where he can gain the proper influences—physically, morally, and socially."

"So he has no belief in God?"

"No, he has no belief in God! He believes religion is the result of someone's imagination, and that it makes man out to be a weak, imbecilic animal, and a miserable hypocrite!"

"In this article, it talks about a place called New Harmony, and it is in Indiana. I've not heard of the place," James said.

"It's my understanding that New Harmony lies along the Wabash River in southern Indiana. Robert Owen designed the community to house around a thousand to twelve hundred people. The families live in one large building, which forms a square. It seems they have their own private apartments, but there is a public kitchen and mess-room, and they have the care of their children until they are about three. After that, according to Robert Owen, the community will bring them up. His desire is to create an environment of equality where everyone is treated the same, and receives the same wage, or receives it in accordance to his needs.

"I've heard it turned out to be a complete failure, which is no surprise to me. People are not 'emotionless beings,' and certainly Robert Owen is not an emotionless being, nor is he God. Hopefully he'll soon find that out, if he hasn't already. Certainly there are many people who are worthy of the highest aims, but there are also many who are drifters, fortune-hunters, bad-tempered wrongheaded fanatics! In other words, James, people have a mind of their own. They're freethinking, and many times uncompromising, wrongheaded extremists—or in other words, normal but un-churched human beings . . . lacking knowledge of biblical truths."

"It makes one wonder how such a belief system could have found its way in America in the first place," James said, puzzling over what he had just heard.

"Well, I guess if it could happen, it would happen here in America. After all, this is a new country, with unlimited opportunities. And since it's a republic, designed by Christian men, it has, without a doubt, permitted man the freedom to decide his own destiny, and/or to do what he believes is right. Here, in this country, as we proclaim 'the love of God,' that love forces no man to submit to any other, telling him what he can do or cannot do, or for that matter what he can think—no, not even a preacher. Although Christianity has opened that door of freedom, the concept of God's words being absolute, to a man like Robert Owen, must seem repressive. Here in this country, outside the church, a man can think as he desires, but beware, for outside of those biblical teachings is where we are most vulnerable. For though the freedom which Christianity has enabled opens the door to any and all ideas, if we turn our backs on God, it won't be long before we find freedom's door closing.

"You know, James, I talked with a man when I was in the Carolinas, who was French and a Christian. He told me he had been forced to leave France because men of the faith, who were in a minority, were being persecuted there. The vast majority of *French* men, he said, were 'rationalists,' contemptuous of Christianity. Why? Well, their thinking was based on what he called the 'Age of Enlightenment,' which was, 'that the human mind needed to be liberated from its rigid state of ignorance.' Do you know anything about deism, James?"

"No, don't believe I do."

"Well, the deists don't believe in the God of the Scriptures. They reject the divinity of Christ, His sacrifice on the cross to atone for our sins, and His resurrection. The concept of man's fallen and sinful nature is repulsive to them, and most certainly 'absurd.' 'Reason' is their god! Anything not based on logic or rational thought they reject. But, it's interesting to note, that the French Revolution proved just how wrong their thinking was. Built on their belief system, that revolution became a bloodbath by comparison to our American Revolution. Our revolution, James, was fought by men with a deep, abiding faith in Christ, and resulted in more freedom than man has ever known! On the other hand, the French Revolution caused chaos and repression. Instead of gaining freedom, they got that dictator, Napoleon.

"This nation's government was created by men who had a profound belief in the Bible. They realized—but not only did they realize, they believed—that they needed to allow themselves to, first and foremost, be governed by God; for if they did not, they would most certainly end up like the French, being ruled by a dictator!

"President James Madison made a profound statement when he told us that America's future is not based upon the power of government but upon each and everyone one of us to govern ourselves according God's laws, those simple Ten Commandments. We, of course, must first believe in the Divine Designer of those laws, for if we fail to govern ourselves according to His just laws, we will most certainly be ruled by man's unjust ones."

"Interesting, Mr. Scott, and it certainly has been a pleasure meeting you. Will you be going to the debate next spring?"

"Well, I would like to, but much depends on it."

As the conversation continued, James learned that Walter Scott had a tremendous influence in carrying the faith into a large region in northeastern Ohio called the Western Reserve. "Many New Englanders are now coming west," Walter Scott said, "and have settled in that section of the country. I found myself roaming the hills and the valleys there, preaching and teaching salvation to those people, encouraging them to come to a deep and abiding faith in our Lord."

James learned that Walter Scott had been an inspiration to scores of men who themselves became preachers of the "simple gospel," and now, Walter was excited to learn that James had a desire to do the same.

"I want to encourage you, James, to learn the Scriptures, and to let that be your guide. I am a diligent Bible student myself, and my suggestion is to memorize a chapter a day. That will put you in possession of the entire New Testament in less than a year. The gospel is threefold; facts, commands, and promises. Facts are to be believed, commands are to be obeyed, and the promises to be enjoyed. We teach faith, repentance, baptism, remission of sins, and the gift of the Holy Spirit. And I am happy to say I have baptized more than a thousand people this year alone. It has been a true blessing and a joy to see the people of this great country coming to know the Lord."

⚍

That evening, after a full day of hard work, James sat before the campfire with his brother along the Scioto Trail, devouring the salt pork and beans Aileen had sent with them. John wanted to talk, but James struggled to give his brother his full attention, as he could not keep from thinking about Walter Scott and what he had said. Other thoughts filled his mind as well, but Robert Owen came to the forefront, for he certainly was a mystery. It was sad to think of all those people whose lives would be influenced by such a man. Did any of them believe in God, he wondered? He knew people who said they believed, but he questioned just how much knowledge they really had of the Christian faith. "Deist?" Yes, many were deist. They had a belief in a supreme being, but that being, whoever it was, was as remote from their lives as he could be, and unfortunately, their faith stopped there.

Yes, people may say they believe in God, but sadly have no concept of what God is like. It must seem to them that God is either dwelling in a shadow, or in such a glorious, penetrating light that He cannot be approached. These men have to feel hopeless, as they struggle to make this world what they think it ought to be. Yet the apostle John tells us in the Bible that Jesus is the embodiment of God. When we know Jesus, we see God displayed in full light; the shadow is gone, the darkness dissipates, and those days of guessing are over.

⚍

James did have an opportunity to be with Alexander Campbell again, but it wasn't until the following fall of 1830. Alexander had been touring churches in southern Ohio, and had gone to almost every town, many times visiting homes where large families had gathered. Realizing it would be extremely difficult to find the time, if only for a moment, to talk with Alexander, James hurried, as he left one of those meetings, to walk with him to his gig.

"I can't put into words how excited I am to see you again," James said, as he cautiously approached Alexander, fearful Alexander would not remember him.

Upon hearing James' voice Alexander turned suddenly, looked straight into his eyes, and then embraced him. "James, I have thought and prayed for you often, my brother. How are you? And how's the ministry going?"

James, hiding a sigh of relief, hesitantly began to give Alexander a brief rundown of the times where he felt the hand of God move in his life—the encounter he had with the men along the riverbank, the heartfelt prayer for Abigail Barton, and a few other times when he had shared the faith—but he hesitated to tell him of the difficulties he struggled with, and how he longed to preach the Word but the opportunities were slow-coming.

"James, I want to encourage you to keep the faith; and remember, preach the gospel only."

"Yes, I have tried to do exactly that; however, the field is sparse. I have had the privilege of baptizing a few, mostly my own family, but then God has of yet to open very many doors. I've thought of you often, and longed for an opportunity to be with you, to just have a good talk. Regrettably I was unable to attend the debate in Cincinnati, and I've often wondered how that went, and if there were many in attendance."

"The church was filled to capacity, with at least a thousand. There were so many people that we had to turn some away. They even stood in the aisles, and I have to say, Robert Owen is a likeable man, good and caring in many ways. It's just sad that he, in his youth, was turned away from believing in Christ because of conflicting views in the church."

"I could see that happening. How the cares and hardships of life could be daunting to someone like Mr. Owen, for I certainly had my share of times like that."

"Man's concerns, James, are not the common, everyday problems of this life, nor are they the day-to-day worries we all deal with. No, those problems are as nothing compared to: Who are we? Where did we come from? And where are we going? Are we merely mortal beings put on this earth like weeds to wither and die forever, simply animals struggling to survive life on a planet to nowhere, bumping into each other as we go? Or is there life beyond this one?

"It was never the intent of the Christian faith to rule the world with a set of laws, laws to control people. No, Christianity is a belief that governs by love. Our belief in Christ creates a love in our hearts that only God can put there. That love, James, teaches us how to live with each other in freedom. No man-made institution can exist without a dependence on something or someone, for it's impossible to go through this world without being responsible. But the question is: Will we be responsible to man or to God, a God who loves us unconditionally, who gave His very life for us? Furthermore, it's impossible to expel the idea of God from the human race, for the sun, the moon, and the stars, everything around us testifies to His existence! We may as well hold back the ocean, keep the sun from shining and the winds from blowing, than to banish the thought of God from our lives. It just does not work!" Alexander said, as he stepped into his carriage. "James, it certainly is good to see you again, and I'm sorry we can't spend more time together, but I am late now getting to my next meeting, so I must say farewell. I will be praying for you, my brother."

As James watched Alexander pull his carriage away, he thought, *What a treasure to be with this great, reverent man of God, and how privileged I am to have known him. Certainly, our meeting had to be by God's design.*

Chapter 24

James was up by four o'clock. He dressed quietly. Nancy was still sleeping with the baby, little Mariah, nestled in her arms. The other children were sleeping as well, all six, snuggled in beds across the cabin floor. As he looked at them, his mind was suddenly filled with memories of another night, many years before, when he encountered children of another family sleeping across a cabin floor. *That was the first time anyone ever called me Preacher!* James reminisced, *That had to be, at least, fifteen or sixteen years ago.* Well, he need not dwell on those days, weeks, and years now. This day was enough, and it would be a busy one. So with the list in his pocket and the old oil lamp in his hand, he quietly closed the cabin door behind himself and made his way to the barn. Even though there was much to get done before the day was over, he would be back in an hour or two, for no matter how busy he might be, morning worship with the family always took priority. He cringed for a moment, contemplating how he might tell them that soon they would be leaving Ohio and their home for good.

The McDowell and Mercer families were going to Indiana, to the Adams New Purchase to settle, and wanted their brother and elder in Christ to go as well. They could not, nor did they want to, leave their preacher and good friend behind, but they had also heard that spreading the gospel in the Indiana wilderness was very much needed, so they pleaded with James to go with them.

"We need you, James, and we feel certain our Lord needs you there as well! Indiana is a land for the taking, or so we've heard. All a person has to do is stake out a claim and live there, work the land, and it becomes his; however, our plan is to buy some. If you will go with us, we'll help you build a cabin on some of our land and help you clear it as well. You can preach on the Lord's Day, and any other day," they told him, also making certain he understood that he was not to worry; they would provide the way.

To James it was an answered prayer—for there, in a new territory, he hoped he would have a chance to preach the way he felt his Lord had called him to. Many times he had regretted the bad feelings which seemed to have formed between him and the Foster family, simply because he refused to be a part of the Methodist Episcopal Church, and that had caused him much distress. His good friend Jacob Barnes had moved on, since a circuit rider of that church could not be in the same area for more than two years, but there were other men who followed—men James did not have the good fortune to know as he had known Jacob Barnes—and those men were protesting, saying his work was infringing upon theirs. The Fosters were his biggest concern, for they certainly had been wonderful friends throughout the years, yet they too were discouraging him, since all of the Foster families had stayed loyal to the Methodist Church.

Perhaps, then, it was time for him to move on, to leave Jackson County and his Ohio home. Proclaiming the "simple" gospel in a new area—a wilderness where it, nor he, had ever been before—was kind of exciting. But telling the family . . . well, that would be another concern.

It wasn't so much his own family he worried about, but what would John and Ruth think? Over the years there had been such a close bond between them all. He had had the good fortune, with lots of prayer, of convincing them of their need to be baptized by immersion, and had ministered to them numerous times. What a blessing to him that was, and he knew in his heart that it would hurt knowing he was leaving, but he had to be faithful now to the One who called him to preach. For he felt, with some certainty, that he was being asked by one higher than man to carry the gospel of Christ into the Indiana wilderness. Perhaps then, this was where God was leading him.

Nancy sat braiding her hair when James entered the cabin two hours later. He silently slipped up behind her, bent down, and kissed her neck.

"I have something to tell you my 'Little Pine,'" he said, "and I think you should be the first to know. We're leaving!"

"Where we go?" Nancy wanted to know. "Will the children go, too?"

"No, I mean, we are all leaving Ohio for good, and will be traveling with William McDowell, Joseph Mercer, and their families into the Indiana territory."

Nancy sat with her mouth opened. She could not believe it! "We leave for good?" She asked, as it kind of excited her. *I might see other Indians, Shawnees, I not see for a long time,* she thought.

"Yes," James said, "and there is much to be done before we can go, so I will need for you to get the children ready. Pack up anything you feel we must take, but keep in mind we cannot take everything. Most of the furniture will have to stay. I can make new beds, tables, and anything else we might need when we reach our new home. It will take time, but I promise you I will get it done. And, Nancy, Big Red is getting older now, almost twenty years old, and he will have to pull the wagon, so we can't carry much," James told her, hoping she would understand.

That morning, as his family was gathered around the big oak table, James told them the news. Not knowing how the children would react, he was actually surprised to see they were excited about going, but when they told him they wanted to take all of their dolls, wooden guns, and other toys, he said, "I'm sorry, but you will only be able to take one, one favorite toy apiece, as there will not be room in the wagon for any more than that. Also, you may have to walk most of the way, and it is a very long, long, long way!" James told them, with a smile on his face.

⌒

He knew that John and Ruth would be saddened when they heard the news that he and the family were leaving. He had told them many times, and with regret, about the bad feelings that had formed, and it seemed, would not go away, between him and many of the men who were already saturating the area with the gospel. "Not that they have been unkind to me. But they certainly have not encouraged me. Of course most of them are circuit riders from the Methodist Episcopal Church," James said.

"We've realized, James, for some time now that you have a real heart for proclaiming the gospel," Ruth said, "so we do understand and wish you the very best."

"Yes, my brother, go then, and God bless and keep you. We'll miss you, but pray you will be able to do, in a new frontier, what you feel God has called you to do," John said, as Ruth stood by his side, agreeing.

⌒

It was late summer in 1841. The day finally came when James and the other men had the canvas-covered wagons loaded and ready for their journey west. They had decided to take four wagons, although only three families were going. The extra wagon would carry food and water, along with the other supplies they might need or find necessary on their trip. Corn meal, bacon, eggs, and dried meat were on the list, along with potatoes, beans, and rice. There were other food items as well, and a large barrel of water, just in case it became unavailable. The cows Ol' Nellie and Jen had been fastened to the back of James' wagon, with cows trailing some of the other wagons as well. They hoped the cows would supply them with enough milk as they traveled west. With the help of the dogs, the men would take turns herding the sheep and the goats. Observing the whole scene, James could tell the animals had accepted and were content with their state of affairs.

The men told him that they had made certain the hammers, axes, and saws were with them, along with nails and numerous other items they would need when they reached their destination.

"The grinding stone is especially important. It's heavy, but we certainly can't do without it," Joseph Mercer said.

"Yes, and there's only enough room in the wagons for some of the children to ride, but not all," William McDowell said. "They'll have to take turns walking." They encouraged the older children to do most of the walking, as there were fifteen of them, all of various ages. James, counting the children, realized he had the most, as William McDowell had two, Joseph Mercer six, and his seven made up the rest.

Two of the older boys took turns driving the extra wagon; however, they had not gone far when James became aware they were in trouble. One of the wagon wheels came loose, and then a hitch from another wagon started squeaking. It took time for them to fix the wagons, but it was not long before they were back on the road again.

The children—laughing, playing word games, and other endeavors of the mind—did fine in the morning, but as afternoon approached James could see they were growing weary. Many of them, needing rest, began crying, causing others to break down into sobs as well. Some were under the age of five, along with the babies not yet a year old. What a trying time it was, and James could tell it was wreaking havoc, not only on his nerves, but most of the others as well, especially the women. It was putting patience in short supply, stirring the soul, causing him to finally say; "Let's stop and rest awhile. I feel we need some nourishment, and perhaps a prayer, or two."

They had traveled not more than five miles the first day, taking the road along the river. Three days later the sun, still sending down some rays of light, was fading fast as they approached the town of Chillicothe. In the distance James could hear singing coming from some unknown source. The words to the song were muffled and difficult to understand, but the closer they got, the clearer the words became; however, they still were being sung with a strange inflection—a kind of twang.

> Steal away, steal away!
> Steal away to Jesus!
> Steal away, steal away home!
> I ain't got long to stay here!
> My Lord calls me!
> He calls me by the thunder!

The trumpet sounds in my soul!
I ain't got long to stay here!
My Lord, he calls me!
He calls me by the lightnin'!
The trumpet sounds it inna my soul!
I ain't got long to stay here!

As they drew closer, James saw a Negro in the distance, sitting beside the roadway with his legs crossed. He was swaying back and forth with every other word he sang, his head turned up as though contemplating heaven. James could see he had closed his eyes, but when he heard the wagons coming, he opened them, jumped to his feet, and ran into the woods, leaving James wondering what it was all about.

James learned, from some men they met along the road, that Chillicothe was the state's first capitol. "It was named after the Shawnee Indians who once lived there, but now it's becoming a well-known station for the Underground Railroad, as slaves are escaping from the South. Since the Northern states abolished slavery after the Revolutionary War, it's now become a symbol of freedom for them. Following what they called the North Star, many have crossed the Ohio River and traveled up the Scioto to Chillicothe on their way north to Canada," one of the men said.

James knew Ohio was a free state, as slavery had been abolished by its state's constitution in 1802 when it was first formed. He also had learned that across the river in Kentucky, the Negro was not free. However, he did not realize that the state of Ohio was aggressively seeking to bar any of the Negros attempting to escape from Kentucky. "But as time has passed, many of the freed Negroes who now live in Ohio are helping slaves from Kentucky and other states to escape. Soon, there'll be hundreds coming through Chillicothe by way of an Underground Railroad, which isn't a railroad nor is it underground," the fellow said.

Surely they must know that with the help of the state's white abolitionists, many will be escaping, going north into Canada, and to freedom, James thought.

Later James was to learn that the spiritual song the Negro was singing had been used in Virginia ten years prior by a slave, who, along with the help of other slaves, had incited a revolt against a group of slaveowners who ended up losing their lives. The Negro had used the song as a signal to others. Although the revolt eventually failed—and the slave convicted, sentenced to death, and hanged—the song was still being used.

The sun lay low on the horizon when they decided to stop the wagons and spend the night along the river. James and the other men, hoping to find someone who could tell them the best way to the Adams New Purchase, met an old gentleman resting by the roadside who seemed to know the way. He told them, "If you continue your journey you'll go right through Chillicothe and eventually to Columbus, our new state capitol. From there you can take the Cumberland Road, or National Pike, as it's now being called. They say it's finished through Ohio and Indiana, but I've heard it stops in Illinois. Take the National Pike to Harmar's Trail in Springfield. The trail goes northwest through the state to Decatur, Indiana, a new town not far from the Ohio border in the Adams New Purchase. I was there last year, and that's how I went. I didn't have a problem, so you'll probably be alright too."

They would soon learn that Harmar's Trail went on to Fort Wayne, but ended there. It was an old road that followed an Indian path, and had been used by George Rogers Clark and other prominent men before, during, and after the Revolution.

That night, James found to be a restless one, for he could not put the image of the Negro from his mind. Where had he come from and how did he get here? What kind of life had the fellow lived? What would he, James Scott, have done if had he lived his life as a slave? He had heard rumors of the brutal treatment at the hands of the slaveowners that many Negros had to endure. They were severely beaten, he had been told, and even taken from their families, to be sold like cattle to other slaveowners.

I couldn't have done it either! No, not in a country that prides itself on being free. James was now deep in thought. *Yet, didn't the Bible say, "Slaves, be obedient to those who are your masters"?* That was surprising to him, for he certainly could not have lived under a cruel slave master. *However, God does want us to live at peace, no matter what our circumstance, and look what Christ, our example, had to bear! He was taken, like a slave, and underwent excruciating cruelty, yet never said a word, but endured it!* James, thinking about the slave, suddenly remembered a scripture, "But I say unto you, love your enemies, bless them that curse you, do good to them that hate you, and pray for them which despitefully use you, and persecute you! Resist not evil: but whosoever shall smite thee on thy right cheek, turn to him the other also" (Luke 6:27–29) . . . *and so many times in the Bible, we are asked to love our enemies!*

Well, that Negro certainly knew who Jesus was, for the words of his song conveyed that, but just how much does the poor fellow know or really understand? James wondered, as he closed his eyes.

He had almost drifted off into a deep sleep when he heard singing again, but this time it was a different song, and more than one person was singing:

Swing low sweet chariot
Comin' for to carry me home,
Swing low sweet chariot
Comin' for to carry me home.

I looked over Jordan, an' what did I see,
Comin' for to carry me home,
A band of angels comin' after me,
Comin' for to carry me home.

If you get-a dere befo' I do,
Comin' for to carry me home,
Tell all my friends I'm comin' too
Comin' for to carry me home.

Where was it coming from? James wondered, as a feeling of anxiousness flooded over him. He had to find out, so slipping on his trousers and some old moccasins, he quietly left the campsite in pursuit of the unknown.

Soon, James was looking at a group of anxious people, concealed in a wooded area along the riverbank. There were five of them; two had light skin, but the others looked African, or Negroid.

"Don't be alarmed; I didn't come here to hurt you or to divulge your hiding place, only to tell you, I am with you, I understand, and I want to help if I can." He could see fear written across their faces.

However, they assured him that they were free people, helping a passenger escape to a station further north. "We sing, hoping to sidetrack the local authorities, as we're waiting for news that the fellow had made it," they said, thanking James for his concern, wanting him to know they appreciated his willingness to help.

With some feeling of relief James turned away, and was walking back toward the wagons when suddenly he heard a horse in the distance. Now his curiosity got the best of him, he had to know: What was the rider going to tell them? He hoped it would be good news!

The night was a long one, but the next morning, as the wagons were preparing to leave, James took William and Joseph aside.

"I have something to tell you, and I pray you'll understand. Last night I heard singing again, and got up out of bed, wondering where it was coming from. I followed the sound to a thicket of trees along the riverbank and found there some people who had helped a man, a slave from the south, escape; however, the fellow never made it. He is right now hiding in a cistern in the yard of a Baptist church in town, a station on the Underground Railroad. I told them, if it met with your approval, we would pick him up on our way through town, and take him to Columbus to the home of a man, or conductor as they called him, who has helped other runaways. But I have to tell you: This is dangerous, because it is against Ohio and US law. Anyone caught hiding or helping a slave could be put in jail, or fined a thousand dollars. But my conscience just couldn't let me turn my back on the plight of this poor fellow. However, it's up to you two. Do you want to help him?" James asked, half-pleading, half-praying.

"Just how dangerous, James, will it be?" Joseph asked.

"I have no way of knowing, but I do know that my Lord has called us to help each other in times like these. Turning my back on the plight of this fellow is like turning my back on God. I simply cannot do it." After a few more questions, Joseph and William reluctantly said yes, they would do it.

An hour later, the wagons were ready to leave the campsite. They made their way into Chillicothe. It was mid-morning, and there was lots of activity in the town. Praying he would not be noticed, James drove his wagon to a log building, apparently newly built, with a sign over the door that read "First Baptist Church." He would stop there, take out one of the blankets, and place it around and over the head of the runaway, or passenger as they were called, until he was safely in the wagon. There he could hide in a large trunk they had cleaned out for that purpose. James prayed he would fit.

Relieved that all had gone as planned, James, traveling the dusty road, soon caught up with the other wagons, as they had gone on ahead. It was a fifty-mile trip to Columbus, and he knew Big Red, along with several of the other horses and all the cows, sheep, and goats were good for only ten or twelve of those miles—that is, if they stopped along the way to let them rest. Traveling at that rate, it would take several days before they reached the town.

The first night, while they were gathered around a campfire along a deserted road leading to Columbus, James and his passenger had time to talk. Paulo was hungry, for days passed since he had eaten. James, anxious to hear his story, sat patiently, watching him devour the salt pork and beans they gave him. Paulo had almost finished eating when he began to tell his story, and there was much to tell. Most of it was sad. With tears in his eyes he said, "I had to leave my wife and baby, cause if I'd stayed, they were goin' sale me, which meant I would have been taken away from them anyway."

As James listened to his sad story, he wondered, again, how a loving God could permit such things to happen. Yet he too had suffered, and at the hands of others. He could relate, as he remembered the pirates, the crashing of the pirates' sloop, his father's death, and the months, years spent on the island. But he also knew his Heavenly Father was in control, that He did care, and that He would send those who were willing to go to help people like Paulo. James felt the need to convey such thoughts, to encourage his new friend, to let him know God would see him through this, and for him to keep the faith.

"Paulo, we are never as close to God than when we're in a valley. For it seems as though it is at those times of greatest need that God becomes most real to us. He becomes our companion, our support, as we travel a weary road." Compassion spread across James' face as he conveyed those thoughts to his new friend. Remembering the days he spent on that deserted island now came flooding back into his mind, as James looked at Paulo. Yes, he knew about valleys, and what it means to need God.

Several days later, with the sun fading fast in the western sky, they approached Columbus. Paulo had been told that the conductor's house stood at the edge of town along the National Pike. Waiting until the sun was completely gone from the sky—and now under a full moon, which was sending down enough light to illuminate their way—they stopped at what they hoped was the right house, or station. Paulo had been told a lighted lantern would be hanging outside to identify it; however, this house didn't have a lantern. The yard was dark, and the house looked deserted. Could it then be further on, down the road?

How strange, for the group felt certain that this house was the correct one. Now James wondered what they might do next as they stood there, bewildered. He suggested they agree in prayer that if they were to find the correct place, God would lead them.

"All we can do is to continue going the same direction. Perhaps it is further down the road," James told the group, as he lowered his head and began to pray.

A half mile later, they saw it; flickering among the leaves of a tree hung a lantern. Paulo told them he had been given a secret code to help identify him to the agents along the way; however, the man hesitated, uncertain whether to accept him or not, as he could see that many of the people with him were white.

"I'm sorry, but you have to understand, there's usually only one, or two at the most, and they're always Negroes."

James began to explain their situation, and after a while the man, still uncertain, finally accepted Paulo and the secret code.

With relief, James and the others, saying their farewells, dispatched their cargo under the conductor's care and continued along the pike, looking for a place to camp for the night.

Grateful that all went well, James bowed his head and began to pray, "Lord, I want to thank you for not only letting us help Paulo, but for your guidance, directing us to the right place. Now, as we pray, we ask that you be with him, helping him find his way to his final destination. And be with his loved ones he left behind; and may they, if it be thy will, all be reunited someday. We ask this in our Lord's name, Amen."

Chapter 25

"The Adams New Purchase is five thousand, eight hundred miles of unorganized land in north-central Indiana," John Runyon said, as he looked at his fellow travelers.

They met John Runyon on Harmar's Trail, near a clearing where two houses stood. James saw him first, after passing a wooden sign with the word "Sidney" chiseled on it. He and the others had traveled but a few miles that day, having crossed the Miami River the day before after riding through a huge barn-like bridge on the National Road.

With the Sidney sign behind them, they had gone but a few feet when James saw John's three wagons in the distance. Pulling back quickly on the reins, he yelled, "Whoa, Big Red," for he suddenly realized the wagons, not moving, were blocking the way.

Leaning over the side of his wagon, James greeted a tall man with a puzzled look on his face standing by the roadside. John Runyon apologized for blocking their way, introduced himself, and then asked James and the other men if they could help him with one of his wagons, as a wheel had come loose.

"Well, we certainly know what that's like. We've had the same thing happen to us several times," Joseph Mercer said. "We'll be glad to lend you a hand."

Several hours later found James, John Runyon, and the other men sitting around a campfire exhausted, talking. John

Runyon captured their attention, for as he talked, James and the other men, seeing his enthusiasm, leaned forward to hear more.

"I heard the government bought the Adams New Purchase from the Miami and Potawatomi Indians not too long ago. They signed a treaty in St. Mary's, Ohio, not far from where I lived. They say it's a vast forest, and the land is unchartered. I also heard that any man, no matter how poor he is, can become a landowner there. All he needs to do is to mark out his territory in the fertile soil of the vast forest, or on the rich river bottomland, and occupy it. He can go where he wants and take whatever he can find, as long as it doesn't infringe on the rights of others or the Indians who still lived there.

"It's my understanding, the original aim of the government was to survey the land and sell it to real estate companies, but people, they call them squatters, want to buy the land directly from the government. So they passed the 'Preemption Act' to protect those people and guarantee them the right to claim the land before it's surveyed. After a person lives on it for at least fourteen months, he can then buy up to one hundred and sixty acres for as small a price as one dollar and twenty-five cents per acre. However, he has to legitimize his claim by living on the land and then working to improve it.

It was difficult for James and the other men to take it all in, but they certainly found what John was telling them exciting.

"Yes, and I hear the rivers and creeks are teeming with the finest of fish," he continued. "And they say every sort of animal can be seen in the forest. Hogs are as wild as deer, and there are plenty of them in those woods. They run like a deer, too, and can scale a fence like a dog, or so I've heard. Turkeys and rabbits, raccoons and bears are there as well. It's a land of plenty, and with a little hard work our barns can soon to be filled with a rich harvest."

After more conversation James said, "Well, it looks like we all are going in the same direction, to the Adams New Purchase. And, I must say, the closer I get the more enthusiasm I have, and now it seems, we're probably only a few weeks away,"

"Yes, I think you may right, and I heard that the government, if they haven't already done so, will be dividing the purchase into counties. Adams County, named after President John Quincy Adams, is the closest. My aim is to purchase land there, if it's still available," John Runyon told them. Obviously he knew a lot about the area, as he couldn't quit talking, and now it seemed he wanted them all to know about it as well.

James soon learned that John Runyon was only a few years older than he, and that John and his wife Mary had seven children. Four were under the age of nine, but three of them were much older. His son Benjamin was married and had a young child of his own, but his son Daniel, who was twenty-five, had not yet found a mate. Joseph, the youngest of the three, was seventeen. John told them that he was originally from Virginia and had grown up there, but came to Ohio in 1833 to farm land in Champaign County.

"After a few years, we became dissatisfied with our Ohio farm and longed to try our fortunes farther west. So we packed up our belongings, loaded them on those wagons, and left our farm to never look back.

"We started out with one horse and four yoke of oxen, accompanied by our son Benjamin, but soon realized we would need more than that, as there were household goods we didn't want to leave behind." John told them. "As it turned out, we were obliged to leave a good amount behind, even though we took those three wagons."

After more conversation, the group decided to travel together. James and the other men were thankful that John Runyon made that decision, as he had a good amount of knowledge about the place where they were going, and it seemed they all were headed in the same direction.

It was mid-September when the wagons approached St. Mary's, Ohio, where the United States Government had signed the treaty with the Miami Indians that John Runyon had talked about. "They paid them a perpetual annuity of fifteen thousand dollars for that tract of land," John said.

Hopefully, a portion of that land would soon be home for James and the other weary travelers. They had heard that Decatur was the only town in that section of the Purchase, having been established there five years prior, in 1836. And that soon it would become the capitol of the newly formed Adams County. They found out that information would be available there about the land, but it would take at least another week or more for them to reach the town.

The days were growing slightly shorter, with a cool breeze being felt most mornings. It had been raining off and on for several days; and when it wasn't raining, the days were nonetheless dreary, with a constant threat of a shower hanging over their heads. They stopped the wagons when it did rain, which allowed the horses and ox team time to rest, but which also forced their families to crowd together under the oiled canvas covers to keep dry. When it wasn't raining, they had to encounter the mud-filled road, which slowed the wagons, putting a stress on the animals.

Two days later the sun came up, bringing with it a promise of a beautiful day. Now with their spirits riding high, the group took off again, hoping they would make several miles that day, sensing they were getting closer to the Indiana border.

It was mid-afternoon. The caravan of wagons was moving along the road at a steady pace when suddenly, out of nowhere, a man came riding toward them. He was waving his hands, as though he wanted the wagons to stop. Joseph Mercer, whom the group had elected to be the wagon master for the day, saw the man first, and slowed his horses down until they had all but stopped. He could tell the fellow was upset, for he had a frightened look on his face

"Ho!" the man shouted, as he pulled back on the reins of his horse. "Howdy! Did ya' know there's a swamp ahead? A huge swamp—ya' can't get over it! There are bottomless mud holes everywhere!" He was looking back, pointing toward the direction from which he came. "The rain's flooded the area, and made it worse, ja!" the fellow told him, speaking English through a German accent.

James, whose wagon was behind Joseph's, looked at the man in shock as he stopped his horse. He could tell the man was terribly distressed.

Joseph Mercer climbed down from his wagon and motioned for James and the others to join him. They needed to hear what this man was saying.

"Howdy," the fellow greeted them, "my name's Otto, Otto Muller. My family and I were headed for Decatur in the Purchase. We thought that was the way to go, but everywhere there's water! Our wagon got stuck! The wheels are knee-deep in mud! I left my family there to go get help! My advice to ya', ya' better not go that way, ja!" He was again pointing toward the northwest.

The group, having gathered around the fellow as he talked, stood, looking at him with amazement and wonder written across their faces. How could this be?

"There's no other way to go but to follow this road," James said.

Yet the fellow looked sincere, so surely what he was telling them was true. His clothes were covered in mud, and he was riding a horse without a saddle. The horse was muddy, too, with mud reaching up its legs to its underbelly.

"How far is it?" James asked.

"Not far, maybe a mile or two."

After more conversation, James, Joseph Mercer, and the other men decided to go with the fellow back to his wagon. They wanted to see for themselves what he was talking about. They unhitched John Runyon's oxen and took them as well, in the hopes the animals could pull the fellow's wagon out of the mud.

As the group approached the area, James could see black water spreading everywhere, and the blackened waters seemed to have no end. The swamp was dark, as it was covered by giant trees so dense they hid the sunlight. Never having encountered anything like it, he stood there, as if bewitched, taking in the sight.

James was to learn later that the pioneers called it The Great Black Swamp, deriving its name from the leaves of the trees and other plant material which fell into the now waist-high water, decomposing and turning it black. It covered hundreds of miles, reaching far into Northwestern Ohio, with a section of it penetrating Indiana. It was a treacherous swamp, a quagmire filled with every danger known to man. Clouds of mosquitoes and other biting insects could be seen in the hot summer months, and well into the fall, along with snakes, water moccasins, water rats, and prowling gangs of wolves and wild cats. It was a fore-boding place, made worse now by the recent rainfall.

Because the band of mosquitoes which now encircled them were indiscriminatingly biting each and every one, James and the men quickly hitched John's four yoke of oxen to Otto Muller's wagon and pulled it free. Soon they were on their way back to the caravan, along with Otto Muller and his family, who were suffering from the tragic event, especially Otto's youngest son, who had received numerous mosquito bites.

That evening, as James and the others were gathered around the campfire confused, disappointed, and most certainly discouraged, they discussed the day's events, desperately trying to find a solution to where they went wrong,

Slowly, as if giving them time to talk, James began to speak. He told them about Noah, about the forty days and nights of rain which God sent upon the earth, and how the water rose and increased until it covered the highest mountains.

"Everything perished," James told them. "The rain came down and flooded the earth for a hundred and fifty days. But the Bible says Noah and his family were saved, because Noah had found favor in the eyes of the Lord. He was a righteous man. God told the people in those days that they would save themselves through their righteousness, keeping the laws that He had given them, but only Noah believed Him. The rest of the earth was corrupt, full of violence, as people were committing every sort of evil act. It would seem God had no choice but to destroy the whole earth, and he did so by a giant flood. Perhaps that black, foreboding swamp is evidence of that flood. A reminder, left behind for anyone who might gaze upon it. As we remember Noah, his family, and the few animals, birds, and other creatures of whom God found, in His mercy, worthy to be saved, let us humble ourselves now before our Heavenly Father and pray. Let's ask His blessings again upon our venture, to guide us, believing He will take us safely where we need to go. Though there seems to be no hope now, nowhere to turn, let us trust in God's guiding hand!" James bowed his head and started to pray, knowing for certain God's hands would be upon them, for he had experienced those hands numerous times during the many tragic events that had filled his own life.

The rest of the men, their wives, and many of the children now bowed their heads as well, as James started to pray. When he had almost finished the prayer, he opened his eyes to look at the group. Every person, except for Otto Muller, had his head bowed. Otto sat with his head up and eyes wide open, as if in disbelief. As James ended his prayer, he wondered if Otto knew his Lord and Savior. He pondered that question for several days, praying God would open the door of opportunity, when he might witness the love of Christ to him.

Meanwhile, James knew they had no other choice but to turn the wagons and take them back to St Mary's, Ohio. However, it was no easy task, for the roadway was very narrow. Trees would have to come down, and their stumps removed, in order for the wagons to make the turn. It would take days to do the job, but he could see no other way.

A vast forest of trees surrounded them. There was every kind of tree within sight—sugar maple, honey locust, buckeye, cottonwood, hickory, mulberry, oak, sycamore, and many, many more covering the ridges, hills, and the area near the road. Soon the slashing rhythm of their axes could be heard for miles, as they began cutting through one tree at a time, felling those that most hindered their way. The trees were huge, with many three, six, even ten feet in diameter, and fifty to eighty feet up to the first limb.

Cutting the trees was not their biggest concern; for after the trees came down they had to be chopped into sections in order to move them from the area. The tree stumps which had been left in the ground were huge, and they too had to be removed.

It took days to complete the job, and evenings found James and the others exhausted, sitting before the campfire bewildered, trying to understand how they could have been so deceived as to have gone the wrong way. James had felt certain they were on the right road, because there was no other road. *How, then, could we have gone wrong?* He was pleased, though, for the men had expressed their thanks to him, and were certainly glad he was there to encourage them, praying and teaching them the glorious truths of the Bible; for James had told them, "If we will allow God to take the lead, I feel certain we'll find a way to continue our journey west toward the town of Decatur."

"It would seem that God blesses those who are faithful," James reassured them. "If we will but believe and remain faithful, God will bless us, and the road to Decatur will be there."

However, very early the next morning, just as he had awaked, James faith was shaken a bit, when he found that Nancy was gone. He could not find her anywhere. She was not in the wagon or near the campsite where the children were sleeping. *She must have gotten up before dawn; I didn't hear her. I wonder, where could she be?*

"Have any of you seen your mother?" He said to the children who were just beginning to wake up.

"Father, I saw Mother leave early this morning just as the sun was coming up. She was walking down the road, back toward the swamp," Sophia said, as she leaned across the other children to get his attention.

James, realizing he had to find her and that it might take some time, said to James Jr., "Go tell the men I've gone to find your mother, and that, hopefully, I will be back soon. Tell them not to turn the wagons until I get here."

Walking down the road toward the swamp, he had gone more than a mile and still had not seen her. *Why,* he wondered, *would she leave the campsite? This is a dangerous place; she knows that.*

He had not gone much further when he decided to turn around and go back, praying that wherever she was, the Lord would be with her and that she would return soon—and hopefully, give a sensible reason for why she left.

As he walked back down the road, he had not gone far when he saw her. She was sitting on one of the fallen logs hidden among the trees and the underbrush. He could see that her head was down, as if she was praying.

"Are you alright, Nancy?" James said, as he came closer, for he could tell she had been crying.

She looked up, surprised to see him, and then said, "Father and my brothers and the other men could be in that swamp. You know they, along with the rest of the Shawnees, went north to fight with Tecumseh; but after Tecumseh was killed, I heard they may have gone into that swamp to get away from the white men, and now are probably dead."

"How do you know that, Nancy?"

"Anna told me."

"I wonder how Anna knew," James said as he put his arm around her shoulders, and then, for some reason, as if perhaps encountering God, he looked up into the sky, and just as he did, he saw a beautiful bird fly by. It looked like an eagle. Suddenly he was reminded of a scripture he knew so well and had clung to many times in his own daunting life. The scripture now filled his mind, and so he said to her:

"Nancy, we must pray that wherever your father is, if he is still alive that he will come to the knowledge that God is real and will protect him. There were many men in the Bible God used who went through great suffering, but they believed God, for He told them, 'they that wait upon the Lord shall renew their strength; they shall mount up with wings as eagles; they shall run, and not be weary; and they shall walk, and not faint' (Isa. 40:31).

"And now we must cling to that as well, for we all have gone through some troubling times in this sin filled world, but God has always been there for us, as long as we are there for Him. We must have faith, Nancy, and never give up believing," James said, putting his arm around her again as they walked back to the wagons.

With James' reassuring worlds, it wasn't long before Nancy was back at the campsite helping the other women, preparing the morning meal and getting the children ready for the day ahead, for she knew it would be a long one.

James knew, or perhaps hoped, that Nancy might pray, as she worked, for her father and the others, wherever they were. For if they were still alive, he prayed that God would place people in their lives who could tell them about Jesus.

By mid-afternoon the men had the wagons turned, and they were on the road again. They would make their way back to St. Mary's, Ohio, for they saw no other way to go. Perhaps in St. Mary's they might gain some knowledge of where they had gone wrong and find the correct way. There was a growing concern, for fall was now upon them. Soon the weather would be turning colder, as the autumn season advanced.

The first day the group traveled only a few miles, having spent the morning turning the wagons. The next day would surely be a better one, James hoped, as they pulled the wagons down the dirt-filled road. Traveling along at a steady pace, they had gone about five miles, and seemed to be making great time, when suddenly he heard some of the older boys, who were walking beside the wagons, yelling.

"Here! It's here!" James Scott Jr., his brother Hiram, and Joseph Runyon's excited voices could be heard now above the roar of the wagons.

"Father, stop the animals!" Joseph Runyon started running toward the first wagon. "It's here, the road, it's here!"

John pulled back quickly on the oxen's ropes and turned to see his son pointing back toward the west.

A large tree had fallen, stretching its trunk and massive leaf-covered boughs across a path. Unless one was looking specifically for the road, it would have been easy to pass by it, and that is exactly what happened. The wind from the stormy weather had blown the tree down, and now it lay with all its foliage covering the fork in the road—a fork which turned northwest, toward the town of Decatur.

Thankful now to God, and more than thankful for James' faith and prayers, the men bowed their heads, as James took a brief moment to praise his Heavenly Father. Soon they had removed the tree and the wagons were back on Harmer's Trail, carrying James and the other weary but happy travelers to, what they hoped would be, their final destination.

Chapter 26

"**H**ypocrites! They're just plain hypocrites! Ja! You Christians, or people who call themselves 'Christians,' say one thing, but then do another. They ain't a'actin' like they ought, or what they say you should act like, or be. Hypocrites! Ja! They're just plain hypocrites!"

Seriously desiring to explain some biblical truths to Otto, James stood looking at his new friend with compassion in his eyes.

"Well, Otto, you're probably right. Yes, we Christians can at times say one thing, and then turn around and do just the opposite, but let me tell you why that happens. You see, it was never God's desire for us to behave like hypocrites. For in the beginning when God made the first man Adam and then from Adam made Eve, his wife, He placed them in a garden, a beautiful place, a place where there was complete harmony. There certainly wasn't any discord or hypocrisy in that garden. It was a paradise. But, God, in his loving mercy, gave Adam and Eve a free will. He made them independent from Himself, but warned them to be careful, and not use their independence to disobey Him, for you see there was forbidden fruit in that garden. In making that fruit, God gave Adam and Eve the ability to choose. But of course, in order to give Adam and Eve the ability to choose, God made evil a grave possibility. For you see Satan, who is the great deceiver, was also in that garden. Was it by God's design? Yes, I do believe God permitted it, for nothing happens without His will. Eventually, Eve believed Satan, and convinced Adam to believe him as well. Disobeying God, they took a bite of that forbidden fruit, knowing not that, from that day forward, their eyes would be opened and they would be outside that garden struggling with evil in this world in which we now live.

"As you know, it's a world full of hardships, struggles, and strife—a place where the evil one lives, constantly tempting us to turn our eyes and hearts away from God. So now, since we have a free will, which God permitted, and a nature that is prone to sin, we will stumble and many times fall or, as you say, speak one way but then do the opposite. The great question is: Is there anyone who can save us?"

James stop for a moment to look fully in Otto's eyes, wondering if he understood what he was saying. Otto, staring at him intensely, seemed to be taking in every word, and so James continued.

"The Bible tells us that from the beginning man has constantly broken God's laws, but God told him that if he would make a sacrifice to show he was truly sorry, he would be forgiven. That sacrifice was to take the life of an animal or a bird, for by killing that animal, man could make amends for the evil, the wrong he had done. It was a difficult sacrifice, and so man continued to struggle, and has to this very day. But now we have a new life in Christ Jesus, for you see, God, in His loving mercy, came to earth and sacrificed Himself for us. He died a horrible death on a cross. It was the final sacrifice. For the Bible tells us Jesus did not come into the world to condemn the world. He came to save it. Now, through faith in Christ, our sins have been washed by his blood, and are made whiter than snow.

"Will we still struggle? Oh, yes, we will continue to struggle, and so I guess you could call us hypocrites, but now we have a Savior, Jesus Christ. For, He tells us in His Word, 'If we will confess our sins, He is faithful and just to forgive us our sins and cleanse us from all unrighteousness.'

"Hypocrites! Ja! We are that, for sure," Otto said, taking in every word James was speaking.

"However, we do need each other, for the Bible tells us to not forsake ourselves from gathering together. We need the prayers of the saints; our brothers and sisters in Christ. We need to support each other, and learn from the rulebook, the Bible, how to live our lives while we are on this earth. Will we fail at times to do it? Yes, we most certainly will, but as we pray for each other, and study the Good Book, we will learn to do it less and less. And always remember, Otto, God will bless those who are faithful to Him, and we certainly don't want to miss out on those blessings."

The next morning, James, standing under an old oak tree with its leaves turning yellow, put his arm around Otto's shoulders, softly asking him if he would like to accept this wonderful gift, which a loving God has for him.

With sadness in his eyes, Otto shook his head. "Yes . . . ja."

Otto had lost his little son. Jessie was only two years old when the family had been attacked by the mosquitoes from the Great Black Swamp. All the rest had survived, though they too had received their share of bites. But Jessie was just too young. His little body could not stand up under the massive attack. The difficult part was having to bury him and leave his little body behind. Oh, how sad it was for Otto and his family, but James was there to comfort and to pray with them.

"Jessie isn't there, in that ground," James told them, "for the Bible tells us that God takes the little children up to heaven to be with Him. Yes, his body is there, but Jessie's spirit is in the lap of Jesus, for Jesus said, 'Let the little children come to me, and do not hinder them, for the kingdom of heaven belongs to such as these.' Blessed are those little ones, for they are now with God, and so it is with Jessie."

It was still difficult for Otto and his family to let little Jessie go, but with James' reassuring words the task became easier.

"God asked us to have faith like these little ones," James reassured them, "and then we, too, will one day, be in heaven with Jessie."

It was the Lord's Day, and it was warm for an October morning, when James, standing in the waters of a little stream that flowed into a larger river, baptized Otto and his family. Now before the eyes of many witnesses, and under the observance of the greatest witness of all—the One who does not want any to perish but for all to come to repentance—Otto professed his faith in his Savior and Lord Jesus Christ.

As James walked back to his wagon, a feeling of satisfaction covered him. As he prayed he also wondered, *Was that, God, by Your design?* It seems the circumstances, however bad they were, had led to this man to salvation; and God had used him, James, at just the right time, for that to happen.

The beautiful October leaves now covered the ground in a thick blanket, as the caravan of wagons approached Decatur, Indiana. It was November 5, 1841, and it was cold, but the bitter air did not damper James' spirit, or the spirits of the other weary travelers, for they all had, at last, reached their final destination, and the excitement they were feeling was like lightning exploding in the air! Now to find the "land office," for there, they had been told, they could examine the plat book to determine where land was available, and register their names.

The road James and the others had taken through the country certainly did not lack in interest, for the occasions were numerous when they could still see the gloom of the Great Black Swamp. In future years James would remember the swamp, and its murkiness, as he conveyed his experiences to others. "That swamp seemed to stretch endlessly towards the northeast on the other side of a river the pioneers called the Saint Mary's."

The Saint Mary's flowed west toward Decatur, but now lay north of the town. As they drove the wagons through Decatur, there were numerous homes lining the dirt road. Fascinated now to see a little bit of civilization, James studied each home. Some were log-built, several framed, and at least two constructed of brick. He along with the other men had learned, from a gentleman they met on the way, that Samuel Johnson, a prominent man in the Purchase, had given the land for what would eventually become the newly formed county seat.

"Mr. Johnson did so with an understanding there would be enough acreage for at least three or four churches, a public square, and an acre or two for a graveyard. But land has also been set aside for a seminary, a school to teach young men in the faith," the gentleman told them.

James found it fascinating . . . a school to educate students in the Christian faith! Then he remembered what his friend and teacher Alexander Campbell had said, "Christianity is a belief governed by love, and that love teaches us how to live at peace with one another. It defeats Satan and sets the captive free!"

Well, if they don't hear it in church, they certainly need to hear it from somewhere. And, is it possible that God might just find a way for me to preach in one of those church buildings? It was wishful thinking, but then it didn't hurt to dream.

Parking the wagons beside the road at the edge of town, James and the other men made their way back to the center of Decatur, where a logged house stood. "That building was built to one day hold court in, but for now serves other purposes," the gentleman had told them. "You should be able to find out there where the land is that's for sale."

Entering the logged house, they learned that the entry book was arranged by townships. Looking at the book and a map showing where land was available, James and the other men agreed it would be best to locate in the southwestern section of the county, for it seems it was at that location, in a township called Hartford, where there was more land that had not been taken.

"Once you're registered and make a payment, the acreage will be yours," the secretary told them. "We put the transactions in this book—" He looked down at the book he was holding. "—in chronological order, according to the date, receipt number, and your name. After that you can apply for a payment schedule—that is, if you don't have the full amount now—to pay for it."

Listening to the secretary talk, a twinge of concern went through James, since he knew he was now at the mercy of his brothers in Christ, for he had no money. Leaving his Ohio home in complete faith, with only ninety-five cents in his pocket, he confided to his family, "We must remember, God is a part of this, and I believe He will provide, for has He not said in His Word; 'Every good gift that you receive comes from My hands. I am your provider. I will meet your needs'? I've tested those hands many times, and found it to be true, but now it seems we'll be testing the mighty hand of God again. Will He be found faithful? I believe He will, but only time will tell."

Both William McDowell and Joseph Mercer had encouraged James to make the journey. They assured him he would always have a home with them on one of their farms, or perhaps on both, that is, if they bought land adjoining. But now there was John Runyon as well.

"James, I love you like a brother," John Runyon told him, as he placed his hands on James' shoulders and looked him straight into the face. "Over these weeks, months that I have come to know you, I've treasured your faith and the biblical knowledge you possess more than I can say. I'm purchasing a large plot of land for myself and my two sons, but I want to buy acreage for you as well, and would consider it a privilege, my brother, if you would oblige me by accepting my offer."

"John, what can I say? 'Thank you' just doesn't seem enough to express how grateful I am. And certainly, my feelings for you have grown as well. In many ways you remind me of my own brother John, whom I love and miss now more than I can say."

Both Joseph Mercer and William McDowell had become aware of the camaraderie that had developed between the two men, and although their plans had also been for James to build a cabin near them, on their land, they conceded when they heard that James might accept John Runyon's offer.

"Well, whichever farm I end up on, fellows, I want you to know, it will only be a loan. Eventually I'll be paying for it, as I don't believe in receiving money, no matter how it's given, for the biblical services I rendered. I minister only because I've felt the call, and for my love of Christ, and those in which the Lord has placed under my teaching. But for now, it's all in the hands of our Heavenly Father, as we still have a long way to go before we can call the land home."

Chapter 27

Within the week, the wagons pulled out of Decatur. James and the men were anxious now to find the land and set up temporary housing until more permanent ones could be built. Winter was coming—in fact, it was just around the corner—and they knew life would become difficult as they faced the frost and icy chill. Finding food and staying healthy would be a challenge. The threat of wild animals, which roamed the forest in the wintry cold searching for a good meal, was another major concern for James as well as the other men, as they sought to protect their families and the domestic animals they brought with them.

James' new friend Otto had stayed behind, since he and his family were going north to find his brother. "I'm thankful, James, to have known you, and the faith you possess. I hope we'll meet again someday. Ja!'" Otto said, then watched James pull his wagon out of Decatur. As James waved goodbye, he prayed the Lord would use his German friend in a mighty way.

The group took the road back south they had traveled, knowing a trail would have to be cut through the forest in order to reach the land. How far that road needed to go, they would have to wait and see.

"Thar's a river in the area, so water's available, but how far away that river goes, I ain't certain," an old pioneer they met along the way, told them. "And thar's' Indians thar too, only a short distance from where you'll be a goin'. They ain't no longer a threat, though. I reckon one of these days they'll be a'leavin', but for now, after signing a treaty to cooperate with the United States government, they seem to be a'livin' at peace with their white neighbors."

It took James and the men weeks to clear enough trees for the wagons to pass. Five miles of underbrush and forest had to be cut before they could reach their final destination. It was now the dead of winter, and the cold, harsh air seemed to be penetrating their bodies to the core, even as they worked.

The women, having been pushed beyond their limits, were sorry now they had made the journey, for not only were their living conditions deplorable, but many of the children were sick.

"James, will you pray for us?" they pleaded. "For the children have a fever, and some have even broken out with measles."

Ague, which caused a terrible shaking, had also taking its toll, so James prayed, trying now to encourage the women, certain that his prayers would make a difference. He was more than thankful that Nancy and Anna Mercer were with them, as both ladies were native-born, and had remedies only the Indians knew about, remedies which did seem to help.

"We'll make it through the winter," James told them, "I feel certain of that! God would not have brought us this far, had He not planned to see us through to the end."

Expressing his thoughts one evening, as they sat around the campfire, he told them about Moses in the Old Testament. "Moses and the Hebrew people were being pursued by Pharaoh and were trapped between his mighty army and the Red Sea! They didn't know what to do, as they felt certain their lives were over, but God told Moses, and I repeat those words for us to hear, now, 'Fear not, stand firm and see the salvation of the Lord, which he will work for you today . . . the Lord will fight for you, you have only to be silent' . . . and believe! So you see, we must believe that there are better days ahead," James told them. "We will finish the race, but we must have faith in our Lord and Savior that it will happen!"

The women and children were forced to stay in their wagons as James and the other men worked, but now that they had at last reached their destination, more permanent shelters were needed in order to see them through the harsh winter. Helping where he could, James watched with admiration as some of the men, the ones who seemed to know what they were doing, fashioned a temporary lean-to, a sort of shed, to their wagons. He saw them using two forked posts or trees that supported a cross timber; and sloping down from there, they laid a large log, against which was placed poles or saplings, and it was all finished off by brush and mud put against the sides.

The next day, following their instructions, James and some of the men who had also been watching were able to do the same to their wagons. Eventually all of them had shelters, using pelts from the wild animals they caught to line the interior and to make mattresses and blankets to sleep on. The lean-tos faced south in a semicircle, away from the cold north wind, and large log fires were kept burning day and night in order to keep them warm.

"I hope the fires will keep those animals from coming too close to the campsite," Nancy told James, as they listened one night to their mournful cries.

The wintry nights were long, and even though the fires were kept burning, many times the sound of wolves could still be heard in the forest. The animals usually maintained their distance, but late one night a band of wolves approached the wagons. James and the other men could hear their gruesome cries, which seemed to penetrate the woods with answering howls coming from all directions. The forest seemed to echo with their gruesome cries. The dogs, barking, sprang into action, as if preparing for a fight, but soon came running back, as though panic-stricken, and crawled under the protective cover of the lean-tos, yelping.

"Grab your rifles! I can hear the sharp snap of wolves' teethes! They must be very close to camp," John Runyon said, as he turned to face the darkness. James could see the wolves' eyes now, reflecting light from the campfires. "They seem to be creeping closer and closer, seemingly unafraid," John Runyon said.

John Runyon and two of the other men fired several times into the night air. James wondered if they had killed any, but the howling continued. If the wolves were gone, he couldn't tell, so he and the other men, with rifles in their hands, took turns standing watch throughout the long, cold, wintry night and did so well into the early morning hours.

The next day, several carcasses of wolves were found lying near the wagons. The dogs, with their tails wagging, sniffed the dead bodies as if they were the heroes, the ones who caused their demise. Even so, James was more than thankful the wolves were now gone.

It was late winter, soon to be spring, when James and the men began to build their first log house. Having flipped a coin to see whose cabin would go up first, William McDowell was pleased to learn he won the first toss. Benjamin Runyon's cabin would be next, but not before a field had been cleared. It was early April when they stood looking at their finished product.

"I'm just amazed at what you all have accomplished. It's certainly taken a lot of hard work, and to think there's still more, many more to be built," James said.

"Well," Joseph Mercer noted, as he looked at the completed logged house, "yes, it did take some work, and it isn't perfect either, but then it's our first. I guess with more practice we'll produce better ones."

"I'm satisfied, and just happy to have a place to call home, some kind of house now for my wife and kids," William said. "Someday, when I have the time, I'll improve it."

Looking down the jagged road they were clearing, where the dense forest still stood, James tried to visualize where the next cabin would go up for Benjamin.

"It won't get done for a while, James. No, probably not until late summer, not until we've cleared a field and planted it," John Runyon said.

The Indiana soil was rich, for generations of trees had grown, died, and fallen. Their decaying process had produced rich humus, which now seemed to penetrate the ground for several feet.

"Those trees," John Runyon said, "will have to come down as well, not only to make the roadway, and at the cabin sites, but the biggest job is clearing that," he pointed toward an area where the field would lay.

It was a laborious job. James and the men sweated and strained, cutting trees for weeks, months, many of which were eighteen to twenty inches in diameter. But, even after the trees came down, they had to clear them, and then cut the thick underbrush as well. They girdled the larger ones, preventing them from producing leaves, with the hopes they would eventually die. Many were burned, causing smoke to permeate the air for miles around. However, the fires could not rid the soil of their roots; only time would do that. The smaller trees were trimmed, sectioned, and rolled into piles.

"Perhaps in a year or two we can split some of those timbers to make rail fencing. But the job will have to be done while the wood is in full sap, since the sections will season quicker, resisting the weather and certainly those woodworms," John Runyon said.

Meanwhile the cows, horses, and other animals ran loose for lack of an enclosure, and it wasn't long before James saw the animals playing havoc with the corn crop they had planted in the unfenced field.

James and the men, realizing that the planted and harvested corn would run out long before summer was over, encouraged William McDowell and Joseph Mercer, who had volunteered, to make trips back to Ohio to buy grain and meal. They did so for the next two years, hoping it would get them through until the fields were producing again.

"The Lord is great!" James said, as he stood in the middle of the field he and John Runyon had just cleared.

"Yes, it's been nearly five years now since we claimed this land and put our first cabin up. We still have more to build, but thanks be to God, most of them are up now, and we've cleared enough land to, at least, supply our families with food, and certainly the animals we brought with us," John Runyon said, as they looked out across the open field. "It has been a rough five years, and we'll be talking about it for a long time. But, even though it's been a huge job clearing those trees, I'm still thankful for that forest. Why, if it hadn't been for those woods, and the deer, hogs, and wild turkeys we found there, we wouldn't have had enough food to get us through these five years."

"Yes, John, it has been a blessing, and I've certainly enjoyed those birds too," James said, as he saw a sparrow fly down from a tree to capture a worm from the ground they had just plowed. "And my, all those fish we caught in that stream that runs from that river they call the Wabash. What a blessing that's been, too."

"I so appreciate you, James," John Runyon said, as he put his arm around James' shoulders. "I'm glad, my brother, to have you as my neighbor."

James' friendship with John had grown steadily through the years, and when he finally made the decision to locate on John Runyon's land, he did so with Joseph Mercer and William McDowell only mildly objecting.

"I knew, fellows, you would be disappointed since, before we left Ohio, we'd planned on my being on your land," James told them. "But, I am thankful we're all neighbors.

"Yes, and I guess it's time to let bygones be bygones," William said, "It was never my intention to let it spoil our friendship."

"You're so right, Will; we certainly don't have time to fret over that!" Joseph Mercer said.

If James didn't see his neighbors during the week along the dusty road they had cleared, or in the fields working, he certainly saw them on the Lord's Day, for not a Sunday went by but that he was, at one time or another, in each and every one of their homes. It wasn't unusual for him to spend the entire day there, preaching and teaching, not only in their cabins but in a few others as well. Many times he left before the sun came up, with his family knowing full well he would not return home again until it was well below the horizon. But those days never got started until he had first ministered to them, his own family.

Many days found James alone with the Lord, either studying his Bible, meditating as he read the Word of God, or talking to his Heavenly Father. It wasn't unusual to find him asking God to increase his flock. *"Thank You, Lord, for I am gaining more and more confidence that You have truly called me to minister, not only to these families, but I am trusting, there will be more to come."*

⸺

On rare occasions the isolated pioneers would gather together, devouring the delicious food the women had prepared, reminiscing, recalling the days when they first traveled to the Indiana wilderness. During those times they always insisted James have a word or two to say about the biblical truths they all had grown to love, and of course they never left without a prayer. Often their singing could be heard across and down the old dirt road they had cut through the forest, with young Joseph Runyon's banjo ringing in the background.

'Mid pleasures and palaces though we may roam,

Be it ever so humble there's no place like home!

A charm from the skies seems to hallow us there,

Which seek through the world, is ne'er met with elsewhere:

Home! Home! Sweet, Sweet, Home!

There's no place like Home!

There's no place like Home!

⸺

The years had now passed, and James' reputation was unfaltering. People came to know him as a man whose mind was always open to receive the truth as written in the Bible, and one who embraced all Christians as brothers. He was a dedicated trailblazer for Christ, praying for the coming of one church as he carried the gospel far and wide.

However, he was not the only one who had so dedicated himself; there were other men as well, men who likewise, saw the need and had devoted themselves to saturate America for Christ. So it seemed inevitable, that from time to time, these men, who resided on the frontier of the Indiana wilderness, would collide.

One Lord's Day morning, as James was off preaching in a logged house called The Limberlost Church, such was the occurrence. He had been invited to preach there by a group of people who heard of his dedication to the faith. "We need you, James, for we've heard you have a desire to set aside differences and unite people in the name of Christ, and we respect that and think it's a praiseworthy accomplishment!" the men told him, as they stood at his cabin door. "The church building is located in Redkey, about twenty miles from here. It was built by a Presbyterian minister, but we've been told that many denominations have found a place to worship there over the few years since it was established, so we see no reason why you couldn't preach there as well."

"I'll pray about it," James told them, "and let you know soon."

As James closed the cabin door, he felt a surge of excitement, and wondered how those men knew about him. *Perhaps it is the hand of God, for I have to admit, it would be a privilege to actually preach in a church building, and it's certainly an opportunity to expand the ministry.*

James did accept their offer, but on that particular Lord's Day morning there seemed to be stringent opposition to this man known as a "Campbellite Preacher of the Simple Gospel," or in other words, a follower of Alexander Campbell, the great "Reformer," as the Presbytery knew him.

James' sermons were long. It was not unusual for him to preach two or more hours, even though it seemed he had not preached nearly that long. This Lord's Day morning was no exception. Looking out over the congregation, he was amazed at how many people were there, and it seemed as if they all sat mesmerized by his message. As usual, he veered little from God's holy Word, and was well into his sermon when two strangers entered the small logged house.

"We're sorry to interrupt this meeting, but you, sir," they looked at James, "are not welcomed here, so we have to ask you to please take your people, and move on. Leave these premises!"

James, surprised by their request, discreetly answered them with a Christlike love and concern reflecting in his voice, "I am sorry you feel that way. We will most certainly leave, but before we go, I would like to pray for you, for this building, and the people who brought me here, if that meets with your approval."

"We see no reason why you cannot pray," they said.

James wondered what the two men might be thinking, as he bowed his head. *Perhaps they're thinking, "His prayer won't hurt, but for that matter, it won't help either!" Well Satan, if it is your aim to divide and conquer, I know it's Christ's desire to unite in love,* James thought, as he reached out with a Christlike love in his heart and began his prayer. When he finished, he opened his eyes to see the men standing at the door with a perplexed look on their faces. Soon he, and the other worshipers, walked quietly out of the door.

Within an hour, the group found another building, an old barn which had been built on a neighboring farm. They nailed some boards to the sides to keep out the wind and the rain, which was now coming down intermittently, and insisted James continue his message.

James, not realizing at the time that the old barn would one day become a very prosperous church—one proudly proclaiming him as its founder—continued his message. Getting the Word of God out to the people was more important to him now than a mere skirmish. However, that skirmish, along with the old barn, would forever be etched in his memory—and would cause him, in the days ahead, to many times humorously refer to it and himself as a "barnstormer."

But for the time being, James continued to struggle; however, he was determined never to give up. With true Christian courage he refused to let such circumstances damper his spirit. He knew he could not always be in control, yet he knew God would hold him accountable for how he responded to such circumstances, and the people those situations brought under his influence.

He knew it would take time to work through such episodes, as he continued to struggle, making prayer the top of his priority list. Certainly those incidents could be cause for concern, and injurious at well; yet he knew nothing was wasted in God's providence, for God was able to take those difficulties and bring from them a blessing, as he had experienced that many times in his life. He saw how his Heavenly Father had taken impediments and made from each a stepping stone. *Yes, as long as I keep my mind and heart on Christ, difficulties such as these will never become a barricade, and I will be found faithful! For no man or circumstances that come into my life will ever keep me from propagating God's holy Word!*

Chapter 28

"It's just too bad there is confusion, doctrinal points of differences in our churches!"

"Yes, but we must keep in mind that Satan does his conquering through division! Therefore, I believe, we must do as Jesus commanded, and keep on loving one another, for that is the one emotional need Satan is defenseless to conquer! For did not Christ Himself tell the people, 'Love your enemies, bless them that curse you, do good to them that hate you, and pray for them which despitefully use you, and would persecute you,' and did He not do that very thing as He let His accusers lead Him to the cross, where He bore our burdens, our transgression?"

James was talking with John Chambers, one of the elders and founders of the New Hope Christian Society, which would eventually become the Chambers Christian Church. It was 1854 and John Chambers, along with Ebenezer Thompson, had helped organize the group, which met in a log school house in the southeastern part of Richland Township in Madison County, Indiana.

Several months before, James had received a letter from a Nancy Scott who resided in the same area, and was also a member of that group:

James P. Scott, reverend and elder in Christ,

I write this letter on behalf of the New Hope Christian Society, and anticipate that I may, somehow, persuade you to consider coming to Madison County for a visit.

We have heard of your dedication to the truth of the Word of God, and wondered if you would have an interest in spreading the gospel here in central Indiana, as we are in need of a man of your reputation.

I am writing this letter on behalf of Hiram and Hannah Chambers, John and Mary Chambers, Susan Chambers and myself, Nancy Scott. Unfortunately my husband Sigismund is no longer living, but he too was one of the founders of the Christian society.

Please contact us as soon as possible, as we are anxious to get your reply.

Yours sincerely,

Nancy Scott

Ebenezer Thompson had family who lived in Adams County and attended one of the many churches James had started. Ebenezer's family could never say enough good things about James, so when Ebenezer told them that his church in Madison County was looking for someone of James' reputation, and although they would not want to see him leave the area, still they could not resist recommending that the church contact James.

"He is a great and holy man of God. You would do well if he would agree on coming to Madison County, for I feel certain he could help establish a church there."

The New Hope Christian Society had asked Nancy Scott to write the letter, not knowing if James would comply. However, James was interested, and it wasn't long before he was saddling his horse and making his way to the county.

As he stood talking with John Chambers, he had a strange premonition that this was where God was calling him, for he was awed by the conversation he was now having with this young man.

"We have had growing concern with the way people are responding to the biblical truths they are learning," John told him. "Why, they can't even come to an agreement over the name of their churches. Some want to go by the 'Christian Connection' and some call themselves the 'Church of Christ,' while others claim to be just 'Christian.' It all gets confusing."

"Yes, it is too bad," James said, "and unfortunately there are people who also want to spread their own opinions as fact, when their views many times have nothing whatsoever to do with salvation as written in the Bible. We do have a right to our opinions, but to convince others that what we say or believe is biblical truth is just not right. Opinions on subjects not revealed in Scripture are merely man's personal views, and no person has the right to pass them on as 'truth'! Yet, it is still possible to remain in full Christian fellowship and in the same church, even though our viewpoints may not coincide. We may differ on many things, but if we are united on the essentials, we can still work and worship together as brothers in Christ. We all want liberty on what we believe, on our interpretation of Scripture, but can we not give that same liberty to others, and still remain brothers? We need to reach out in compassion, in love, and understanding, and defeat the devil of mistrust, hatred, and division. Remember what the Bible tells us in 1 Corinthians 13: Though I speak with the tongues of men and of angels, but have not love, I have become sounding brass or a clanging cymbal. And though I have the gift of prophecy, and understand all mysteries and all knowledge, and though I have all faith, so that I could remove mountains, but have not love, I am nothing. And though I bestow all my goods to feed the poor, and though

I give my body to be burned, but have not love, it profits me nothing."

As James conveyed his thoughts to John, he remembered his trusted friend Alexander Campbell: "James, all of us who are followers of the meek and lowly Jesus, all who kneel at the same cross, all who live in the hope of life beyond the grave . . . are brothers! Then who is a Christian? Everyone who believes in his heart that Jesus of Nazareth is the Messiah, the Son of God, repents of his sins, and obeys Him in all things according to his measure of knowledge of His will. I cannot make any one duty the standard of Christian state or character, no, not even immersion. It is the image of Christ the Christian looks for and loves; and this does not consist in being exact in a few things but in general devotion to the whole truth as far as he knows."

"We must," James said, as he talked with John Chambers, "keep that spirit the Bible, especially in the book of Acts, talks about—and pray that our fellow believers, as well as those unbelievers who are our neighbors, would be touched by the truth as expressed in His Word, showing the world that God sent His Son for our salvation. We must never let that spirit die, no matter what sinful man does in his struggle for power, using unscrupulous methods to gain or to maintain control and positions of influence, which can cause confusion and division. Love and love alone is the answer."

~~

James, feeling dumbfounded when he read Nancy Scott's letter, could not imagine how a church, in a county so far away, knew about him. *How could they have known that I've been considering, for some time, the need to establish churches, many churches in Indiana, and that I have so dedicated myself, encouraging all believers to unite under the lordship of my savior, Jesus Christ?* James puzzled, as he stood and looked down Bear Creek, where he had gone many times to pray. *My ability to start the few churches I have has not only taken courage, but much prayer, time, and certainly willingness to do so, yet the prospect of going to "many" lays heavy on my heart.* It seemed as though, on one of those rare, quiet moments, God had put an image in his mind, for he could see the spires and the steeples of many churches spreading across the Indiana skyline.

He had prayed through the years that God would use him. With little knowledge, other than what he learned reading his Bible, he had many times stepped out in faith, trusting God. Leaving his brother and his family behind in Ohio, he took the long journey to Indiana, confident that God had called him, for he left with little money in his pocket. Now he owned a small farm, and had organized a church of believers called the Christian Oral Church, near Bear Creek. It was a short distance from where he lived, having been started within a few years after arriving in the county. The church was now fifteen years old, holding services in various school houses the pioneers had built. He knew it would not be long before they would be worshiping in a framed building of their own, for the elders had been planning that for some time. They had saved, through the fifteen years since its founding, a considerable amount of money for the new church building, having the biblical understanding that they were never to be in debt.

Now though, James was being asked to travel to another county, many miles south, to help start yet another church. He would have to sell his home, the farmland, and move all of his family. *Pulling up roots will be no easy task, as the children are older now, and have friends they won't want to leave behind. It'll be difficult for Nancy, too, as she has complained of not feeling well, and, it seems, has felt that way for some time.* Since there were no doctors close by, it had been a struggle for her. Because she was tired most of the time and seemed to be constantly cold, most days found her in bed, too weak to get up.

He would have to pray about it, as he had done many times in the past, letting God take the lead. For did not God say in His word, "Those who wait upon the Lord shall renew their strength; they shall mount up with wings like eagles, they shall run and not be weary, they shall walk and not faint" (Isa. 40:31)? *Just like that eagle, relying on the wind to power its wings as it soars the heavens, so now I must rely on God to give the strength and lead the way. Certainly if this is where He desires me to be, He will provide the means, and if He does, then surely I must go. . . .*

As he prayed, it seemed as though God was putting an image in his mind, for he could see Paul on that road to Damascus. Eventually, and emphatically, Paul would preach in the synagogues that Christ was the Son of God! He would preach it before much of the known world at that time, even to his death!

Certainly Paul, too, had a lot to consider. Remembering now the scripture in Philippians 4:6–7, James began to recite it to himself, "'Be careful for nothing, but in everything by prayer and supplication with thanksgiving let your requests be made known unto God. And the peace of God . . . shall guard your hearts and minds through Christ Jesus.'

"Yes, but before that, the Lord tells us to rejoice in Him, to be gentle as we deal with others, to remember how near He is, and to pray earnestly, to count our blessings with thanksgiving and to center our hearts, our minds on what is true, noble, just, pure, lovely and praiseworthy!

"Well, I will take the first step, trusting my Lord will lead me!" James said, as he closed the barn door and walked to the house. His first step would be telling the family, getting their input, and from there he would make his final decision.

Chapter 29

The long, broad frames of the two-seated buckboards were coming down the road crowded with people, along with numerous wagons and carriages, as far as the eye could see. There were people walking as well and others on horses, with one or two riders sitting astride their saddles. A steady flow graced the old dirt road, a road that had been built more than thirty years before by the sweat and toil of the pioneers who first came to the county.

The elderly preacher, wearing his black Prince Albert frock coat, double-breasted and skirted well below the knee, with buttons from the waist up to the broad lapel where a matching cravat was folded loosely about his neck, watched the wagons, horses, and buggies pull into the church grounds. As he stood there beside the small window of the white-framed church building looking out, he could not help but wonder from where they had all come, for he had never seen so many people. Glancing at his Bible, he bowed his head and began to pray,

"Oh God, only You could have done this! For without Your grace, I am unworthy to lead these people. But You have found in Your mercy to bless me, to make of me a 'living sacrifice,' holy and acceptable to You. Take me now, oh my Lord, use me to save these You have brought under my care. Bring to my mind those wonderful words of wisdom found only in the Bible, that I may tell them what You, and You alone, would have me say."

One by one men, women, and children entered the building, anxious now to not only see but hear this legendary man, this Campbellite preacher of the Simple Gospel, who had been gone for more than ten years but was back now, to take his place again in the pulpit. As the people took their seats, they began to sing, and the melody resonated for miles across the open fields. The only other sound to interrupt the quiet tranquility of the countryside was the birds singing in the trees that encompassed the churchyard.

> Blessed assurance, Jesus is mine!
> O what a foretaste of glory divine!
> Heir of salvation, purchase of God,
> Born of His Spirit, washed in His blood.

> This is my story, this is my song,
> praising my Savior all the day long;
> this is my story, this is my song,
> praising my Savior all the day long.

It was 1874, and it was spring. The flowering trees, which were now in full bloom, had not completely extended their growth to the point where they blocked the sun; it was shining in all its glory and did so, as with a promise to help pull the leaves from their buds. They, along with the farmer's fields, were springing to life, as a bountiful display of green was sweeping across the land replacing the deadness of winter.

James Scott, with his marvelous physique, rose to grace the pulpit. His gray-blue eyes shown with wonderment as he looked out across the faces of the blessed people who were now seated before him. They were his friends and neighbors, people he had not seen for a long time. With affection in his voice, he began to speak, for his mind was full of precious memories.

"Good morning, my dear brothers and sisters in Christ. I pray this Lord's Day morning finds you all well. My, it's good to be back at old Christian Oral Church and see so many of you here today. As you may know, I have been in Madison County for several years. Four of my children are now living there. Mariah, my youngest daughter, was recently married to a fine young man, William Davis, and my sons Hiram and James, as well as my daughter Sophia, are still in Madison County. Regretfully, my dear Nancy is there too, laid beneath the ground, but we know her spirit is in the arms of Jesus. For, 'the wind bloweth where it pleases, and thou hearest the sound thereof, but canst not tell whence it cometh, and whither it goeth: so it is with every one born of the Spirit' (John 3:8) . . . and so it is with my beloved Nancy.

"I know many of you have lost loved ones as well—fathers, husbands, and sons in the war. I heard that more than twenty-four thousand from Indiana lost their lives serving in the Union army. Most of those men were volunteers, men who were willing to lay down their lives to help others, to free those who had been enslaved, and to keep these states that have united together. Many more wanted to go, I'm sure, but were turned away for one reason or another, or simply were not needed. As we mourn the dead, let us remember that truth written in Scripture, for the wind bloweth where it pleases, and so goeth the Spirit of the Lord, 'for they that worship Him must worship Him in spirit and in truth' (John 4:24). 'Flesh gives birth to flesh, but the Spirit gives birth to Spirit' (John 3:6). Our concern now should be to stay faithful to Him every minute of our lives, so that someday we too will hear the words, 'Well done, my good and faithful servant,' and gain the privilege of seeing our loved ones again on that golden shore.

"In my younger life, I never thought much about the Spirit of the Lord, or about church. My father and I were at sea most of that time. But when you find yourself alone on a deserted island in the middle of a vast ocean, not knowing if you will ever get off that island to see those you cherish, God becomes very real to you. I felt His guiding hand many times as I dwelt in that deserted place, and certainly He was there the night a schooner put down anchor at the edge of a coral reef and rescued me.

"While I was on that island, I became aware of Him, the living Stone, rejected by men, but chosen of God and precious to Him. I could relate, for I felt rejected, as I struggled to live in that foreboding, deserted place. But unbeknownst to me, God was using that opportunity to build in me a spiritual house, a holy priesthood, to become a spiritual offering, acceptable to Him through our Lord and Savior, Jesus Christ. Amen! Jesus said, 'I've come that you may have life and have it more abundantly.'"

James paused for a moment. He looked out across the faces of the people crowded into the small building. They were listening intensely to every word he spoke. Suddenly a thought flashed through his mind: *These people, having heard God's Word, will pass those words on to their children, and with a prayer their grandchildren will hear them as well, and with that knowledge will build one of the greatest of nations that has ever existed upon this earth.*

"I certainly didn't feel I had an abundant life," James continued, "living on that deserted island, but as I considered God,

He impressed upon my mind that He is alive and that He came, compassionately atoning for my transgressions. Now, I no longer have to suffer the penalty for my sins, and certainly with that knowledge, I must confess, He has given me an abundant life. So, when we think of Him today, we must realize our thoughts of Him will influence every area of our lives, for it is all too easy to bend our thinking of who God is to suit ourselves, or the situation we may find ourselves in. Even those of us who are mature believers face this temptation. But the Bible is our guide, for it is God's instructions. We must look to it and learn, praying that the Holy Spirit will guide our thoughts as we struggle to live in this evil world. Let us consider and be thankful for the saints who have gone before, many of whom were persecuted for their faith, as they guarded the faith, and gave their very lives, so that we today may have access to these ancient words. And, may we never take them for granted! As we consider their sacrifice, let us speak only where the Bible speaks, and where it is silent, let us be silent!

"Jesus came to show us the way, but the gate is narrow, and the way is straight! We must carefully follow Him and do what He says. Listen, my children, and learn. Listen and do what He tells you. The Bible warns us, 'Be not deceived; God is not mocked: for whatsoever a man soweth, that shall he also reap. For he that soweth to his flesh shall of the flesh reap corruption; but he that soweth to the Spirit shall of the Spirit reap life everlasting.' (Gal. 6:7–8). Beware, for the devil prowls around like a wild beast, deceiving the very elect themselves.

"The apostle John tells us that in the beginning was the Word, and the Word was with God and the Word was God. God, by His word, spoke the world into existence, but that Word which created the world, giving it order, became flesh and lived among us, and they called His name Jesus. He came to teach us that He is the way, the truth, and the life, and that no man comes to the Father except through belief in Him, because He is God! In Him is life and that life is the light of men. We will never know what our lives are truly like until we look at them in the light of Jesus, for our faith will be determined not by what we say we believe, but by the results of our actions. So let us not grow weary in doing good, for at the proper time we will reap a great harvest, if we do not give up. Therefore, as we have opportunity, let us do good to all people, especially to those who belong to the family of believers.

"Scripture says that God is love, and that love is the light of men, and no greater love has any man than one who is willing to lay down his life for another. Christ came to do just that! He suffered and died on a lonely cross, carrying the penalty for our sins, as he hung there, bled, and died. Now, as we consider what He did for us, let us live our lives in accordance with His Holy Word." James took the Bible in his hands, and lifted it high into the air.

"This book," he continued, "tells us that Jesus is the Truth, but what is truth, and why is that word so important? Why do we need to know the meaning of 'truth'? Well, the rest of that scripture goes, 'and the truth will set you free'! We certainly want to be free, for we have experienced the glorious light of freedom in this country now for several decades. We could not imagine ourselves without it, but do we really know, or under-stand from where that freedom came? The Israelites certainly didn't. Listen to what happened to them.

"In the book of Deuteronomy, God told the Israelites to 'keep the commandments of the LORD thy God, to walk in his ways, and to fear him. For the LORD thy God bringeth thee into a good land, a land of brooks of water, of fountains and depths that spring out of valleys and hills; a land of wheat, and barley, and vines, and fig trees, and pomegranates; a land of oil olive, and honey; a land wherein thou shalt eat bread without scarceness, thou shalt not lack any thing in it; a land whose stones are iron, and out of whose hills thou mayest dig brass' (Deut. 8:6–9). Is that not what He has also done for us, here in America?

"But He also told them, 'When thou hast eaten and art full, then thou shalt bless the LORD thy God for the good land which he hath given thee. Beware that thou forget not the LORD thy God, in not keeping his commandments, and his judgments, and his statutes, which I command thee this day: Lest when thou hast eaten and art full, and hast built goodly houses, and dwelt therein; And when thy herds and thy flocks multiply, and thy silver and thy gold is multiplied, and all that thou hast is multiplied; Then thine heart be lifted up, and thou forget the LORD thy God, which brought thee forth out of the land of Egypt, from the house of bondage; who led thee through that great and terrible wilderness, wherein were fiery serpents, and scorpions, and drought, where there was no water; who brought thee forth water out of the rock of flint; who fed thee in the wilderness with manna, which thy fathers knew not, that he might humble thee, and that he might prove thee, to do thee good at thy latter end; And thou say in thine heart, My power and the might of mine hand hath gotten me this wealth. But thou shalt remember the LORD thy God: for it is he that giveth thee power to get wealth, that he may establish his covenant which he sware unto thy fathers, as it is this day. And it shall be, if thou do at all forget the LORD thy God, and walk after other gods, and serve them, and worship them, I testify against you this day that ye shall surely perish. As the nations which the

LORD destroyeth before your face, so shall ye perish; because ye would not be obedient unto the voice of the LORD your God' (Deut. 8:10–20).

"It was 926 BC. Solomon the Great had just died, and with his passing went the dream that Israel would become a great power. For two generations that dream had fostered a reality, built by two great and godly men, Solomon and his father King David. Now another generation was emerging, godless men who would crush the power of this great nation by their tribal dissension and split the nation into two separate kingdoms—Israel in the north, with Judah claiming the south. Eventually Israel would fall to the Assyrians, while the Babylonians would take over Judah. Two hundred and fifty years after Solomon's death the kingdoms were no more. Many kings claimed the throne of that split nation. Most had turned their backs on God, and looked to and sought to worship other gods; and as they did, they fell into disrepair, just as God had told them they would. Eventually they found themselves taken over by other nations. God was no longer a part of their lives, for they had rejected Him, and continued living without Him.

"In the years before their destruction, King David, a godly man, lived. He walked and talked with God.

"King David ask God this question, 'LORD, who shall abide in thy tabernacle? who shall dwell in thy holy hill? He that walketh uprightly, and worketh righteousness, and speaketh the truth in his heart He that backbiteth not with his tongue, nor doeth evil to his neighbour, nor taketh up a reproach against his neighbour. In whose eyes a vile person is contemned; but he honoureth them that fear the LORD. He that sweareth to his own hurt, and changeth not. He that putteth not out his money to usury, nor taketh reward against the innocent. He that doeth these things shall never be moved' (Ps. 15).

"The nation which David ruled was a nation of godly people, and so it was with Solomon, his son. God blessed Solomon, and gave him great wisdom. Because of these truths, he was at peace with all of the surrounding nations, and had more wealth than any person had ever known; but Solomon, in his later years, became proud and began to disobey God by marrying women of other nations. God had warned the people not to marry those women, for well He knew that if they did, they would soon begin to worship their gods, and that is exactly what happened to Solomon. Though God did not forsake the nation of Israel while Solomon was living do to the promise He had made to his father, David. He did, however, turn his back on that nation at Solomon's death, for the people Solomon had ruled continued turning their backs on Him by worshiping other gods.

"Now as we struggle to live in this day, we must be careful to not repeat their mistakes. For as surely as we do, becoming a proud people, turning our backs on God, and worshiping other gods like the god of wealth or money, we too will fall! God will most certainly lift His hand of blessing off of this great land; and when He does, we will find ourselves as the Israelites did, surely destroyed! Listen, my friends, and learn. We cannot become wise without God's hand upon us. When we begin to think our wisdom is due to our learning, pushing God from of our lives, we will most certainly fall!

"Jesus came that we 'may have life and have it more abundantly'—but to have an abundant life, we must understand truth. This great mystery of truth unlocks when we come to know the Bible, for he tells us in His Word that He is the way, the truth, and the life, and that no one can come to the Father except through Him. When we know Him, we begin to understand truth. For truth stands in the darkness of this evil world and dissipates that darkness with its glorious light. Suddenly, we have a choice. We can either continue living in darkness, or choose to live in the light. As we begin to understand and act on that knowledge, choosing to follow Him, we find ourselves living as free people. Jesus told the Jews who had believed in Him, 'If ye continue in my word, *then* are ye my disciples indeed; and ye shall know the truth, and the truth shall make you free' (John 8:31–32).

"No ropes or laws will bind us! We have been set free, as God's glorious light begins to shine through the darkness of this sinister world! Oh, my brothers and sisters, this is so important to understand, for if we do not realize from where our freedoms came, we will most certainly, one day, lose them just as the Israelites did. They went from bondage to spiritual faith, from spiritual faith to great courage, from courage to liberty, from liberty to God's blessings, which produced for them an abundant life. But then they took those blessings of God's for granted. Becoming a proud people, they turned and worshiped other gods, claiming it was their fortitude, their wisdom that produced for them an abundant life. In time they became complacent, and their complacency produced laziness, which caused a dependency upon those who would rule over them. Soon they found themselves in bondage again; struggling in the darkness of this evil world, for God's glorious light of freedom was gone.

"God told the people through the prophet Hosea, 'According to their pasture, so were they filled; they were filled, and their heart was exalted; therefore have they forgotten me' (Hos. 13:6).

"Listen my children and learn, for these ancient words have been written for our learning. Do we want to repeat their mistakes? We are living in a dark, sinister world, and the Bible says that men love darkness because their deeds are evil. Peter tells us in 1 Peter 2:16 to live as free men, 'not using your liberty for a cloke of maliciousness, but as the servants of God.'

"Jesus said, 'Not every one that saith unto me, Lord, Lord, shall enter into the kingdom of heaven; but he that doeth the will of my Father which is in heaven. Many will say to me in that day, Lord, Lord, have we not prophesied in thy name? and in thy name have cast out devils? and in thy name done many wonderful works? And then will I profess unto them, I never knew you: depart from me, ye that work iniquity.' Therefore whosoever heareth these sayings of mine, and doeth them, I will liken him unto a wise man, which built his house upon a rock: And the rain descended, and the floods came, and the winds blew, and beat upon that house; and it fell not: for it was founded upon a rock. And every one that heareth these sayings of mine, and doeth them not, shall be likened unto a foolish man, which built his house upon the sand: And the rain descended, and the floods came, and the winds blew, and beat upon that house; and it fell: and great was the fall of it' (Matt. 7:21–27).

"Oh, my dear friends, let us not become weary in doing good, for at the proper time we will reap a rich harvest if we do not give up! We must always remember that the one who sows to please the Spirit of God, from that Spirit will reap eternal life! Therefore, as we have opportunity, let us do good to all people! Amen!

"And Jesus said, "Greater love hath no man than this, that a man lay down his life for his friends. Ye are my friends, if ye do whatsoever I command you' (John 15:13–14).

"Oh, what a friend we have in Jesus! Let us sing that song now. . . ." James began singing, with his voice ringing out heavenward. The people followed, and soon all were proclaiming:

What a Friend we have in Jesus, all our sins and griefs to bear.
What a privilege to carry everything to God in prayer.
O what peace we often forfeit, O what needless pain we bear,
All because we do not carry everything to God in prayer.

Have we trials and temptations? Is there trouble anywhere?
We should never be discouraged; take it to the Lord in prayer.
Can we find a friend so faithful who will all our sorrows share?
Jesus knows our every weakness; take it to the Lord in prayer.

Are we weak and heavy laden, cumbered with a load of care?
Precious Savior, still our refuge, take it to the Lord in prayer.
Do your friends despise, forsake you? Take it to the Lord in prayer.
In His arms He'll take and shield you; you will find a solace there.

Blessed Savior, Thou hast promised Thou wilt all our
burdens bear
May we ever, Lord, be bringing all to Thee in earnest
prayer.
Soon in glory bright unclouded there will be no need
for prayer
Rapture, praise and endless worship will be our sweet
portion there.

The message echoed across the open meadows, as they
sweetly sang. Only their voices could be heard, for there was
not an organ or any other musical device in the building to
muffle the lilting reverence of the sound. It was a prayer, from
the people's voices only, to a loving God.

"The God of the Bible is a God of love," James continued,
"for the word 'love' is mentioned over one thousand times in
Scripture. Every one of the commands of God's is backed by
love. In the New Testament, Jesus tells us, 'A new commandment I give unto you, That ye love one another; as I have loved
you, that ye also love one another' (John 13:34). Then He set
the example, when He gave His very life for us. Now, because
He did that for us, can we not live our lives for Him? For in so
doing we will live them more abundantly. What a great command, but, perhaps, the greatest command of all, is to love the
Lord with all our hearts.

"'Finally, brethren, whatsoever things are true, whatsoever
things are honest, whatsoever things are just, whatsoever things
are pure, whatsoever things are lovely, whatsoever things are of
good report; if there be any virtue, and if there be any praise,
think on these things' (Phil. 4:8).

"Love one another, and treat people as we would have them treat us, to give our lives, if necessary, as He gave His for those who are suffering or have no freedom. For He tells us no greater love has any man than he who is willing to lay down his life for another. For we now know, the greater gain will be our home in heaven.

"We are living in Satan's dark world. The only thing that keeps Satan at bay is our faith in the Light, for that Light dissipates the darkness of evil, and it is the only thing that does. The Bible says Satan comes as an angel of light, deceiving the very elect themselves. He is a liar and the father of lies and his greatest lie is to convince us that he does not exist.

"But we will do well to remember, that 'the wrath of God is revealed from heaven against all ungodliness and unrighteousness of men, who hold the truth in unrighteousness; because that which may be known of God is manifest in them; for God hath shewed it unto them. For the invisible things of him from the creation of the world are clearly seen, being understood by the things that are made, even his eternal power and Godhead; so that they are without excuse: Because that, when they knew God, they glorified him not as God, neither were thankful; but became vain in their imaginations, and their foolish heart was darkened. Professing themselves to be wise, they became fools, and changed the glory of the uncorruptible God into an image made like to corruptible man, and to birds, and fourfooted beasts, and creeping things. Wherefore God also gave them up to uncleanness through the lusts of their own hearts, to dishonour their own bodies between themselves: Who changed the truth of God into a lie, and worshipped and served the creature more than the Creator, who is blessed for ever. Amen' (Rom. 1:18–25).

"Oh my people, we must always remember, God will not force His will upon us! We are free to believe Him or not. But in everything we do, we will be either turning this world into a heavenly place or into hell. There are no other choices. Remember, the Bible says for us to be sober-minded; to be watchful, for our adversary, the devil, prowls around like a roaring lion, seeking someone to devour. Resist him, firm in your faith, knowing that the same kinds of suffering are being experienced by your brotherhood throughout the world.

"I can only imagine what the Galilean Sea was like that beautiful day Jesus climbed up the side of the mountain which overlooks it, sat down, and began to teach. There was a multitude of people there that day, yet each and every one could hear him. That within itself was a miracle, as He taught them saying: 'Let your light so shine before men, that they may see your good works, and glorify your Father which is in heaven. Think not that I am come to destroy the law, or the prophets: I am not come to destroy, but to fulfil. For verily I say unto you, Till heaven and earth pass, one jot or one tittle shall in no wise pass from the law, till all be fulfilled. . . . But I say unto you, Love your enemies, bless them that curse you, do good to them that hate you, and pray for them which despitefully use you, and persecute you' (Matt. 5:16–18, 44).

"Remember, He causes the sun to rise on the evil and the good and sends rain on the righteous and the unrighteous, for as He blesses America because of those who have stayed true to Him, evil men will gain from those blessings as well—but only as long as the faithful outnumber the unrighteous. When the equation changes and evil men become greater, this country will fall, just as the Israelites did. There were seven thousand men who had never bowed to the god Baal, yet they suffered along with all those who were unfaithful.

"So let us remember, and may we never forget, what Jesus told the people who were gathered there, that day, on that Judean hillside, 'Enter ye in at the strait gate: for wide is the gate, and broad is the way, that leadeth to destruction, and many there be which go in thereat: Because strait is the gate, and narrow is the way, which leadeth unto life, and few there be that find it' (Matt 7:13–14).

"Oh, my dear friends, I have looked far and wide, I have traveled the world, but I am pleased now to tell you I have found that *narrow gate*. My prayers are that you and your children, and your children's children, will find it as well . . . and that someday I will meet you all in that glorious heavenly home."

James bowled his head, closed his eyes and began to pray silently, when suddenly he heard a man singing:

> Our fathers' God to Thee,
>
> Author of liberty,
>
> To Thee we sing.
>
> Long may our land be bright,
>
> With freedom's holy light,
>
> Protect us by Thy might,
>
> Great God our King.

Soon others joined him, and before long the whole congregation was singing. Opening his eyes, James saw the man standing at the back of the church. Suddenly the room was full of people standing, rejoicing, as they sung;

> My country, 'tis of thee,
>
> Sweet land of liberty,

Of thee I sing;
Land where my fathers died,
Land of the pilgrims' pride,
From ev'ry mountainside
Let freedom ring!

Be strong and very courageous. Be careful to obey all the law my servant Moses gave you; do not turn from it to the right or to the left, that you may be successful wherever you go. Keep this Book of the Law always on your lips; meditate on it day and night, so that you may be careful to do everything written in it. Then you will be prosperous and be successful. Have I not commanded you? Be strong and courageous. Do not be afraid; do not be discouraged, for the Lord your God will be with you wherever you go (Joshua 1:7–9, NIV).

Historical Notes

 James P. Scott was the author's great, great grandfather. His daughter Mariah was grandmother to Chester O. Kreegar, the author's father. It has always been rumored in the family that James Scott married a Native American no one of this present generation knows for certain. He lived to be ninety, died on July 19, 1891, and is buried in the Limberlost Cemetery near Bryant, in Jay County, Indiana.

The following article appeared in *The Christian Standard* in 1910 and was written by James Scott's grandson, Hamilton Mercer of Greensburg, Indiana:

A Pioneer Evangelist

If the world should stand a million years, the story of the pioneer preachers never would be written. While *The Christian Standard* has teemed with the life stories of these veteran trailblazers and scores have thus been vividly brought to our notice, any one of who was an honor to the cause, nothing that I know of ever has been said about James P. Scott, who at one time in Adams County, Indiana, called so many out of the sects and the world that they were nicknamed "Scotties."

James Scott, who called himself the "barnstormer," passed to his reward twenty years ago near Geneva, Adams County, Indiana, at the age of ninety years. He passed without pain, and those who watched at his bedside say that it was a happy moment to him when he saw the portals swing back. He was a vigorous preacher up to within a few days of his death, and the infirmities of age or the vitiating powers of invalidism never marred the strength of his marvelous physique.

James Scott was a preacher of the simple gospel for sixty-five years. No record of his baptisms [those he baptized] was ever kept, and no accurate statement of the number of churches he established is available, but there is a record in heaven, a record that is indisputably true to the facts.

Coming to this country from Ireland with his father, Scott located in New York. His father engaged in the export trade, shipping flax in his own vessel to Europe. The boy had been seasoned to the rough sea life by an apprenticeship, which ended about the time he was twelve years old. After he had married, Scott and his father sailed for Europe with a cargo of flax, but were overtaken by a pirate sloop, *The Bald Hornet*. The crew was overpowered and Scott became a prisoner of the desperate robbers of the sea. His father was taken prisoner also and such members of the crew who were not slain in the conflict. On the voyage to one of the islands in the tropics, whither the sloop was bound to escape detection, a fearful storm arose and drove the vessel on the rocks, shattering it and destroying all aboard save Scott. He was cast upon the island, which he found to be uninhabited and remained there after the fashion of Robinson Crusoe for a period of two years when he was picked up by a passing vessel and taken to New York.

Soon after the restoration to his family Scott began to preach, and though he was opposed by his friends, he persisted and with true Christian courage to proclaim the simple gospel, which was then little known. When Indiana was a virgin forest,

Scott and his wife and children came west in a covered wagon, with one jaded horse, and ninety-five cents in his pocket. He arrived in the heart of the Indiana wilderness and settled in Adams County, Indiana. He took off his coat and went to work. At night he studied his Bible by the light of a hickory bark fire and on Sundays preached in the log cabins of his scattered neighbors. He never would take any money for his preaching, but in later years he received many gifts of cash. He was opposed to instrumental music in the church, and so far as is known, there never was a time when he was humiliated by a congregation using the organ while he was present at church. The congregations always respected his feelings in this, out of consideration for the man.

[It was said] that he lost the faculty of estimating time, and the occasions are numerous when he preached for two and one-half hours when he supposed that he had preached not more than half that long. At Redkey, Indiana, he was turned out of a building after he had gotten his meeting under way. The few disciples at that meeting then secured an old barn, nailed on some boards to keep out the wind and rain, and insisted that the meetings continue. The results of that meeting are apparent today as Redkey now has a prosperous church, worshipping in a comparatively new building.

Experiences such as these were numerous in the life of James P. Scott, as was the case in the lives of all the pioneer preachers of blessed memory, and during Scott's last days he often would refer to them in comparison to the time of his old age.

A few years before his death, Hamilton Mercer, who wrote the above article, sent James Scott a copy of *The Christian*

Standard so that he might get a better idea of the condition of the work throughout the country. James Scott told him that he had read every word. He also said, "But it seems to me that there is too much begging for money."

The following picture is of the Limberlost Church and the graveyard where James Scott is buried. The church is no longer standing.

In attempting to tell this amazing story, the author has sought to fill in the missing pieces. Historically, they are true to fact. The information about Alexander Campbell was taken from the following books: *The Christian System* by Alexander Campbell; *The Fool of God* by Louis Cochran; and *Alexander Campbell, Adventurer in Freedom: A Literary Biography* by Eva Jean Wrather. The information about Ireland came from the book *The Story of the Irish Race* by Seumas MacManus.

No one knows for certain if James Scott and Alexander Campbell actually met; however, James Scott was well known to be a Campbellite preacher of the "simple gospel," and because of that fact, this writer has assumed that they probably did meet.

Please note: James Scott was only one of many men who carried the gospel of Jesus Christ across this great land, securing the freedoms which we have enjoyed these many years.

Charlotte J. Reynolds